ADDITIONAL PRAISE FOR
WHAT CHINESE WANT

"What do Chinese want? It's a big question. But marketing guru Tom Doctoroff can handle it. He approaches rough business challenges not only strategically but also psychologically. He catches what numbers don't capture: the heart of a people and how it affects who succeeds and who fails on the mainland."
—Jing Ulrich, Managing Director and Chairman of Global Markets, China, J.P. Morgan

"Tom's unique experience and perspective is a boon to anyone who plans to address the Chinese consumer. Insofar as it is possible to sum the sentiment and unique cultural underpinnings of this mammoth country, Tom has done it."
—Kathleen Hall, Windows Global Campaigns and Product Marketing General Manager, Microsoft

"In explaining what Chinese consumers want, Doctoroff vividly shows us where China is headed as a society and a world power."
—Garrick Utley, Senior Fellow at SUNY Levin Institute

"*What Chinese Want* is required reading for any business person that deals with Chinese nationals or companies. It will help you quickly learn what was so hard for me to understand during my five years of living in China: China *is* very different from the West, and Tom Doctoroff will explain what you need to know to succeed there."
—Miguel Patricio, President of Anheuser-Busch InBev for Asia Pacific

"The scale of potential opportunity in China is staggering. But business people who want to succeed in China often feel like they have landed on a different planet. Tom Doctoroff's book offers a very insightful, down-to-earth analysis of both what's driving growth in China as well as a nuanced analysis of the psychology of Chinese leaders and people. Anyone who wants to succeed big time in China will find his book very helpful and interesting."
—Dr. Ramesh Tainwala, President Asia Pacific and Middle East, Samsonite Group

"Tom Doctoroff's *What Chinese Want* succeeds in linking the most dynamic facets of the modern Chinese commercial and consumer landscape with the unique and timeless characteristics of China's people and culture."
—John Quelch, Distinguished Professor of International
Management, Vice President and Dean, CEIBS
(China Europe International Business School)

"This is a breakthrough work on the modern Chinese consumer. Rooted in a long and successful career in China, Tom Doctoroff's book gives a concrete, in-depth, and simple explanation about how this mysterious land really works that will begin to change the world's biased understanding of a great country."
—Pierre Xiao Lu, author of *Elite China*, professor of marketing at
Fudan University in Shanghai, and Founder of
China Market Institute Consulting

WHAT CHINESE WANT

CULTURE, COMMUNISM, AND CHINA'S MODERN CONSUMER

TOM DOCTOROFF

palgrave
macmillan

WHAT CHINESE WANT
Copyright © Tom Doctoroff, 2012.

First published in 2012 by
PALGRAVE MACMILLAN®
in the United States—a division of St. Martin's Press LLC,
175 Fifth Avenue, New York, NY 10010.

Where this book is distributed in the UK, Europe and the rest of the world,
this is by Palgrave Macmillan, a division of Macmillan Publishers Limited,
registered in England, company number 785998, of Houndmills,
Basingstoke, Hampshire RG21 6XS.

Palgrave Macmillan is the global academic imprint of the above companies
and has companies and representatives throughout the world.

Palgrave® and Macmillan® are registered trademarks in the United States,
the United Kingdom, Europe and other countries.

ISBN: 978–0–230–34030–5

Library of Congress Cataloging-in-Publication Data

Doctoroff, Tom.
    What Chinese want : Culture, Communism, and China's modern
consumer / by Tom Doctoroff.
        p. cm.
    Includes index.
    ISBN 978–0–230–34030–5
    1. Consumers—China—Attitudes. 2. Consumers' preferences—China.
    3. Marketing—China. 4. China—Economic conditions—21st century. I. Title.

HF5415.33.C6D634 2012
658.8'3430951—dc23   2011041408

A catalogue record of the book is available from the British Library.

Design by Newgen Imaging Systems (P) Ltd., Chennai, India.

First edition: May 2012

10 9 8 7 6 5 4 3 2 1

Printed in the United States of America.

CONTENTS

Part Six   Epilogue

IMAGES

FOREWORD

Sir Martin Sorrell,
CEO, WPP

Over the past few years, China watchers have seen a change. The country's business people, politicians, and academics display a new spring in their step. It isn't arrogance, merely greater confidence. I see it everywhere I go—at conferences, at the World Economic Forum in Davos, and traveling in China.

There are good reasons for this newfound swagger. Yes, the Chinese people's admirable ability to listen and learn is still there. But they rightly feel they have a little less to learn from us these days—especially after the largely Western financial crisis of 2008. The scales have fallen from Chinese eyes. We messed up; they didn't. Now they are less inclined to take lectures on economics, politics, or human rights from Britain or the United States.

This new attitude provides ample opportunities for sly humor. When David Cameron announced that he was considering controlling social media to prevent a repeat of August 2011's rioting and looting in Britain, an editorial in a Chinese newspaper remarked, with evident relish, that it was good to see the British government understands that the Internet has to be moderated during times of crisis.

Although they would never put it so bluntly, the Chinese don't think we're quite as good as we think we are. This should hardly come as a surprise. As Western countries struggle to maintain any sort of growth, the Chinese economy surges ahead.

While we agonize about containing our state debt, Chinese banks and companies pour money into the rest of the world. When Wen Jiabao, the Chinese premier, pledged to buy further Euro zone sovereign debt, the reaction was not one of concern about undue Chinese influence but relief. His pronouncement that Western countries should put their houses in order sets the tone for the new Chinese engagement with the world.

Wherever you go, you see the power of the renminbi. The People's Republic is still a net receiver of foreign direct investment, but its acquisitions abroad are catching up. China needs food and, even more important, Russian and Middle Eastern oil and gas, because it has few energy resources of its own.

The Chinese are expanding their influence around the world, even beyond the 800,000 Chinese people already living and working in Africa. Throughout the Mediterranean, central Europe, and farther afield, Beijing is on a global acquisition spree. Swedish car companies, Greek infrastructure, an oil firm in Canada, a mining company with assets in Central Africa—all snapped up by China in the past few years.

Even in the unlikely territory of Iceland, the Middle Kingdom is making its presence felt. Huang Nubo, a Chinese businessman and poet, has offered $9 million for 300 square kilometers of wildness, 0.3 percent of the country. He says he wants to build a $100 million hotel, but some suspect ulterior motives.

Huang is not the only Chinese businessman benefiting from his country's unique melding of carnivorous market forces and central state planning. The ranks of Chinese billionaires are swelling. A recently published rich list identified 270 billionaires flourishing in the Middle Kingdom, topped by Liang Wengen, a construction equipment tycoon with a net worth of about $11 billion. This is only half of it. The Hurun Rich List estimates that there may be the same number again, but they keep themselves and their assets from public scrutiny.

This new money has not gone unnoticed. In Britain, high-end retailers purr at the prospect of their custom. Mandarin-speaking sales assistants are employed in top department stores, and boutique staffs in Bond Street receive lessons in Chinese etiquette. Prada's recent IPO was not held in Milan—its home base—but in Hong Kong. It knows where its customers live.

China is also an essential part of the future of WPP, the international marketing services company of which I am CEO. We have been there since 1987, through our acquisition of agencies J Walter Thompson, Ogilvy, and subsequent other companies, and there are now nearly 13,000 people (including associates) in Greater China. WPP's business in China is larger than all the other international marketing services groups, combined, and China's share of our global business is growing every year.

Chinese influence is not merely confined to investment, trade, and retail. Beijing rightly expects the voices of its more than 1.3 billion people to be heard in global politics, underscored by greater spending on defense. The Chinese military's budget is a fraction of that of the United States; that China's is expanding at a time when Western nations are cutting nevertheless causes twitches. Some suspect the massive Icelandic land acquisition to be more a question of China's strategic interests than a leisure project.

If you are reading this book, you do not need to be convinced of China's impending preeminence. The only thing in doubt is exactly when. It is already the world's number one consumer of energy; it is only a matter of time before it has the largest economy by gross domestic product. Estimates suggest that that could happen as soon as 2019, while others think it will take longer.

But, even so, many people fail to be persuaded that China can be anything more than a volume producer of low-priced generic goods under the guidance of the Chinese Communist Party. Proper creativity and the spark of innovation still reside, they insist, in the mature democracies of Europe and the United States. China has no services, it is argued, and few internationally recognized brand names or luxury goods.

This is to forget that as recently 150 years ago, China had the upper hand in technology and manufacture. The West's ascendancy is a comparatively recent development and, it seems, a temporary one.

We have been here before. My father was in electrical retail. He used to buy from Hong Kong, which he regarded as cheap and cheerful. Japan was the same, until brands like Sony came along.

Sooner or later, the same will happen in China. It is a matter of time and incremental evolution. The Chinese are ambitious and diligent: they will succeed, first developing in a way that is right for their home market and then competing in developed markets.

Millward Brown's 2011 BrandZ survey has already placed twelve Chinese companies on its list of 100 Most Valuable Global Brands. The state-owned China Mobile is at number nine in the global survey, ahead of Amazon and Walmart, and at number one in Millward Brown's ranking of China's most valuable domestic brands.

Inch by inch, Chinese brands will take their place on the world stage. One is Haier, the electrical goods manufacturer, which already counts as its customers 70 percent of the US undergraduates who buy air conditioners. Another is Geely, the carmaker that bought Volvo. There will be a slow but sure climb up the value chain.

While the Chinese may now believe they have less to learn from us, we have much to learn from them. Any Western company with ambition knows it has to be in China, one of the few markets offering potential for growth, with its rapidly expanding middle class, which will soon be larger than America's.

But to think of the country as merely another territory that can be decoded through translation is arrogant and potentially business killing. Even to think of it as a single territory risks failure. Mao often had to travel with a linguist to understand the many tongues and dialects in his sprawling kingdom.

For a Westerner, China's subtleties of philosophy, religion, and community, its thinking—order, harmony, conformity, balance, pragmatism—are fundamentally different. Some will choose denial and avoidance over trying to grasp how the Chinese approach the world. But to assume that a 5,000-year-old civilization sees everything as we do is a fundamental mistake.

For nearly two decades, Tom Doctoroff has lived and breathed China. His first title on the subject, *Billions*, offered readers highly original and thoughtful insights into the Chinese consumer—all in his concise, respectful, yet witty style. Every paragraph glinted with gems of wisdom.

This, Tom's new book, looks at China from a cultural standpoint, examining how timeless Chinese truths inform modern society, business, consumer habits, and geopolitics. Tom's writing is both authoritative and sensitive. He understands the Chinese mind.

Doctoroff argues that China and the West have inherently different strengths and weaknesses and—if leaders keep their cool and America accepts that it will no longer be the only tiger on the mountain—we can happily coexist. China will always need partners and so will we.

There have been many books about the Chinese economy but few on the motivations of its people, which are shaped by a worldview radically different from the one we know in the West.

As Beijing finds its new place in the world, any Western person or company seeking a productive relationship with the PRC must start with an understanding of what makes the Chinese tick. That is the goal of Tom Doctoroff's book. No Western business person should book a flight without reading it.

PART ONE

THE CHINESE WORLDVIEW

1

MODERN MIDDLE KINGDOM: OLD PIPES, NEW PALACE

What makes Chinese people tick? To secure a peaceful, productive twenty-first century, we in the West must achieve a deeper understanding of their motivations and behavior. The Chinese are often described as inscrutable, even by some who have spent long stretches of time in China, but this is misleading. Despite China's growing significance on the world stage and an explosion of new Chinese material and lifestyle opportunities, local culture remains intact and, to those with cultural curiosity, knowable. China is modernizing, but it is not becoming Western, nor is it in the throes of a debilitating spiritual or cultural disorientation. In order to establish a productive relationship with the Chinese people, we—business people, politicians, students, and tourists—must reorient ourselves to engage with a profoundly different worldview.

China's economy and people are evolving rapidly, but the underlying cultural blueprint has remained more or less constant for thousands of years. As the nation races toward superpower status, it will nonetheless remain quintessentially Chinese—ambitious yet cautious at the core. In this sense, the country doesn't necessarily threaten to eclipse its Western counterparts. China's social structure and cosmological orientation yield strengths and weaknesses that complement, rather than debase, our own Western worldview.

SNAPSHOT

The Chinese have always wanted to advance, to win the game of life, albeit without upsetting the apple cart. This tension leads to three key interrelated and eternal characteristics of Chinese culture that are, directly or indirectly, relevant for practically all marketing strategies:

- a fatalistic, cyclical view of time and space characterized by meticulous interconnectivity of things big and small;
- a morally relativistic universe in which the only absolute evil is chaos and the only good is stability, a platform on which progress is constructed; and
- a view of the family, not the individual, as the basic productive unit of society.

These characteristics translate into quintessentially Chinese adaptive and dysfunctional traits that unify past and present, poor China and prosperous China.

On the plus side, the country has a unique ability to

- mobilize resources for critical strategic undertakings at the national level;
- study other cultures' competitive advantages while adjusting them to suit Chinese circumstances; and
- progress, slowly but surely, toward rational, pre-defined objectives.

Less productively, China continues to be handicapped by

- conformity that discourages bottom-up innovation, and
- an underdeveloped civil society—that is, institutions designed to impartially protect the economic and political interests of the individual.

The contemporary, street-level manifestations of China's cultural blueprint include

- anti-individualistic social cohesion, underpinned by individual identities inextricably linked to the nation and clan, the latter still the elemental unit of Chinese civilization;

- top-down, patriarchal management of business and industry, reinforced by the obligation of CEOs to bow to Communist Party mandarins;
- contemporary consumerism, propelled by the tension between bold status projection and nervous protection of hard-won, easily lost, gains;
- diplomatic pragmatism, characterized by incrementalism and dependence on geopolitical stability.

AN ADVERTISING GUY'S GOAL: EXPLORATION AND DEBATE

To some, advertising executives exist at the fringes of legitimacy. We are neither hard-core business people nor scholars. We do not control the levers of capitalism or offer academic insight. In fact, a few believe our profession is inherently corrupt, profiting from base human desires by transforming them into products pumped out of factories like processed cheese.

On self-deprecating days, however, I remind myself that advertising people exist at the intersection of commerce and culture. Our ultimate goals have always been, first, to identify fundamental motivations for behavior and preference, and, second, to translate these insights into revenue-generating consumer propositions. No matter what the product category or target demographic, insight and profit margin are inextricably linked. In order to transform a mouse into Mickey Mouse, we must be both amateur cultural anthropologists and unaccredited psychologists.

After a four-year stint in Hong Kong, I arrived on the Chinese mainland in 1998. I have been eager to explore the nooks and crannies of modern Chinese life, as many of the firsthand experiences I describe in the later chapters will attest. I bought a classic Shanghai-style house in the heart of the former French Concession, a tree-lined, intimate-yet-lively milieu favored by locals and expatriates alike. I grappled with the teeth-gnashing frustration of home maintenance. I slowly vanquished the prejudices of local neighbors, modest folk who regarded me as an overindulged foreign invader.

Professionally, I have had the privilege of partnering with leaders of dozens of corporations, multinational and local, private and state owned. Directly or indirectly, I have managed, and aspired to motivate, thousands of employees—an aggressive-yet-conservative, inspiring-yet-maddening, starry-eyed-yet-pragmatic group. Together, we have mapped the corners of China's consumer and commercial terrain—from glittering coastal capitals to scrappy, gray, cookie-cutter inland towns. We have infiltrated both Orwellian boardrooms with conference tables the size of squash courts and apartments no larger than a US suburban bathroom.

It is impossible to "manage China" without curiosity, and more important, the willingness to articulate and refine conceptual frameworks. If we lack the courage to formulate operating hypotheses regarding a fundamentally alien worldview, Westerners will be lost. What follows is my take on what makes China Chinese. These theories are, by their nature, generalizations and not necessarily bulletproof. But they have helped me navigate a strange landscape for many years, and I believe they can help others do the same.

MODERN CHINA: CONSTANTS AND VARIABLES

People frequently assume, given my long tenure here, that I have witnessed huge changes. Well, yes and no. Average per capita income—in purchasing power parity terms—has skyrocketed from less than $1,000 per year to more than $6,000. China has become the world's second-largest economy, soaring from industry neophyte in the mid-1990s to manufacturing powerhouse today.

It is also now the world's largest auto market, a phenomenon that has transformed urban and suburban roads beyond recognition. Shanghai's restaurant scene rivals Europe's. If purchases during trips abroad—to, say, Hong Kong or Paris—are taken into account, Chinese consumers are now the most avid buyers of luxury products. Even in lower-tier cities, where the middle class has only recently begun to develop, residents are more worldly and more connected to global forces than during any time in history. China boasts more than 800 million mobile phone subscribers, 500 million Internet users, and 250 million microbloggers (that is, Chinese Twitterers whose number quadrupled in 2011 alone). Connectivity, contrary to media reports, has not been dramatically handicapped by the "Great Firewall," the government's ban on politically sensitive websites and foreign social networks such as Facebook and Twitter. In the realm of pop culture, young Chinese are as intoxicated by *Glee*'s pop cool and *The Big Bang Theory*'s geek chic as their American counterparts.

Diplomatically, China has been integrated into multinational organizations, including the World Trade Organization, the International Monetary Fund, and the G20. Sociologically, the country has also opened up. Divorce rates, almost nonexistent twenty years ago, exceed 40 percent in first-tier cities. Premarital sex, condemned during the 1980s, is now a wedding prerequisite.

China is blessed with an ancient worldview, a cultural blueprint with inviolable constants that nonetheless evolves to accommodate contemporary circumstances. Many observers suggest that the country is in the throes of a spiritual crisis: it is struggling to identify a philosophical and moral center of gravity in the midst of twenty-first-century realities, a disorientation exacerbated by postrevolution ideological swings, including the Cultural Revolution and the contradictions inherent in "socialism with Chinese characteristics" (Deng Xiaoping's description).

I disagree. If anything, the country is in the process of slowly *rediscovering* values that have always set it apart. China has remained a cohesive civilization for more than 5,000 years, through epic ups and downs, from Tang dynasty glory when China *was* the center of the world to Qing era degradation, when the world carved up China. Since the Bronze Age, the country has remained unified by cultural and cosmological truths. It will not abandon them today but rather will leverage them to adapt to changing conditions, both domestic and international.

The 1972 Michelangelo Antonioni documentary, *Chung Kuo—China*, offers a revealing window into these arguments. As his cameras trawl from Beijing to Suzhou to Shanghai to Guangzhou and weave through the countryside, we are transported through time, back several decades to a stripped-down, dusty, and gray nation. Entrepreneurialism, which would have been considered a profane concept, does not exist. Maoist structures, low-tech factories, and utilitarian housing scar the landscape. The contrast with today's China, exploding with neon and color, is stark.

However, by looking into the subjects' eyes, we can still recognize the Chinese soul. The humor, the directness, the wariness, the warmth, the sarcasm, the shrewdness, the knowing wink, the titillated gleam when cash is exchanged, the celebration of small joys…these quintessentially Chinese traits were as evident during the Cultural Revolution as they are today. The film demonstrates the incontrovertible: China is becoming modern and internationalized. But it remains Chinese.

AN EVER-PRESENT CONFLICT: AMBITION VS. REGIMENTATION

Westerners are often disoriented by the seeming paradoxes of contemporary Chinese society. On one hand, the Chinese are cautious and self-protective. They are rule bound, fixated with order, tentative in implementing change, obsessed with preserving face, understated in expressing opinions, and supremely hierarchical. On the other hand, they are ambitious and like to boldly project status, as evidenced by an obsession with luxury brands as tools of advancement. They are also compulsively entrepreneurial, passionate about educational achievement, operatic in industrial aspiration, militantly nationalistic, and driven by success.

Of course, one size doesn't fit all. But there are unifying themes and variations on these themes that reflect socioeconomic and geographic truths. In

Image 1.1   Sean's shy, obedient manner masks determination. One of JWT's hardest working employees, his favorite t-shirt, emblazoned with a Superman logo, is a hint of hidden determination. His style reflects an omnipresent Confucian conflict between ambition and regimentation. (Courtesy Robin Cui)

fact, I am convinced that there is a unifying Confucian conflict—between self-protection and status projection—that brands, by the way, have a fundamental role in resolving. Unlike practically any other country (Korea and Vietnam come closest), China is both boldly ambitious and solidly regimented, with hierarchical and procedural booby traps for anyone who hasn't mastered the system. The tension between upward mobility and fear-based conformism shows up everywhere—in business meetings, in struggles with in-laws, in every new-generation release on the Internet.

The duality can be perplexing. The world is stunned by the nation's epic revolution in its infrastructure and its rise from economic backwater to industrial world-beater. This transformation has been driven by a number of inspiring characters, from Deng Xiaoping, who imposed an economic blueprint upon a chaotic, confused post–Cultural Revolution landscape, to Jack Ma, founder of Alibaba.com, the world's largest business-to-business e-commerce platform.

In many spheres, however, China remains infuriatingly static, blank faced, passive-aggressive, even brain-dead. Decision making within state-owned enterprises is no less opaque than twenty years ago. CEOs continue to toggle between market and political imperatives. The shiny new Boeing 777s shown off by the nation's airlines are misleading. The reality is institutional rot: Carriers are quasi-commercial concerns with strong ties to the military; modern airports are Lego-like, and PA systems blare travelers into submission. Passenger service is an oxymoron; customers are herded onto planes with no departure times; communication between air traffic control and pilots is treated as a state secret.

When the Chinese feel insecure, they retrench, slinking into a self-protective cocoon. Progress comes to a halt; eyes deaden. When they feel safe, they go for it, shifting from the back to front foot. Prodigious productive forces are set in motion. Confident China, kissed by the winds of economic transformation, wants to take off. Fearful China, still awakening from Leninist hibernation, suffers from chronic learned helplessness.

The tension between ambition and regimentation begs two questions. First, how did the conflict come into being? And, second, how does the nation adapt to the contradictions within its own society? These polarized instincts have co-existed since time immemorial and reflect enduring truths of Han civilization—that is, the culture of ethnic Chinese who represent 92 percent of modern mainland China's population. They explain why China is at once inspiring and maddening, rising and falling, the promise of the future and a vestige of the past. As to how the nation adapts, it comes down to striking a balance between the two forces and advancing within the system, not outside of it. So what do the Chinese want? They want to succeed by mastering convention. Challenge to order, natural or societal, is a fool's errand. Ultimately, in order to win, all Chinese need to maintain stability.

THREE TIMELESS TRUTHS

As a result, the Chinese worldview can be distilled into three perpetual yet shape-shifting and interrelated truths:

1. A fatalistic, cyclical view of time and space characterized by meticulous interconnectivity of things big and small
The Chinese excel at logic and linear reasoning. Verbal refinement, in their view, is a lovely asset but not an invaluable one. As such, the Chinese government is populated by a vast legion of statistically obsessed technocratic engineers who have orchestrated—in a step-by-step, top-down manner—a prodigious reformation of the country's transportation, energy, distribution,

Image 1.2 Articulated in the *Book of Changes* about 2,500 years ago, the *ba gua* limns the cyclical interconnectivity of everything from the stars in the sky to sand by the sea. The complexity of China's cosmological design requires years of study to master. (Courtesy ImagineChina)

and housing infrastructure. China, assuming bugs—political or otherwise—have been purged from the system, is a well-oiled, glorious machine. As Miguel Patricio, Asia's chief of beer giant Anheuser-Busch InBev, puts it, "The Chinese Communist Party, on its better days, is a ruthlessly efficient corporation."

The impulse to study, diagram, and prognosticate societal—and cosmological—design is ancient. The *Yi Jing*, or *Book of Changes*, is one of the oldest of the Chinese classical texts. It contains an intricate divination system, the *ba gua*, comprising four masculine (yang) and four feminine (yin) elements that can be combined into sixty-four hexagrams that progress cyclically, shifting from yin to yang and back again. It explains everything from the stars in the sky to the sand by the sea and is instrumental in promoting alignment between heaven and Earth. The earliest version of the text, written on bamboo slips, dates to the latter half of the Warring States period (mid-fourth- to early-third-century B.C.E.) and manifests itself today in predictive readings of all sorts: palmistry, phrenology, feng shui, numerology, and astrology. It explains why the Chinese people, despite the opportunities created by economic development, remain fatalistic, eager to manage destiny but not to challenge their place on Earth.

Critically, the *Book of Changes* centers on the dynamic balance of opposites, the evolution of events as a process and acceptance of the inevitability of change. Even today, the Chinese worldview shuns absolutes of any kind—legal, moral, psychological, economic. Happiness, and success, can occur only when an individual achieves harmony with the surrounding world, which is composed of many variables and few constants. Change, and the wisdom to adapt to its inevitability, is one of the enduring hallmarks of Chinese identity.

2. A morally relativistic universe in which the only absolute evil is chaos and the only good is stability, a platform on which progress is constructed
So the world is ever changing, sharpening an insecure, and pervasive, self-protective instinct. The challenge of balancing opposites, let alone aligning heaven and Earth (that is, cosmological and secular laws) is monumental. In this context, China has always struggled to adapt to the elements. Historically, a suboptimal crop could result in millions of deaths. Every year, the Yellow River burst its banks, often flooding broad swathes of countryside. Earthquakes—omens of celestial displeasure—strike frequently, with pitiless wrath. After the 2008 Sichuan earthquake, a disaster that killed more than 80,000, a shell-shocked nation grieved for seven days—television stations broadcast only in black and white—and then picked itself up and proceeded with the business of preparing for the Beijing Olympics, as if calamity were an inevitable fact of life.

In an unsafe, topsy-turvy universe, stability is prized above all else. All philosophical frameworks indigenous to China reinforce the sublimity of order and the evil of chaos. Consider:

Legalism. This was the governing principle that enabled China's first emperor, Shi Huangdi, to brutally unify the country more than 2,000 years ago. The country's legal framework was built upon threat of punishment, not protection of rights. The Chinese expression "In order to scare the monkeys, you need to kill a chicken" says it all: to prevent turmoil, the interests of a few must be sacrificed for the greater good. Profoundly utilitarian ripples of Legalist philosophy reveal themselves across the Chinese landscape. For example, it helps explain why most people support the death penalty despite the widely acknowledged absence of an independent judiciary and due process of law.

Daoism. Dating from the sixth century B.C.E., Daoism emphasizes *cosmological* order. As I have discussed, the *ba gua* reveals heaven's blueprint. It promises disaster—bad crops, tidal waves, impotence, and indigestion—if humans and nature are not in sync. Daoism, however, is not purely passive. It also promises gain if life is lived according to principles of the Dao. In order to flow, human beings, like water, must assume the shape of that which surrounds them. Harmony with nature is a means to an end, a prerequisite for forward momentum.

In twenty-first-century urban China, Daoist manifestations are everywhere: the enduring appeal of kung fu; the veneration of nature; the ubiquity of bathhouses and spas that fuse over-the-top rococo style and nature; and the admiration of round things, including double eyelids, full moons, and the number eight (8). The influence of Daoism can also be seen in Chinese medicine and in the popularity of feng shui in office design.

Confucianism. The strongest influence in Chinese society, Confucianism, also extols stability as the antecedent of forward momentum. Confucian thought is rooted in a complex code of conduct that explicitly and micro-analytically details, and addresses, the relationship between individual and

Image 1.3 Red banners sporting imperial proclamations—this one urges citizens to build a harmonious socialist society—are ubiquitous. They are one manifestation of the government's patriarchal role vis-à-vis the masses, reinforced by a deeply entrenched Confucian ethos. (Courtesy ImagineChina)

society. The *wu lun,* or five key relationship dyads—between father and son, husband and wife, older brother and younger brother, friend and friend, and ruler and ruled—define the mandates of social intercourse. Confucian thinking reinforces the inviolability of duty and responsibility, as well as a regimented, often ritualistic, approach to daily life. The Chinese are ambitious, socially mobile, and dynamic when liberated from the shackles of insecurity or doubt, but in order to advance, one must accept convention, not rebel against it.

The gravitational pull of Confucian dark matter can be felt everywhere: obsession with face (or status projection) because of its importance in professional and social advancement; submission to authority, particularly during times of crisis or uncertainty; fixation with titles and business cards, the latter exchanged ritualistically; emotional and financial investment in luxury brands, markers of hierarchical achievement; reverence for professors and business tycoons; submission to parental expectations on matters ranging from what car to buy to whom to marry; subjugation to the Communist Party's autocratic implementation of its macroeconomic growth model; slogans emblazoned on red banners promoting "eight honors," "eight shames," and "three represents." (The last are former General Secretary Jiang Zemin's 2002 articulation of the Chinese Communist Party's omnipresent role in Chinese society. They are now enshrined in the constitution. The Communist Party must always guide the development of (a) China's advanced productive capacity, (b) the progressive orientation of China's advanced culture, and (c) the fundamental interests of the broad majority of the people.)

Legalism, Daoism, Confucianism—all propagate China's only morale absolute: stability is good, chaos is bad.

3. A view of the family, not the individual, as the basic productive unit of society

The tension between regimentation and ambition—a pervasive "Confucian conflict" that manifests itself at every level of society and dictates consumer dynamics in every category, from cars to computers to sanitary napkins to shampoo—results in deeply rooted anti-individualism. In China, there are huge egos, yet refusal to go with the flow has always been, and continues to be, a nonstarter. The individual is not the basic productive unit of society. It is the clan. Paternal authority is almost absolute, no matter how successful the son.

The need for acknowledgment is fundamental. Face, the respect or deference from others a person can claim, is the fuel of forward movement. It is traded at boardroom tables when business deals are struck. It is a social bank account. You spend it, save it, invest it. When you take away face, you take away someone's fundamental sense of security.

Image 1.4   Blogger, author, and racing car driver Han Han represents a rare breed of outspoken individualism. He is idolized by many but emulated by few. (Courtesy ImagineChina)

Western individualism encourages each of us to define him- or herself independent of external expectations. We admire Bill Gates and Steve Jobs for the courage of their convictions even more than for their material success. In ambitious China, self-driven identity is an exotic, alluring aspiration, but it is also dangerous. The pursuit of happiness, frivolous without financial gain, is an adolescent escapist fantasy, unacceptable after marriage.

Even the post-1990s singletons run with the pack. Yes, they may be trendy, neon-haired fashionistas who adulate self-made icons such as racer-cum-author-cum-blogger Han Han, Alibaba's Jack Ma, NBA star Kobe Bryant, and, most recently, Jeremy Lin, the New York Knicks point forward, a Harvard-educated Taiwanese American who has emerged from nowhere to take the NBA by storm. Yes, they flock to the Internet to express deeply held convictions, railing against corrupt officials and hegemonic superpowers denying the inevitability of China's rise. However, they do so only when it is safe. Online, they are shielded by virtual anonymity, a digital invisible cloak. At work, employees will resign if pay and title do not increase every eighteen months, but no one expresses opinions with which the boss disagrees or offers recommendations that are not fail-safe.

Standards of success are defined by society, not by the self. In 1992, Deng Xiaoping went on his famous Southern Tour and declared, "To get rich is glorious!" Many Westerners assume China, at that point, embraced a free-market individualistic ethos. Nothing could be further from the truth. Rather, Deng defined asset generation for the motherland's glory as the ultimate achievement.

TIMELESS STRENGTHS

An interconnected, anti-individualistic, protection-based worldview yields enduring adaptive traits, and China has them in spades. These assets will enable the country to sustain its current growth model well into the future.

1. Mobilizing resources for critical strategic undertakings at the national level

For centuries, China has awed the world with its monumental undertakings, harnessing resources from all corners of the country to advance the interests of the nation. Some of these undertakings have been defensive, such as the construction and fortification of the Great Wall during the Han and Ming dynasties. Others, including the engineering of the Beijing-Hangzhou Grand Canal during the Sui dynasty, enhanced labor productivity. All, however, were made possible by a centrally directed administrative structure designed to mobilize resources, both human and material, over vast swathes of time and space.

Critically, individual interests—economic and legal—have always been subordinated to collective imperatives.

This same capacity to operate on a near-biblical scale is behind China's emergence as a modern economic superpower. When the system works, it really works. During the 2003 SARS epidemic, neighborhood tea ladies morphed into dragon queens, monitoring the movement—by plane, train, or automobile—of every resident in every house; meanwhile, more than one million so-called volunteers swept through the countryside to lock down hospitals and educate rural residents about high-risk behavior. For six weeks, an entire mask-wearing nation was practically under house arrest.

More darkly, China's one-child policy has also been enforced by a network of neighborhood watchdogs who report second pregnancies to local officials charged with meeting district birth targets.

The urge to project national greatness and unity focuses minds and resources. The 2008 Beijing Olympics were executed seamlessly against an architectural and infrastructural backdrop that had been transformed, almost beyond recognition, with new airports, wider "ring roads" that encircle the city, five-star hotels, entertainment districts, and modern taxi fleets. In advance of the 2010 Shanghai World Expo, ten subway lines were completed on time and under budget; Shanghai now boasts one of the largest public transportation networks in the world.

Mobilization is also a key element of long-term economic and industrial strategy. Every decade, 10 percent of China's population relocates from villages to cities. To liberate human capital, tens of millions of workers are shifted from low-end agricultural jobs to high-productivity industrial ones. The National Expressway Network Plan, approved in early 2005, will connect the capitals of all provinces and autonomous regions with Beijing and with each other. Half of the projects in the almost 53,000-mile network are already underway.

Finally, the government has identified—and pledged funding to—several strategic industries in which China is to become a world leader: information technology, energy-saving and environmental protection, new energy, bioscience, high-end equipment manufacturing, and energy-efficient vehicles. The country's bureaucracy, just as command and control today as it was a thousand years ago, is trying to orchestrate a new golden age.

The key question is whether China faces a sudden slowdown in growth if it fails to undergo urgent economic and political reforms. Rising social tensions, choking pollution, a lack of public services, and an overreliance on exports and investment are evidence that growth has come at an extremely high cost and is unsustainable in the long term. But at the same time it could be argued that the current phase has some distance still to run. Urbanization rates remain low, slightly over 50 percent; efforts to boost growth in western China have only recently succeeded in raising incomes in lower-tier cities; and the countryside, particularly inland provinces, will be a source of relatively cheap labor for years to come. Most experts believe China's choppy-yet-steady growth will continue apace, albeit at rates marginally lower than the past decade's given the party's desire to gradually rebalance the economy by increasing domestic consumption.

2. Studying other cultures' competitive advantages while adjusting them to suit Chinese circumstances

China rigorously analyzes the world and applies the strengths of other cultures in a Chinese context. Chinese Buddhism, fused with Daoism imported from India, was widely embraced during the Tang dynasty to balance Confucian pragmatic secularism. Trade between Islamic Arabia and China reached its peak during the Mongol Yuan dynasty, itself a foreign power that ruled by assimilation. China's long and interactive relationship with the various steppe tribes and empires paved the way for a large sustained Islamic community within China. Muslims served as administrators and generals. Even during the tumult that preceded the xenophobic Qing dynasty's collapse, progressive leaders such as Kang Youwei attempted the Hundred Days' Reform, with most policies inspired by those of foreign industrialized nations, including Japan.

Communism was, of course, a European import, tailored to suit China's agrarian reality; the first generation of Chinese Communist Party leaders was educated in Moscow. More recently, Jiang Zemin pursued membership in the World Trade Organization to integrate China into the framework of international institutions and also impose external pressure on government officials to, paradoxically, "reform from within," as the apparatchiks like to say.

China is still obsessed with importing and applying expertise from abroad, particularly in the business realm. Foreign joint venture agreements, painstakingly negotiated, focus on technology transfer more than share valuation or long-term profit considerations. Once equipped with Western technology, domestic companies leverage government subsidies and easy access to capital to push down production costs and expand global market share.

Chinese executives come of age during "learning tours" in US business capitals. Bootlegged books by Western CEOs, from Lee Iacocca to Jack Welch, fly off the shelves. (General Electric is *the* role model for all Chinese conglomerates.) Since the 1980s, hundreds of thousands of Chinese have earned advanced degrees at American and European universities; today, the government is calling in its chits, as returnees are drawn back to China, lured by professional gold.

The mainland business of JWT, a communications agency and the company I have led since 1998, also benefits from China's openness. Ten years ago, all of our clients were multinational; in 2010, 50 percent of revenue was generated by local enterprises, both private and state owned. Contrary to perception, even state owned enterprises are willing to pay a premium to gain access to global branding models (whereas in Tokyo, for example, Western agencies remain barbarians at the gates).

China learns from the world, but it rarely cuts and pastes foreign expertise. Everything is adapted to suit Chinese imperatives. Western principles of corporate governance are twisted to fit a Han reality of limited shareholder rights. Copycat Internet sites incorporate features demanded by Chinese surfers, such as enhanced social networking and high-speed entertainment downloads. The rest stops that line China's American-inspired highway system are low-end and gigantic, better for accommodating tour buses than passenger cars.

3. Progressing inch by inch, step by step, toward rational, predefined objectives

China loathes the concept of breakthrough—anything abrupt is anathema. Every radical change, from Zhu Di's Ming dynasty maritime adventurism to Mao's industrialization of the countryside during the Great Leap Forward, ended in tears. But the country is brilliant at implementing gradual reform. The ancient proverb "Dripping water pierces a stone; a saw made of rope cuts through wood" is revealing: in Chinese eyes, haste does more than make waste; it triggers pandemonium.

From automobiles and tennis shoes to nursing home equipment and computer processors, Chinese corporations' slow but sure crawl up the value chain has been relentless. Every state-owned enterprise plays a long game. Twenty years from now, many will have become multinationals, thanks to careful planning. They will microscopically analyze the landscape to uncover hidden risks, from protective lobbyists to growing anti-Chinese nationalism. Similarly, the renminbi will rise—China has no choice, given the need to stimulate consumer spending—but fear of unemployment spikes dictate that, by Western standards, its appreciation will be agonizingly measured.

Looking in the rearview mirror, China's sweeping infrastructural transformation has been revolutionary. But each mile of high-speed railroad has been laid down meticulously and planned a decade in advance. (There have been setbacks. A collision near Wenzhou killed dozens and probably resulted from corruption and poorly enforced safety standards.)

On the diplomatic front, Deng Xiaoping cautioned the nation to "hide your brightness, bide your time" for fear of upsetting the geopolitical order China relies on for economic growth. His warning will not soon be forgotten. A rising China will "cross the river by feeling the stones," inching forward, occasionally overreaching but quickly correcting course, toward its rightful, pragmatically harmonious place on the global stage.

Despite their passion for status, Chinese consumers do not splurge, particularly on risky big-ticket items. Automobiles are usually paid for in cash. Down payments on real estate are often more than 50 percent of the purchase price. Within the household, the milestones of legitimacy have always been crystal clear: Men must *wu shi you wu er zhi yu xue* (set your heart on learning by fifteen), *san shi er li* (be successful by thirty), *si shi bu huo* (have no doubt about yourself by forty), *wu shi er zhi tian ming* (know the mandate of heaven by fifty), *liu shi er er shun* (hear only the mandate of heaven by sixty), *qi shi er cong xing suo bu yu ju* (follow your heart's desire but without transgressing the norms by seventy), and, from birth to death, *guan zong yao zu* (honor and bring glory to ancestors).

Advancement through life stages is equally scrupulous. Young men will not introduce girlfriends to parents unless marriage is in the cards. Family planning is precise; unexpected children are few and far between. Eulogies consist of recitations of the deceased's progression from greenhorn to master of her or his domain.

TIMELESS LIMITATIONS

Will China rule the world? No. The West and the People's Republic of China (PRC) are yin and yang. Our strengths are their disadvantages. Confucian regimentation and an insecurity-driven worldview have always prevented the Chinese, both individually and as a nation, from fully leveraging formidable assets. They are constrained by conformity that militates against bottom-up innovation and by an embryonic civil society in which economic interests remain institutionally unprotected. Neither bodes well for long-term self-sufficiency. China will always need partners, if not friends.

1. Conformity that militates against bottom-up innovation

China has always been weak in inculcating a pioneering ethos. The four great inventions of ancient China—the compass, paper, gunpowder, and printing—were not replicated in Europe until the end of medieval times. However, scientific breakthroughs, common within the confines of the imperial court, were rarely secularized for the benefit of the common person. Across immense sweeps of history, life in the fields remained unchanged for the teeming masses. Despite technological breakthroughs as far back as 771 to 476 B.C.E., the Spring and Autumn Period (e.g., use of cast-iron tools), some modern-day farmers in Hubei still plow fields with buffalo.

Historians debate the roots of this stagnation, but all hypotheses are shaped by anti-individualism. Historian John K. Fairbank argued that China's political system was hostile to scientific progress. Scientist Joseph Needham believed that Daoism was antithetical to the humanist rationalism that gave rise to the Enlightenment and the Industrial Revolution. Sinologist Mark Elvin's "high-level equilibrium trap" postulates the Chinese population "was large enough and workers cheap enough" to not require agrarian mechanization.

Chinese individuals are, of course, capable of creativity—advertising agencies thrive, and artist colonies have popped up in practically all major cities—but they remain largely neutered. Popular filmmakers such as Zhang Yimou, Jiang Wen, and Lu Chuan battle omnipresent, vaguely defined censorship rules; directors across all media are relentlessly ambushed by ultraconservative regulators; the rock scene, punked out and nihilistic, is buried underground.

Commercial innovation in China has always been, and continues to be, a question of top-down diktat, not bottom-up entrepreneurial self-expression. This is manifested by the following characteristics:

Infrequent innovation. China is not—and may never be—a fertile ground for conceptual exploration, leaving it reliant on imports of new ideas and technology. It is true that China's rulers frequently give lip service to the importance

Image 1.5   Commercialized creativity and innovation are limited. One example: most local athletic shoe brands sport a logo suspiciously similar to Nike's swoosh. (Courtesy JWT)

of original thinking. At the November 2011 Asia-Pacific Economic Cooperation (APEC) CEO Summit, Hu Jintao, the PRC's paramount leader, proclaimed, "China has huge market potential and capital. China will work hard to turn itself into an innovation-driven country so we can transition from 'made in China' to 'created in China.'"

The transformation will be easier said than done.

Regression to the mean is everywhere: cookie-cutter television series; indistinct Canto- and Mando-pop musical fare; newspapers and magazines saturated with bland propaganda that neither provokes nor intrigues; rubber-stamped airport designs scarred, from Xiamen to Chengdu, by identical low-end building materials; cheaply produced household appliances sporting random bells and whistles; ubiquitous pirated mobile phones; dozens of sneaker brands adorned with clunky variations of Nike's swoosh; a dynamic luxury scene that has never produced a Chinese label; undifferentiated, bombastic advertising that dulls the senses; a brandscape that thrives on scaled commoditization rather than differentiation.

China's education system is partly to blame. Though meritocratic, it is stultifying, ultraconformist, and all about learning by rote. Americans compose original essays on "my summer vacation" or "my favorite book" almost as soon as they learn the alphabet. Students here do not ask questions in class, let alone challenge the teacher. At university, they are conditioned to "receive wisdom," even in highly interpretative majors such as literature or mass communications. Class participation counts for nothing. When fresh graduates enter the workforce, their lips are sealed and their bosses go unchallenged. New ideas are suppressed and professional development is limited, leading to frustrated ambition and chronic job-hopping among young people.

Organizations are not equipped to generate and commercialize new ideas. Corporations are rigidly hierarchical, with power concentrated in the hands of imperial CEOs whose priority is balancing market demand and political requirements. Procurement departments are pay-to-play black holes. In faction-driven offices, self-starters are reduced to drones, afraid of expressing unconventional opinions lest they become ostracized from the power structure. Marketing departments are beholden to sales mandarins, most of whom view low price, not added value, as the ultimate competitive advantage.

Entrepreneurs do not have it easy, either. Even during lending binges, banks favor large state-owned enterprises that have strong ties to the central government. Small- and medium-sized businesses are therefore perpetually starved for capital. As 2011 drew to a close, Wenzhou, a city in which most economic activity is privately generated, was in the throes of an ominous debt crisis and credit crunch. Manufacturers were forced to seek loans from back-street lenders at usurious rates, sometimes approaching 90 percent. Many bosses skipped town. Meanwhile, Andy Xie, a noted Shanghai-based economist, called Wenzhou's lending practices a Ponzi scheme.

Stunted services. The woeful state of China's service sector is the inevitable consequence of a power structure that frowns on independent thinking and autonomous decision making. Services account for only 40 percent of economic activity; in India, services' share is 55 percent, despite a much lower gross domestic product (GDP). China has made laudable progress implementing large-scale, technologically proficient solutions to enhance mass-market efficiency: branches of the major banks can be found on every corner in every city; airline reservations are now made online; e-ticketing is pervasive; mortgage applications have been standardized; and the stock market is fully accessible to individual investors. But genuine, personally responsive service is nowhere to be found except, only intermittently, at the very tip of the socioeconomic pyramid.

Image 1.6 Service in China is still scripted, armylike and robotic. Among airline, restaurant, and retail staff, individual initiative is rarely encouraged. This is a picture of morning training outside a department store. (Courtesy ImagineChina)

A genuine service ethos requires the courage to go off script, probe into customer motivations, tailor individual responses, and even make mistakes. It also requires challenging past practices and experimenting with empirically untested solutions. In framework-fixated China, the qualitative dimensions of world-class service are scarier than bungee jumping. Hence the blank stares that greet unfamiliar requests at five-star hotels and the swarms of saleswomen at high-end department stores who accost customers without first asking what they want.

The founder of New Sun, a relatively large local ad agency in Guangzhou, is confident China will, one day soon, develop and market a revolutionary product like the iPad. Sorry, but that is extremely unlikely. It is not just a problem of lax protection of intellectual property; it's that, in China, there is no Steve Jobs of Apple or Mark Zuckerberg of Facebook. Creative mavericks are personae non gratae—they are eaten by the system and absorbed back into the bloodstream of the body politic. The PRC's anti-individualism culture does not, and will not, celebrate originality. Even Jack Ma, Alibaba's iconic leader, based his business-to-business e-commerce platform on traditional Chinese strengths: efficiency maximization and scaled resource mobilization.

2. An embryonic civil society in which economic interests remain institutionally unprotected

Where to begin? Unruly fans marring the 2012 Beijing launch of Apple's iPhone 4S; untrained judges; rampant kickbacks within provincial party organs; pervasive protectionism that corrupts local judicial decision making; epic eminent domain abuses by real estate companies in bed with district-level apparatchiks; unenforced environmental regulation; ill-defined property rights; a Communist superstructure with few mechanisms for self-discipline; rogue officials who strong-arm office relocations in exchange for tax breaks; fatal fires in Shanghai skyscrapers; patchy intellectual property protection; milk tainted with melamine; thousands of deaths in Dickensian mines; more than a dozen Foshan city passersby ignoring a two-year-old toddler who lay in the street, critically wounded by a hit-and-run driver; rural child kidnappings and reports of child slavery.

Civility exists on two planes: interpersonal and societal. In China, both are full of potholes. On an interpersonal level, there has been significant progress in recent years. The happy combination of economic growth, global commercial engagement, an influx of foreign expatriates, and digital connectivity has made the Chinese less fearful of the outside world. Elevator etiquette has improved; line cutting occurs less frequently, at least in coastal cities. Many restaurants have nonsmoking sections. Philanthropy is becoming more popular, whether it is business moguls warming up to the notion of donating chunks of their fortunes to charity or the general public offering financial support in the wake of disasters. Drivers are slightly less aggressive; crossing the street during rush hour is no longer quite the death trek it was a few years ago.

Still, standards of interpersonal propriety are low. In crowded planes, business people blare into mobile phones. Spitting on the street is rampant. Most relationships remain quid pro quo, predicated on mutual interest or familial obligation, not mutual respect.

On a societal level, there are few institutions to safeguard the economic and legal interest of individuals. Civic organs—from commercial courts and stock markets to the media and consumer protection agencies—explicitly serve the interests of the Communist Party, itself in self-protection mode. They are therefore inherently unreliable. The schizophrenic attitudes of the masses toward the party—faith in its ability to both advance collective interest and sustain a rising economic tide versus skepticism of its willingness to defend the little guy—result in a curious blend of personal anxiety, anger, and long-term confidence. This codependent, love-hate relationship explains the juxtaposition of stratospheric savings rates and willingness to purchase cars that cost more than 100 percent of yearly income, and Internet users who rail against both corrupt officials who abuse the masses and American politicians who inhibit China's rise.

The power structure, intent on maintaining dominion over strategic affairs of state, breeds a population trapped in protracted adolescence, tentative about engagement with the broader world. This mind-set, reinforced by both the weakness of contemporary institutions and a fixed belief that individual interests should be trumped by the need for stability, guarantees that civil rights in line with global standards will be elusive for decades to come. The fabric of Chinese society will remain brittle, stunting the evolution of dynamic capital markets, an independent judiciary, intraparty checks and balances, market-driven health care, transparent commercial lending practices, nongovernmental organizations (NGOs), corporate boards of directors, an independent media, and other entities that maximize economic and individual productivity.

CHINA TODAY: PRESENTNESS OF THE PAST

"If you want to know your past, look into your present conditions. If you want to know your future, look into your present actions." This Chinese proverb states an obvious truth: Ingrained behavior will not be swept away by *American Idol* and *Prison Break* fan clubs or even the winds of digital revolution. Tomorrow's China will reflect the present. Today's China, and the street-level manifestations of its culture, will reflect the past.

China is becoming modern and internationalized. But the fundamentals of the national identity are hardwired. China, eminently pragmatic, is still gun shy—it will not aggressively rock the boat. The country will be engaged with the world, but it will lead only if narrow self-interests can be advanced. The reasons include:

1. Anti-individualistic social cohesion, underpinned by individual identities inextricably linked to the nation and clan
Chinese society is racing forward, but it is not cracking up or spinning off its axis. The traditional pillars of individual identity—the family and the nation—remain robust. True, there are stresses that disorient people. Families are torn apart by geographic dispersion as sons and daughters, at all socioeconomic levels, wander far from their hometowns in search of better jobs. Digital technology has created a new generation of socially stunted video game addicts unplugged from offline reality. The imbalance between male and female births, and a resulting surfeit of single men, exacerbates both digital dependency and anxiety about a future without wife or family, still the epitome of

failure in a society built on clans, not individuals. Money is a new god, sanctified by a government that has forfeited ideological purity to shepherd the masses toward an illusory materialistic high ground. Religion, meanwhile, remains a dangerous balm, particularly in the countryside, where membership in illegal underground organizations, mostly Christian, put millions of adherents at great risk.

Cautious optimism. Yet the Chinese do not feel helpless. A rising economic tide, one that has already lifted 200 million out of poverty, has resulted in disorientation but not despair. Despite the gulf between rich and poor, residents of lower-tier cities sense they are at life's starting line and thirst for a piece of the action. Incomes are rising in China's hinterlands, thanks in part to government tax incentives and massive infrastructure investment. There are few blank faces. Eyes sparkle. Foreigners still elicit giggling curiosity. Factory workers, thousands of miles from home, saunter hand in hand through factory gates. Young men release frustration on ubiquitous basketball courts. Modest, though modern, restaurants teem with activity, a cacophonous delight of bantering, bragging, and gossip.

Family ties. What sustains China during an era of tumult? Aggregate optimism—faith that, despite setbacks, the government's strategy is working—is one important factor. But, more subtly, most Chinese are not lost. The family, the most important societal unit by far, is intact. Divorce rates have spiked, but husbands who abandon their wives and kids are still scorned. (One former colleague whispered to me, "Have you heard about my scandal? I remarried.") Educated Chinese are marrying later—the average age in primary cities is about twenty-seven for men and twenty-five for women—but practically everyone exchanges vows before thirty. All children, regardless of income or class, send money to parents as a token of respect and out of a deep sense of obligation. And, even as the number of nursing homes increases, a son's or daughter's greatest shame remains what is regarded as abandoning elderly parents in institutions.

National pride. Chinese define themselves not only as citizens of the People's Republic of China but as apostles of a great Chinese civilization. National affiliation, and growing confidence in their country's place in the world, is a tremendous stabilizer. Pragmatically, it fuels faith in future financial stability. Emotionally, it bolsters individual identities. The aforementioned Confucian conflict—the tension between restrictive regimentation and relentless ambition—yields both repression and an unquenchable thirst for achievement and acknowledgment. But at least frustrated individuals can project their personal dreams of glory onto the nation. Every achievement—from the success of the Olympics to sustained year-on-year 10 percent GDP growth—is deeply satisfying. Of course, there is a fine line between patriotism and nationalism.

Underlying individual insecurity, not to mention relentless propaganda regarding foreign suppression of China's ascent, often leads to jingoist outbursts, particularly against the Japanese, an equally nationalistic people. Online chat rooms are hornets' nests of zealotry, suggesting that the new generation is angry. But this is a dramatic oversimplification. China wants to engage with the world, and as long as its people don't feel rejected, nationalistic indignation will not boil over.

Entrenched anti-individualism. China remains deeply anti-individualistic, with the country and clan as the key pillars of identity. Rebellion against the system is a nonstarter. Various youth subtribes intermittently bubble to the surface of contemporary urban life: popular affiliation groups like "vegetable males" (Chinese metrosexuals), "Taobao Maniacs" (online shopping aficionados), and "Art and Culture Gangs" represent a level of heretofore unseen self-expressive drive. Yet societal acknowledgment is still tantamount to success. Liberal arts majors will always be considered inferior to those with engineering or accounting degrees. Few dare to see a psychologist for fear of losing face or being branded sick. Gays still walk voluntarily into prison marriages. Failure to have a child is still a grave disappointment. Travel is still more about status than enjoyment.

Paternalistic government. Will China discover democracy? Not any time soon, despite the hopeful projections of some Western political scientists and economists. The concept of one person, one vote is a theoretical abstraction in China, not a compulsion that reflects individuals' view of their rightful relationship with society. Sons do not sass fathers; subjects do not challenge sovereigns. Of course, local protests—against land usurpation, eminent domain abuse, taxi fuel prices, and so on—happen every day in this huge country but are quickly put down and pose no real threat to the establishment. (One of the most dramatic uprisings against unlawful land seizure occurred in Wukan, a town in Guangdong province, in September 2011. In December, after senior officials had fled the scene, police forces laid siege to the city. In the end, however, provincial authorities and residents reached agreement on compensation and protesters pledged loyalty to the party.)

Chinese fear chaos; they are unable to imagine social order without autocratic control. They can hypothetically grasp the link between efficient resource allocation and leadership accountability, but no one has ever articulated a clear roadmap of political reorganization, one that yields stable, bottom-up representation. This includes Liu Xiaobo, the imprisoned winner of the Nobel Peace Prize; much of his "Charter 08," a peaceful call for democracy and human rights, is naive, lifted directly from the U.S. Declaration of Independence. Assuming the system does not come apart at the seams—and there is no immediate reason to suggest it will—the government will do nothing more than tinker with self-disciplinary reform, and likely will not be fundamentally challenged.

2. Top-down, patriarchal management of business and industry, reinforced by the obligation of CEOs to bow to Communist Party mandarins

There is no evidence to suggest the party is *fundamentally* reconsidering its traditional approach to growth. In fact, cultural factors preclude dramatic departure from China's management modus operandi.

Macroeconomically, the key strategy is still urbanization, which entails massive infrastructure investment and the upgrade of nonproductive rural workers into higher-productivity manufacturing workers. Factories are being built on rural farmland, as are transportation networks to ship raw and semi-finished goods between lower-tier cities and the coast. The party believes China can, as a whole, maintain its low-cost labor pool for at least the next twenty years, particularly in inland provinces. Wage hikes are not resisted: they conform to the wider economic objective to boost domestic consumption; they facilitate the movement of industries to lower-cost locations in the interior; and their impact is to some extent negated by the fact that China's workforce is larger and more skilled, and its logistical resources more developed, than those of its regional peers.

In many ways, China's key strengths—the mobilization of resources and scaled markets—are inconsistent with any leap up value chains, although this is the government's stated objective. As noted in my discussion of the nation's "timeless strengths," the Chinese model is appropriate for incremental creation of value. From green technology to autos, favored companies are on the verge of international expansion, but no industry has had anything close to a paradigm shift in terms of setting global standards of innovation.

Microeconomically, the development of strategic industries—anything that shapes the lives of the masses or impacts raw material production and supply—is orchestrated by the government. The "big four" banks, the "big three" airlines, the "big three" telecom operators, and the "big three" oil and gas firms are all, directly or indirectly, wards of the party. Even in more fragmented industries—steel is a good example—the major players are state controlled. Leadership selection, geographic domination, and new technology usage rights are determined within the inner sanctum of the party's Central Steering Committee. Sectors burdened with overcapacity, such as automobile manufacturing, will be restructured within the next few years, following protracted negotiations between rival power factions.

The heavy hand of bureaucracy can be felt everywhere: mammoth lobbies, omnipresent security forces, wall-to-wall propaganda banners, and dour facial expressions. When CEOs speak, they adopt the same style—booming cadences that crescendo to staccato falsetto when key points approach or applause is required.

Companies in nonpriority industries are laboratories of experimentation. Free of ties to the state, they are evolving from producing cheap products to creating value-added brands. Winners include the sportswear chains Anta, Lining, and 361; home appliance behemoth Haier; computer manufacturer Lenovo; a string of fashion and apparel firms, including Lilang, Tangshi, Metersbonwe, and Jasonwood; and various newly established tech-sector players such as Sohu, Baidu, Tencent, and Alibaba. These companies often struggle to obtain bank loans, so they operate on private investment and, ultimately, stock market listings. Anta's story is not uncommon. In 2004, it generated about US$150 million in revenue and its products were available in one thousand stores. By 2010, revenue was up tenfold and the group had more than 10,000 retail outlets, both owned and franchised, mostly in lower-tier areas, small cities with limited average annual income per capita.

Despite relative freedom, the majority of private enterprises are managed in a quintessentially Chinese fashion. They bear many of the same strengths and weaknesses as state-owned firms: distribution scale, low prices as a competitive weapon, broad awareness but low consumer loyalty, limited innovation, and inconsistent brand imagery. Resources are not harnessed against a strategic vision. Sales barons, driven by short-term considerations, are powerful and hold sway over thousands of reps. Corruption is endemic within procurement departments. There is limited investment in market research or in-depth consumer insight. Authoritarian CEOs are self-protective, maintaining their place at the top by issuing ambiguous instructions that trigger anxiety among underlings. CEOs also divide and conquer by propagating rival power factions. Corporate structure is both hierarchical and Balkanized, discouraging creative thinking and challenges to convention.

The Chinese business model, adopted in both state-owned and private concerns, is appropriate for a nation mobilized to urbanize. It suits a culture with faith in the efficacy of top-down, command-and-control leadership. Nothing on the horizon suggests China's paradigm is about to run out of steam. Yes, the upper middle class demands increasingly high levels of product innovation and service, but they account for only 5 percent of the population. For the next two or three decades, China is determined to get the basics right. The country's business modus operandi is rational; it also complements Western strengths (fluid markets, vibrant venture capital, collaborative networks, and an eagerness to nurture new thinking). If the West continues to sharpen its advantages, China poses no threat to American and European prosperity.

3. Contemporary consumerism, propelled by the tension between bold status projection and nervous protection of hard-won, easily lost, gains

Buffeted by globalization and modernization, Chinese social structures, rooted in societal acknowledgment and diffused insecurity, endure. Mainland consumer behavior, characterized by simultaneous status projection and risk avoidance, reflects these truths.

Status and public consumption. In China, consumers regard brands as tools for success, not self-actualization or fulfillment. Publicly consumed products command huge price premiums relative to goods used in private. All leading mobile phone brands, for example, are international. Even in tier-five and tier-six cities, Nokia still commands a 30 percent market share, despite significantly higher retail prices relative to local competitors. Sony's Handycam, a product brandished outside the home, boasts 50 percent market share. However, Sony televisions are still niche products, since it's likely only the family will see them. The leading household appliances are, without exception, cheap domestic brands such as Haier, TCL, and Changhong.

The "public display" imperative leads to fundamental positioning differences from Western markets. Benefits should be externalized, not internalized. Even for luxury goods, appeals to individualism do not work. Automobiles should make a statement about a person on the way up. Sport cars—"thrill vehicles"—are not big sellers. BMW has successfully fused its global "ultimate driving machine" proposition with a Chinese declaration of ambition. Passat, Honda, Toyota, Ford, and Buick are also positioned as status vessels. Even beer must *do* something. In Western countries, letting the good times roll is enough; in China, pilsner must bring people together, reinforce trust, and optimize opportunity for mutual (financial) gain.

The importance of public display is also a critical consideration in shaping business models. Starbucks in China is not a comfortable environment in which to relax and sip coffee. To conform to local tastes, the company broadened the sandwich menu, identified prime real estate, and expanded average store size. From day one, it successfully established itself as a public place in which professional tribes gather to proclaim affiliation with the new-generation elite.

Insecurity and price sensitivity. Every day, the Chinese confront shredded social safety nets, a lack of institutions that protect individual wealth, contaminated food products, and myriad other risks to home and health. Therefore, consumers' instinct to project status through material display is counterbalanced by conservative buying behavior, regardless of socioeconomic level. Protective benefits are the primary consideration for consumers. Even high-end paint advertising must focus on nontoxicity before it moves on to colorful self-expression. Baby formula commands huge price premiums in both middle-class and mass markets. Safety is a key benefit for Mercedes and Ford Fiesta buyers alike.

The Chinese will never spend freely. Savings rates will always be higher than in the West. There is no question the consumer economy will expand as incomes and purchasing power rise, but price sensitivity runs deep. One anonymous viral email that made the rounds in late 2010 as inflation was gathering pace said it all: "Can't afford to be born because a Caesarean costs RMB50,000; can't afford to study because schools cost at least RMB30,000; can't afford to live anywhere because each square meter is at least RMB20,000; can't afford to get sick because pharmaceutical profits are at least tenfold; can't afford to die because cremation costs at least RMB30,000."

New media, traditional values. Finally, digital technology has not transformed consumer behavior at an elemental level. For all the savvy of youth and the broader awareness of the outside world, Chinese Internet users' underlying conservatism is clear. First, despite the explosive growth of e-commerce, online transactions are still relatively infrequent, particularly when compared to the high levels of digital usage in major cities and, increasingly, smaller towns. According to the China Internet Network Information Center, by 2008, only 25 percent of Internet users had bought something online, and most of those purchases involved offline cash-for-product exchanges. The barriers are not technological; people still do not feel safe making electronic payments. Second, so-called digital liberation is anonymous. Social networking sites such as Sina Weibo (a Chinese version of Twitter) as well as Renren and Kaixing Wang (Chinese versions of Facebook) are popular platforms of self-expression. But even the angriest online protesters hide behind avatars and pseudonyms. To quote one online gaming fan: "I can be gay. I can be king of darkness. I can be whoever I want to be because no one knows who I am." A joint survey conducted by JWT and IAC, a leading Internet holding company, supports the importance of online anonymity. Less than a third of young Americans agree with the statement "I feel free to do and say things I wouldn't do or say offline," and many (41 percent) disagree. Among Chinese respondents, almost three-quarters (73 percent) agree, and just 9 percent disagree.

4. Diplomatic pragmatism, characterized by incrementalism and dependence on geopolitical stability

China will find its place in the world, but the path to geopolitical harmony will be bumpy. There is much evidence of trouble, unnerving veteran China watchers: an opaque military buildup; reversion to platitudes after recurring North Korean military provocation; castigation of countries attending Liu Xiaobo's Nobel Peace Prize ceremony; a blind eye to both Sudanese sponsorship of genocide in Darfur and Iran's nuclear weapons program; over-the-top grandstanding after America's weapon sales to Taiwan; trumped-up charges of American bellicosity when a Chinese plane was downed off Hainan island; monopolistic suspension of the export of rare earths; hysterical anti-Japanese brinkmanship following a naval skirmish off the disputed Diaoyu islands; tetchy border disputes with many countries, including India and Pakistan; and outlandish claims of dominion over the South China Sea; the January 2012 veto of a United Nations resolution to censure the Syrian government for killing more than 5,000 unarmed protesters.

But the country's bark is worse than its bite.

China is, awkwardly, testing the limits of newfound clout. It is uncompromising on certain issues perceived as core national interests—the supply of natural resources or Taiwanese, Tibetan, and Xinjiang separatism—but no one wants to rock the boat. Fearing chaos, China is grappling to demarcate, and avoid, red lines of conflict. As such, North Korea will not be allowed to spark a nuclear arms race, the renminbi will appreciate (albeit slowly—there are domestic interests at play here as well), and China will seek compromises with trading partners on issues ranging from intellectual property protection to luxury import tariffs. As one leader of a large state-owned enterprise confided to me, "In the end, we are afraid of not having any friends."

China's most fundamental interest remains the global stability that has made its emergence as an industrial power possible. This is why it is actively engaged in all major international institutions, including the World Trade Organization, International Health Organization, United Nations, World Bank, G8, International Monetary Fund, and Asia-Pacific Economic Forum. Even the People's Liberation Army, China's powerful military, does not advocate belligerence: for thirty years, no islands have been seized and no borders crossed.

Finally, what about the Sino-American relationship? We do not need to be afraid. In thirty years, the United States will no longer be the world's largest economy, but if investment in innovation continues, it could be the most productive. Anyway, the Chinese do not want to beat the United States; they want to stand beside it, proudly. They are suspicious of America's government but fond of its people. They admire American scale and ambition and adore its pop culture. Young Chinese like to work for open and apolitical American bosses. In the end, the seeds of constructive engagement are already planted but must be painstakingly harvested.

China is evolving, but its trajectory will never collide with that of the West. Fortunes have waxed and waned over thousands of years, but Chinese civilization has remained apart. Enduring fundamentals—morality rooted in stability, anti-individualism, and a microanalytic, balance-obsessed worldview—fuel contemporary growth but preclude China's ascendance as a superpower capable of projecting its values abroad. The country, aware of its limitations, will be content to collaborate with the United States in twenty-first-century prosperity. If America accepts this inevitability, we will all be fine.

PART TWO

TOP DOWN: DOING BUSINESS IN CHINA

2

ANTA AND ALWAYS: AN INTRODUCTION TO CHINESE BUSINESS

Cai Hua, founder of Always, China's most extensive field marketing operation, and Ding Shizhong, founder of Anta, the country's largest sports shoe and apparel manufacturer, are two of the most impressive business people with whom I have had the pleasure of working. Through sheer force of will, they have emerged as iconic heroes of their respective industries. Their companies reflect the current realities, both cultural and operational, of doing business in China.

Cai and Ding both hail from Fujian, an outward-looking province that extends along the Taiwan Strait and was home to China's earliest seafaring emigrants. Cai is a self-made man who started his career as a Procter & Gamble sales representative. Ding took over a small shoe company started by his father. Between 2000 and 2010, both Always and Anta emerged from practically nowhere to dominate their domains.

The development strategies of the two companies are, for better and for worse, quintessentially Chinese. So too are the leadership styles of both men.

National mobilization. In China, bigger is better. Without scale, it is impossible to dominate unwieldy distribution, sales, and retail networks; force order from chaos across a primordial consumer terrain; and achieve low fixed costs and leverage low price as a competitive weapon. Always boasts more than one hundred offices and directly manages, or has access to, a field force of more than 70,000 promoters. Anta, a nonplayer ten years ago, currently ranks among the top twenty mainland firms in terms of stock market valuation and enjoys more than RMB10 billion in annual sales, spread across 10,000 retail outlets, each practically identical in design and stock.

For both leaders, a well-oiled network transcends efficiency. It is a source of deep pride. When Cai Hua gave a motivational speech to his city managers, his eyes filled with tears as he proclaimed his troops a "modern military," the "soul of our machine." His words, mechanistic to Westerners, triggered profound emotion among audience members. In China, scale begets security. Unity yields strength.

Global embrace. Neither company has any desire to export its product internationally, at least not into developed markets. Given the robust growth of lower-tier mainland cities, both Anta and Always are content to deepen their domestic penetration. Anta, historically strong in third- and fourth-tier urban areas, has recently begun a major thrust into second-tier provincial capitals. However, the company's eyes are not bigger than its stomach. It is tentative in developing its business in primary coastal cities such as Shanghai and Beijing (except for an occasional flagship store for image purposes) and has no plans for active marketing support in Western markets within the next five, or even ten, years. Always, for its part, refuses to consider extending its services into Taiwan or Hong Kong, let alone farther afield.

That said, Anta and Always are passionate about learning from abroad and applying those insights in a Chinese context to strengthen competitive advantage. Always entered into a joint venture with Smollan, South Africa's leading field marketing organization, to facilitate deployment of an outsourced sales management capability. When WPP, the communications holding company, purchased a majority share of Always from Cai, he was edgy about enforcing compliance with the rigorous accounting standards of the 2002 Sarbanes-Oxley Act. He and his finance team, however, quickly realized that global standards of transparency could be a competitive advantage locally, particularly since multinational companies had already become Always's largest clients. Anta was one of the first local companies to establish a stable relationship with a foreign advertising agency, well before its initial public offering in Hong Kong. The shoe company has also been relentless in restructuring its marketing and finance operations in accordance with international practices. Finally, Anta has adopted a checklist of global quality standards—it subjects its products to rigorous testing to ensure a favorable price-value equation.

Incremental progression, modest innovation. There are no revolutions in corporate China. As they crawl up the value-added ladder, Always and Anta are committed to building from the base. Anta has streamlined, systematized, and standardized procurement. While the company's wholesale price to cost-of-goods ratio has crept up over time, it has never attempted to position itself as a premium, fashionable shoe. It has introduced a series of innovations—such as "A-Jelly" technology for enhanced "bouncing power"—but there has been no breakthrough along the lines of Nike Plus (shoes equipped with computer chips to monitor heart beats) or NikeID (personalized design). When asked what he most fears, Ding replied, "We must not have a Great Leap Forward. We are still a fragile company."

Likewise, Always sticks to its knitting. The company has gradually transformed itself from a network into a smart network. Promoters are armed with easy-to-input smart phones that measure and monitor store activity in real time. Over the years, service range has expanded to include promoter training, road shows, and point-of-purchase material management. But leadership adamantly refuses to branch into anything disconnected from its core strength of geographic coverage—say, sexy one-off public relations extravaganzas or high-end creative development.

Imperial leadership. Innovation, while valued, is stunted for two reasons. First, it is not a fundamental strategic priority, given the primacy of managing

Image 2.1 Ding Shizhong is the leader of Anta, mainland China's largest sports shoe and apparel manufacturer. The company was founded by his father. Ding is the company's driving force and a passionate advocate for the brand. He rules with a unique combination of imperial authority and informal accessibility. A proud native of Fujian province, the forty-one-year-old is also one of China's wealthiest entrepreneurs. (Courtesy Ding Shizhong)

scale. Second, patriarchal corporate culture militates against conceptual experimentation. Cai and Ding are both physically unimposing, soft-spoken men.
But they rule with an iron fist. They are beloved but feared. Decisions result
from behind-the-curtain wheeling and dealing, and when policies are issued,
they are promulgated as royal proclamations. In a group setting, few dare
to offer new solutions if there is even the slightest risk of transgressing pre-
ordained conclusions. Both leaders project omnipotence. Cai's office is the size
of a football field, complete with an elaborate Buddhist shrine. Within Anta,
Ding's ascension to the National Committee of the Chinese People's Political
Consultative Conference was glorified in local media as tantamount to Christ's
second coming. A private audience in his office—expensive Fujian tea is ritualistically served—commands hushed awe. A recent coup: securing the title sponsorship of the Chinese Olympic Committee, which immediately elevated him to
the highest echelon of the national sports hierarchy.

In the upcoming chapters, we will hopscotch across an array of topics, each
of which reinforces the distinct dynamics of China's patriarchal, cautious-yet-
ambitious business culture, including the cultural barriers that preclude the
rise of innovative Chinese brands; the protective instinct of marketers during
the 2009 financial crisis; boardroom dynamics and the importance of trust
facilitation; the golden rules of marketing in status-driven yet insecure China;
structural obstacles that prevent corporations from harnessing the digital revolution; the rise and fall of Tang Jun, an iconic business leader obsessed with
face; tips on stimulating creativity in a sea of convention; "understatedly grand"
design aesthetics that elicit loyalty among the high and mighty; and a behind-
the-scenes peek into China's *shanzhai* (that is, counterfeit) and illegal DVD
industries.

3

THE RISE OF CHINESE BRANDS: A DISTANT DREAM

When the Chinese company Geely purchased the Swedish carmaker Volvo from Ford Motor Company for $1.8 billion in 2010, it was the highest-profile Western purchase by a Chinese firm in recent years. However, it was by no means the only one. In almost every case, the Chinese acquirer was looking to better establish and develop its brands overseas. The massive decline in asset values in the United States and Europe meant deals could be made for bargain prices.

The purchase, however, is just part of the battle. Whether any Chinese manufacturer of consumer goods is in a position to compete at a price premium directly against established brands in developed markets, sustained by robust brand equity, price premiums, and consumer loyalty, is a separate question. And the answer right now is no. Although some brands—TCL, China Mobile—are making progress in emerging markets such as India, Africa, and South America, they are not in a position to go head to head with Western counterparts on their home turf. Telecom equipment manufacturer Huawei and household appliance manufacturer Haier have made more progress than other domestic corporations. Huawei's products and services have been deployed in more than 140 countries and it currently serves 45 of the world's 50 largest telecoms operators. According to Euromonitor, the market research firm, Haier is the largest kitchen appliance manufacturer in the world and currently generates approximately 30 percent of sales from overseas markets. The company has captured 10 percent of the United States refrigerator market and has set up research and development centers in America, Europe, and the Middle East. However Haier's momentum is still based on an acceptable price-value equation—that is, cheap and good enough—rather than active consumer preference.

Chinese companies, to their credit, are savvy incrementalists. Most know they're not ready to unfurl their flags in the West. But domestically they have crawled their way up the value chain. Cars are getting better. Athletic shoes are becoming more technologically advanced. Food-processing standards are improving. Many local brands have started to forge real consumer equity. The Chinese National Cereals, Oils and Foodstuffs Corporation implemented systems to ensure truly integrated communications and established itself as the country's safest food manufacturer. Anta's China Olympic Committee sponsorship had a three-year roll-out plan centered on a core proposition of turning China into a sporting nation. Even jeans brand Jasonwood has significantly upgraded its marketing staff to provide positioning consistency, both over time and with product development. On a general level, companies have also gradually increased their prices relative to cost of goods, bolstered by product innovation and more robust brand equity.

Many domestic brands also have more or less stable relationships with international advertising agencies. In 2005, five out of the top ten media spenders were local players, most of them fly-by-night pharmaceutical companies that blanketed the airwaves with unfocused ads, only to retreat into obscurity months later. Today, dairy companies Yili Group and China Mengniu, telecom carriers China Mobile and China Unicom, and beverage maker Wahaha are fixtures in the top ten, and they are here to stay.

But success for these brands in developed international markets is a long way off.

KEY EXPANSION HANDICAPS

Competition in developed international markets requires a price premium, rooted in both value-added—not parity—products or services, and strong brand equity. The last can be acquired only gradually over time. In these respects, Chinese brands are still disadvantaged, in many cases grievously so, and not just by a generic fear of anything stamped "Made in China."

Scale vs. value. Focusing on scale without a commitment to innovation implies commoditization, not an unreasonable domestic strategy in a market as large, geographically dispersed, and untamed as China. Distribution clout and competitive prices linked to economies of scale are huge advantages. This is particularly true in large state-owned or state-sponsored sectors such as appliances, banks, and auto and telecom industries. For example, China's major telecom providers were recently restructured into three companies—China Mobile, China Telecom, and China Unicom—offering mobile, fixed-line, and broadband services in order to facilitate the rollout of third-generation services and boost average revenue per user. But managed competition is inherently unhealthy. The decision-making apparatuses of these companies are very rigid.

They are traditional in outlook and management structures, and they frown upon entrepreneurial thinking and the risk taking that generates innovation.

On the flip side, smaller companies, usually private enterprises in the food, fashion, and beverage industries, tend to be more innovative. But they do not have the scale required for international expansion. It is a catch-22: Companies big enough to go global are the most encumbered by commoditized products and services. Companies that grasp advantages inherent in value-added products and services—that is, the ability to charge a premium—lack the critical mass to become global power brands.

Centralized corporate structure. Chinese companies' management structures are not built to encourage global brand expansion. They are sales driven and managed by emperor-kings who rule in a defensive manner. Quite often, instructions are promulgated ambiguously, creating an undercurrent of permanent anxiety at lower levels. Furthermore, many managers create rival power centers under them so competition is horizontal rather than vertical. Ultimately, this is a failing of corporate governance. There is no local management team that reports to an independent board of directors charged with ensuring long-term shareholder growth. As a result, organizational structure is too centralized and planning too short term.

The Japanese and Korean difference. Like Chinese brands, Korean and Japanese marques—Samsung, Toyota, Sony, and so on—are built on scale and have benefited from decades of consistent national economic policy rooted in vertical and horizontal integration. But Japanese and, to a lesser extent, Korean products are also highly innovative, obsessed with details that delight. Why is this so? Japanese business culture is bottom-up and obsessed with perfection. Korean corporations, while ruled with an iron fist, are, unlike Chinese stated-owned enterprises, free to focus on the bottom line and long-term shareholder gains. Unfortunately, Chinese companies have not yet planted the seeds of genuine, consumer-driven innovation. Investment in research and development is neither sufficient nor channeled productively. Market research, imperative for uncovering unmet needs, is conducted sparingly. Corporate culture is extremely hierarchical, thereby minimizing bottom-up innovation. It will be many years before Chinese business opens up enough to drive innovation rather than merely pay lip service to it.

INTO THE FUTURE

It will be another decade or more before companies reform their strategies and structure in a manner consistent with global brand management. Furthermore, we're still half a generation away from a Chinese corporate leader who sees willingness to delegate as a strength, not a weakness.

Therefore, Chinese companies will expand foreign presence in one of three ways: further exploiting narrow markets in which Chineseness is seen as an advantage rather than a weakness (alternative medicine, niche fashion brands in which Asian style carries cachet); forging production alliances with multinationals to provide components or products that compete at lower price tiers but under non-Chinese brand names; and acquiring international brands while retaining the existing Western management.

The latter is a highly risky strategy. Lenovo, for example, bought IBM's personal computer division, hoping to kill two birds with one stone by leveraging China's low-cost manufacturing base while increasing penetration of value-added PCs in the West. Unfortunately, this bifurcated strategy led to schizophrenic management structures, one for China and the other for international markets. When they tried to consolidate the two operations, including an effort to globalize communications, things deteriorated. There were culture clashes. And, more fundamentally, the company was divided between addressing the needs of China and those of international markets. As a result, Lenovo suffered more than its competitors during the global economic downturn, losing market share for high-end PCs in foreign markets. Another management upheaval followed, with the original Chinese leaders reasserting control over all operations. To its credit, Lenovo now realizes that success must start in China. There is no shortcut.

Medium-sized stars. The brands that stand a chance in the medium term will be the ones known as more than simply big Chinese trademarks. Again, this requires innovation, a process that has barely begun. China Merchants Bank (CMB), not among the country's largest financial institutions, has developed a range of innovative products and services for the new middle class. Examples include an iPhone mobile banking service and the multiple-account "All in One" card. To boot, CMB's brand image is young and dynamic. Anta has begun to sign up globally recognized personalities such as tennis star Jelena Jankovic and has also introduced high-tech features such as "hi-arch" shock absorbers and cooling fabric.

Chineseness, even at ultralow prices, simply won't cut it. Any brand capable of sustaining long-term loyalty with a long-term price premium must have a consistent, unique brand offer. This can be rooted in a brand truth, an equity associated with the brand and built up over time (for example, Body Shop equals green), or a product truth, something about the product itself that delivers a meaningful benefit. No large Chinese brand offers either. It will be the midsized brands that make the first splash in overseas developed markets but not until they generate the scale required to manage an international marketing and sales operation. And not until they have a global position, one robust enough to be flexibly adapted in different markets with different cultural orientations.

4

BRAND MANAGEMENT IN CHINA: THREE GOLDEN RULES

The Chinese worldview, not to mention its brandscape, differs profoundly from other markets. In my fourteen years here, I have not encountered a single brand that did not require significant modifications to positioning and marketing before it succeeds in the PRC. This, of course, does not preclude the feasibility of a global brand idea—Nike should breathe a "Just Do It" spirit everywhere. But, to maximize relevance and trigger loyalty that results in a sustainable price premium, global brands must appreciate Chinese cultural and operational realities. At the risk of dramatic oversimplification, there are three golden rules to which marketers must be sensitive before landing on the mainland.

MAXIMIZE PUBLIC CONSUMPTION TO JUSTIFY PRICE PREMIUMS

In China, a Confucian society torn between stifling regimentation and relentless ambition, consumers regard brands as tools for success. Face, the primary currency of upward mobility, is rooted in status projection, generating societal acknowledgment for one's ability to scale the socioeconomic hierarchy. This is why brands that, directly or indirectly, are publicly consumed are able to command huge price premiums relative to goods used in private or within the house. As I highlighted earlier, all leading mobile phone brands are international. The leading household appliance brands are, without exception, cheaply priced domestic names.

Internal vs. external benefits. The public display imperative leads to fundamental positioning differences versus what works in Western markets. As a general rule, benefits should be externalized, not internalized. Even for luxury goods, unadulterated individualism—reinforcing "what I want, how I feel" irrespective of societal consequences—does not work. Bath gels should not promote sensorial indulgence in the shower, they should help the user to start busy days with a kick; beauty products must help a woman move forward and enhance her ability to open doors professionally or control her man. Even mass-market beauty brands should focus on helping lower-income women be admired as a great mom or adored wife. Automobiles should make a statement about a man on the way up. BMW has successfully fused its global "ultimate driving machine" proposition with a Chinese declaration of ambition.

Display and business models. It's worth repeating that public display is also a critical consideration in shaping business models. One more time: Starbucks successfully established itself as a public place in which professional tribes gather to proclaim affiliation with the new-generation elite. Likewise, both Pizza Hut and Häagen Dazs have built megafranchises rooted in out-of-home consumption. (No Chinese is willing to pay $4.50 to eat a pint of ice cream while watching an illegal DVD.)

SIMPLIFY COMMUNICATIONS/BENEFITS TO ENHANCE COMPREHENSION

Simplify, simplify, simplify. Chinese, irrespective of income or geography, are overwhelmed—yet excited—by the explosion of brands, both local and international. Twenty years ago, the public phone was the only way to make a telephone call; today, there are more than three hundred brands of mobile devices, ranging from US$30 basic models to state-of-the-art smartphones. Making matters worse, China's media landscape is extremely cluttered. According a study by WPP's MindShare, a large media-buying and -planning agency, the average Shanghai resident is exposed to three times as many ads in one day as UK consumers. In Beijing, television screens, mostly owned by Focus Media, are ubiquitous—in taxis, elevators, restaurants, building exteriors, locker rooms, and bathroom stalls.

Direct is best. Complicated messages therefore are not easily digested, even among the most brand-literate subsets of the population. Consistent messages must be conveyed directly, requiring as little cognitive processing as possible. Advertising must be ruthlessly single minded about the visualization of key benefits, leveraging demos as creative ideas—that is, slice-of-life formats that dramatize product performances in extreme circumstances and so on. Celebrities must be carefully selected so that their star attributes reinforce a core brand proposition. (In nine cases out of ten, celebrities should be Chinese.

Unlike Japanese, mainlanders are profoundly nationalistic and relatively unfamiliar with Caucasian personalities, with the exception of superstars like Michael Jordan, Lady Gaga, or Jennifer Aniston.)

To conform to the simplicity mandate, heavy mass media—television and print that is passively consumed and seen by many people—is ideal. China's untamed landscape requires that brands be created from scratch; television is flexible enough to forge broad-stroke equity and brand character. Digital media, actively digested, is increasingly critical to deepening engagement and loyalty but, even for high-involvement/heavy search categories such as autos and financial services, mass media will remain the most important plank for years to come.

EXTEND BRANDS DOWNWARD TO GENERATE BOTH SCALE/ AFFORDABILITY AND MARGIN

Margin and scale. To succeed in China, multinational brands must boast both profit and mass-market scale. Most multinationals have little problem charging a price premium because, with few exceptions, Chinese consumers maintain an active preference for the reliability and prestige of foreign brands. The tough nut, however, is establishing a pricing strategy that kills two birds with one stone: sustaining a premium image while creating broad sales reach. Scale, the most potent signal of performance reliability, is critical in a reassurance-driven market such as China. It also forges operational order from chaos, exerting gravitational pull throughout distribution channels and the sales force.

Lower price tiers. The only way to target a broad swathe of price-sensitive consumers is to extend premium-priced brands downward across lower price tiers, always by reducing costs and simplifying benefit structures. At the same time, the risk of negatively affecting quality perceptions of the entire brand must be minimized. This is often accomplished by investing advertising funds in communicating the benefits of the premium variants while relying on in-store and other promotional efforts to push sales of the less expensive items. Colgate toothpaste was an early innovator on the mass-market front. Colgate Total Oral Care premium toothpaste, composed largely of imported ingredients, cost approximately 200 percent more than local brands and maintained a 3 percent share. Colgate Herbal and Colgate Strong, however, used local ingredients, had a lower cost of goods, and were priced slightly higher than local brands. The combined Colgate franchise controls a phenomenal share—more than 20 percent—of the toothpaste market, one with hundreds of regional and national competitors. In recent years, Nestlé and some Procter & Gamble brands—notably Crest—have adopted a similar strategy. So too have higher-involvement categories such as mobile phones.

5

CHINESE RECESSION TACTICS: HOW MARKETERS CAN WIN DURING A DOWNTURN

U nlike much of the world, China didn't experience a postglobal financial crisis recession, but its growth rate lost several percentage points toward the end of 2008 and for much of 2009. Times were toughest for low-end workers and entrepreneurs hit by the slowdown of export industries. While aggregate savings rates in China remained high, confidence suffered because of job insecurity. People looked right, then left, surveying the landscape for clues about when it was safe again to wade back into the water. The key point is that Chinese consumers were held back by anxiety; their Western counterparts were deterred by a lack of cash arising from a heavily indebted economic infrastructure and a steep drop in stock and home asset values. As a result, consumer confidence in China rebounded relatively quickly, while in the United States and Europe liquidity remains a problem.

For a period, though, China's unfettered optimism, even boldness, gave way to caution and conservatism in spending. In this environment, one that has only been exacerbated by the country's historic production overcapacity and lack of a reliable safety net, consumers segued from a surging to a dwelling modality. Relatively speaking, they became less forward looking and more focused on stabilizing the here and now.

MIDDLE-CLASS PROJECTION BECOMES
MASS-MARKET PROTECTION

The Chinese have always been split between projecting status as a means of forward momentum in life and protecting existing wealth. More specifically, the urban mass market, not having benefited as directly from economic reform, has always been conservative, less sure of material stability. The middle class, on the other hand, has traditionally preferred transformative benefits, promises of professional or societal advancement. But during the downturn, trenchant ambition was deferred. Job hoppers stopped in their tracks. The protective impulse, usually a dominant mass-market and secondary middle-class trait, reasserted itself across all levels of society.

Marketers must study this shift when crafting future strategies. A dip in consumer confidence should prompt a recalibrating of the message: products should reflect a new conservative reality without conveying fearfulness; middle-class advertising should have mass appeal but not be down-market in tone.

Establish a new price-value equation. Shoppers, regardless of whether they are psychologically gun shy or genuinely strapped for cash, require a reconfigured price-value equation. It is critical to reinforce affordability without adulterating a brand's underlying equities—that is, the emotional or functional associations built up over time that command a long-term price premium. Given this imperative, brands should reconsider not only their competitive advantages but assumptions regarding their role in life.

Shift from style to substance. Brands, particularly in high-end categories, should highlight inner substance. Rolex, for example, should move from abstract status claims to a core functional message rooted in craftsmanship or precision. Nike must ensure its "Just Do It" spirit is grounded in sports authenticity. In China, Rejoice shampoo advertising highlighted the product's nutritional properties and therefore value. It is important to note that this was done without compromising externalized beauty benefits, always crucial in maintaining the brand's public payoff and price premium.

Turn from selling to helping. Chinese do not like to beg for low prices, but they remain fiercely price conscious. Therefore, discounts must be positioned as bargains, the fruit of resourcefulness, one of the most admired—and adaptive—behavioral characteristics in Confucian society. Nanfu Battery encouraged users not to throw away old batteries but rather to reuse them for less intensive applications. Crest advertising demonstrated how its tubes are packed with more toothpaste than its competitors. The Internet, a medium that makes comparison pricing exponentially easier, can be very useful in enhancing consumers' bargaining power. The websites of fast-food marketers such as

McDonald's offer online-only supervalue gift coupons as well as discounts for products on Taobao, China's leading auction site.

Repurpose from want to need. First, focus on external payoffs rather than internal satisfaction or release. In a back-to-basics environment, celebrating indulgence is risky. Premium yogurt should focus on "delicious digestion that gets you going" rather than pure taste satisfaction. Snow, a leading Chinese beer, focused on easing anxiety associated with mortgages, car payments, and work. Second, advertising should dramatize the consequences of *not using* the brand. GlaxoSmithKline's Panadol, an over-the-counter analgesic, showed nasal discomfort disrupting an audition, neatly linking the product with career advancement. Tempo tissue, a leading player in a price-sensitive category, underscored the danger of not carrying a pack by associating sneezing with social embarrassment. With "Raindrops Keep Fallin' on My Head" playing in the background of TV ads, Lipton tea draws attention to the advantages of mood enhancement during office hours.

Refocus the portfolio. Multinational products have historically been priced too high to penetrate price-conscious consumer segments, rendering most foreign brands aspirational but inaccessible. In the past few years, however, many multinationals have extended brands downward to lower price tiers, increasing total share dramatically. As discussed in the previous chapter, both Crest and Colgate, for example, have expensive "complete oral care" variants that generate single-digit share as well as lower cost-of-goods versions with higher sales. During downturns, wary shoppers, even middle-class ones, need to justify any premium and will gravitate to affordable options. Therefore, all companies should examine the depth and breadth of their portfolios to ensure maximum coverage across economic strata—while taking care not to degrade brand equity. Furthermore, payoffs should shift from projective (status, professional advancement, wealth) to protective (financial security, safety, prevention) without conveying any hint of fearful immobility.

Move from hard to soft sell. In uncertain times, corporate trust is an invaluable asset as consumers flock toward safety. In China, the government, particularly the central government, is trusted more than business (79 percent for the former versus 54 percent for the latter, according to the Edelman Trust Barometer). First, companies can reinforce the reliability of their product by highlighting corporate scale. In China, bigger is always better; benevolence is the privilege of power. Companies must be perceived as big enough to care. China Mobile, for example, began running copy that highlights coverage. A voice over intones, "During critical moments, when precious life is at stake, lean on the world's most extensive network." Bank of China deftly leveraged the size of its branch network to reinforce "life-long partnership, through good times and bad." Second, efforts must be made to demonstrate sufficient means to invest in consumers' well-being. Johnson & Johnson's small-town network of neonatal and pediatric clinics reassure, not to mention inspire, Chinese masses.

Bring the family back together. In Confucian society, the clan, not the individual, is the basic unit of society and the ultimate defense against instability. This is particularly true during times of economic uncertainty, so family cohesion is critical in buttressing peace of mind. Products that forge domestic harmony will be embraced. Ajinomoto, which sells seasoning in China, moved away from its quintessentially Japanese "taste of refinement" and positioned its spices as a "family magnet" that draws loved ones together. Gold Wine adopted a gifting strategy, encouraging robust ties between extended family members. Even China Mobile refocused its businessman-targeted "Go Tone" sub-brand to emphasize long-distance bonding with kids.

Promote confidence. The Chinese really do see opportunity in crisis—and the fact that the country was relatively untroubled by the global recession further predisposes a look toward the bright side. While the benefits of such a broad emotive approach are difficult to link directly with sales, brands should encourage a chin-up mentality to reinforce long-term equity. Anta's "from perseverance to glory" proposition, originally launched after 2008's Sichuan earthquake and anti-Tibet protests, succeeded by strengthening bonding. Diaopai, China's leading local detergent, gracefully fused empathy for the unemployed with hope while, at the same time, incorporating a "more washes for less money" claim.

6

THE CHINESE BOARDROOM: FACE AND FEAR

The headquarters of large Chinese corporations, both private and state owned, look and feel the same. They are immense, majestic, built to impress. The front lobbies are enormous, with fifty-foot ceilings and marble floors. Security is elaborate; receptionists and guards are serious. Upper stories are overbuilt, with rows and rows of vacant cubicles. Ordinary workers cluster in immense, harshly lit rooms like ants on the cusp of a picnic invasion. Any organization worth its salt boasts an expansive museum—usually behind a massive front desk, up a regal staircase—of the company's timeline, starting with the founder's vision and culminating with recent breakthroughs. Photographs of important officials are prominently placed throughout the display.

CEO suites are sanctuaries of power. They are huge, concealed behind hidden doors, equipped with showers, king-sized beds, and the occasional Buddhist shrine. Busts of Mao and photos of Communist Party officials-cum-industrial titans are displayed as testaments to political savvy and networking prowess. The walls are likely adorned with magazine pictorials of the CEO himself. Black leather couches are overstuffed and oversized. Visitors, like children asking for favors, are reduced to supplication.

What awes most is the boardroom. Tables are as long as bowling alleys. Microphones are installed at every chair. Seating must mirror the power structure, with the big bosses smack in the center, flanked by subordinates in descending rank. Nonexecutives never get to sit with the big boys—they hover in rows, pushed against the wall, silent, nodding endlessly. Boardroom design forbids the spontaneous exchange of ideas. Meetings are promulgations masked as presentations. When the leader enters, the pageant begins.

Image 6.1 Most large Chinese corporations project stature through on-site museums, timeline displays of an enterprise's technological breakthroughs. Metersbonwe, the nation's largest youth apparel brand, goes one step further by associating itself with the evolution of Chinese fashion. (Courtesy JWT)

In these conditions, it's essential that visitors do substantive groundwork, not least to ensure that the imperatives of business relationships in China are respected. It is critical for Western expatriates to maintain face, lubricate trust, root proposals in mutually beneficial pragmatism, and demonstrate power and credibility.

Conveying respect. Visitors have an obligation to generate face, the currency of advancement, for the CEO. Chinese rulers derive legitimacy from their assumed mastery of the system, so the worst sin a foreigner can commit is teaching. The phrase "perhaps you don't understand" is suicide. Sermons on price-to-earnings ratios or consumer loyalty are offensive. My most grievous faux pas was asking the CEO of an appliance manufacturer what he thought of Philips's "Sense and Simplicity" campaign. When he confessed ignorance, the room fell into awkward silence. The meeting never recovered. Recommendations should always be delivered *after* senior management buy in—and solely for the benefit of subordinate edification.

Establishing camaraderie. Trust must be lubricated one on one, in the CEO's office or in private dining rooms at round tables. Unfamiliar people or new ideas elicit anxiety, so informal meetings must be set up beforehand by trusted third parties. Email contact gets you nowhere, since executives are uncomfortable with mechanical communication (although, these days, many issue one-way microblog postings). Common business objectives must be established at dinner but only after the ice has melted. Sincere admiration for both the brand and corporation will be well received, but excessive flattery will backfire. For instance, I've found the brand video a useful weapon during warm-ups: A montage of images, complete with stirring music, that capture what, for example, Yili, a milk brand, means to the masses. Speaking rudimentary Chinese goes a long way in signaling respect. Use the translators to ask questions about the leader's background and business philosophy. It goes without saying that anti-China sentiments are toxic. Genuine affection for the country and people is the crucial first step of partnership.

Dreaming realistically. The Chinese dream big, but they dream pragmatically. Business leaders are moved by the beauty of things to come, yet also are self-protective and acutely aware of the country's primordial operational landscape. A famous saying, *gao chu bu sheng han*, can be translated as, "When you are on the top of the mountain, you are unable to stand up to the cold." In other words, the higher your position, the more problems you face. Leaders therefore fear overreach. Proposals, communicated to the CEO before the boardroom meeting, must be rooted in current and future business imperatives as well as empirically bulletproof yet be bold in describing the end goal.

The last is about more than ego. To avoid a commoditization bloodbath on China's brutally price-sensitive business battlefield, sustainable competitive advantage is vital. Industry leaders, engineers with strong ties to the Communist Party, have been groomed on five-year plans, so step-by-step blueprints, loaded with detail, are key to building credibility. Points should be made simply and evocatively—but if they are not grounded from the start, they will be ignored.

Projecting authority. Chinese CEOs want to negotiate with worthy partners. In the boardroom, Western expatriates must demonstrate stature in front of the leader's acolytes. The Chinese are not bottom-up in a Japanese sense, but the buy-in of subordinates is still important. Credentials must demonstrate international expertise and global scale; business cards must be thick and embossed; and expatriates should sport a well-crafted Mandarin name, composed by a copywriter, with a combination of Chinese characters that convey power or wisdom. When presenting, stand up, speak from the diaphragm, focus your eyes on the seniors in the room, use short sentences, and avoid rhythm-killing long translation gaps. Even fluent Chinese speakers should avoid excessive Mandarin to minimize loss of "foreign expert power" and the scent of desperation. Lighthearted correction of the translator, however, is a nifty way to telegraph friendliness and street smarts. A phrase that elicits laughter when spoken in Mandarin with an American accent: "There's nothing to fear under heaven and Earth except a Jew who can negotiate in Chinese." (In the early stages of establishing relationships with clients, I often reveal that I am Jewish. Jews are admired for global cultural cohesion and, even more important, shrewdness in business. Residents of coastal Wenzhou in Zhejiang province, a prosperous trading port with an economy dominated by entrepreneurial start-ups, are proud to be called "the Jews of China." And bookstores overflow with best sellers that "reveal the secrets of the Jews.")

7

TYCOON TANG JUN'S LOST FACE: A CHINESE BUSINESS TRAGEDY

Tang Jun, once an esteemed business executive and role model, has emerged as the star in a quintessentially Chinese tragedy. First, he was exposed as an academic fraud, having falsely claimed to have a Ph.D. from the California Institute of Technology. Then, two weeks later, Tang was implicated in the misallocation of $30 million related to a real estate deal in Jiangsu. Responding to the hubbub, he said, without a shred of remorse: "Losers cheat some people and get caught. Winners cheat the whole world all the time."

Is Tang China's Bernie Madoff? Did he betray the goodwill of the Chinese people? Most admired his transformation from small potato to master and commander, a rare bicultural breed who leveraged stints at Microsoft and Shanda, China's largest online gaming company, to represent the face of modern Chinese business. In the process, he became the nation's highest-paid executive, earning RMB1 billion per year at New Huadu, the conglomerate owned by Fujian native Chen Fashu, the Warren Buffett of China.

To most Westerners, Tang appears morally bankrupt. He built his reputation on, at best, half-truths and, at worse, outright deceit. Further, former colleagues at Microsoft and Shanda describe him as a pseudoleader, perpetually detached, more interested in managing his image among foreign bosses and investors than generating lasting shareholder value.

But many ordinary Chinese have shown a far more ambiguous, and sometimes sympathetic, reaction. Although the case did unleash a tidal wave of

schadenfreude among Tang's poorer countrymen, the masses were more titillated than up in arms. "He was only doing what anyone in his position would
do," was one professional's response. Another said: "Tang Jun got caught. He
pushed it too far. But today it's so competitive. We have no choice but to play the
damn game. Face is everything."

In China, an ambitious, anti-individualistic, and morally relativistic society, integrity is often perceived as a luxury. Despite the brutality of the Great
Leap Forward and Cultural Revolution, Mao is still considered a great leader
because he unified—that is, stabilized—the nation. Even Mencius, a Chinese
philosopher who was the most famous Confucian after Confucius himself and
regarded benevolence as innate, focused his philosophical energies on harnessing the power of goodness to reinforce a well-ordered social structure. Such
moral utilitarianism is felt everywhere in China. From tolerance of corruption
to wide availability of commercialized sex, Chinese are no-nonsense pragmatists. That is not to say they are immoral, but in a culture sans God or heaven,
ends justify means. Corruption lubricates business relationships. Prostitutes
are less threatening to family cohesion than mistresses.

In this respect, winners—people who start, forge, and build things—are
infinitely more respected than good guys. Public endorsement, or face, something Tang Jun was desperate to acquire, plays an important role in amassing
the interpersonal capital to get things done. On the dog-eat-dog business battlefield, face is everything. It lubricates all interactions, personal and financial,
and requires constant replenishment. When it dries up, people not only move
backward; they disappear into a sea of anonymity.

Tang had a master plan. By writing books with titles like *My Success Can
Be Replicated*, he sought to become an icon. By appearing on television shows
and glossy magazine covers, he hoped to achieve guru status, generating social
currency that could be reinvested for future gain.

But even in a status-obsessed country such as China, substance counts for
something. The practical Chinese revere results—they like engineers, technocratic leaders, and concrete structures. Throughout his career, Tang ignored
this truth. He cultivated his image, but in the end, no one knew the man, his
beliefs or his vision. He is an almost preternatural shape shifter, projecting
radically different personae depending on his audience. Deferential to Chinese
bosses and foreign boards, he is a shark with subordinates. Rarely have I met an
individual capable of unleashing both yin and yang with equal vigor and, yes,
aplomb.

Sadly, Tang's fabrications and moral ambiguity came to light before he
could demonstrate tangibly irrefutable value as a business leader. His accomplishments were not self-evident. Had he not billed himself as the incarnation

of Chinese capitalism or publicized his outrageous salary, his transgressions would certainly have been forgiven and probably ignored. But he flew too close to the sun.

So what will become of Tang? He is currently living in Shanghai, out of the spotlight. He may simply fade away. However, it is hoped he will do some soul searching and realize external validation never trumps genuine self-possession. In hyperkinetic, brashly materialistic boom times, China needs a real role model who extols—even if he profits from—this timeless truth.

8

MANAGING CHINA: STIMULATING CREATIVITY IN A SEA OF CONVENTION

The greatest managerial challenge creative agency leaders face in China is forging an environment of self-expression and innovative thinking. Success hinges on liberating the creative juices of local staff across all levels, from junior account executives and copywriters to senior business directors and creative directors. Without mold-breaking ideas, our relationships with clients are doomed to be short and unprofitable.

So far, we have made progress. But it's been hard won and can be easily lost: the order-taking, client-appeasing, faction-driven, and hierarchy-abiding modus operandi always hovers close. These tendencies are reinforced by cultural traits that have not significantly evolved since I arrived in Shanghai in 1998. While exponentially more internationally aware and modern in lifestyle, the new generation has not become individualistic in the Western sense. Society does not—and perhaps never will—fundamentally value challenge to convention. Success is still largely a function of external acknowledgment rather than pursuit of personal vision.

ADVERTISING, CREATIVITY, AND INNOVATION: DANGEROUS TERRAIN

Advertising, as a professional landscape, is dangerous terrain. Many of China's best and brightest stay away, drifting toward the respectability of client-side jobs or owning one's company. Advertising is not safe. Our product is abstract.

Image 8.1   Chinese are capable of stunning creativity. However, in hierarchical settings, it must be carefully cultivated through an ethos of "dangerous silence" or "safe self-expression." This Samsonite ad, executed by JWT Shanghai, was awarded mainland China's first-ever Grand Prix at the Cannes advertising festival. (Courtesy Illusion Co. Ltd. and Samsonite Asia Ltd.)

Despite a renewed focus on measurability and return on investment, there are few objective standards against which creative ideas can be evaluated. Although there is no formula that guarantees success, a critical mass of personnel who possess the courage to persuade is a characteristic of agencies that produce effective creative work. China, however, is a rule-bound terrain on which rational technocracy is prized more than conceptual adventurism.

The country is characterized by a coexistence of conformism and determination, a quixotic combination that has enabled a totalitarian Leninist power structure to lead 1.3 billion people toward superpower status. Subordinates should know precisely what is expected of them, but at the same time, innovation must be rewarded. Creativity of the Chinese variety should be an incremental, not revolutionary, force. Leaders, in advertising or any other value-added industry, must explicitly limn the destination while providing a clear, safe path for getting there.

To liberate latent talent in every Chinese, managers must ensure that subordinates are given enough space to color outside the lines but not so much that they become anxious. Experimentation should be gradual, within the realm of convention.

HOW TO HARNESS AN INNOVATIVE IMPULSE

Here are a few rules that can help leaders in China nurture an innovative, entrepreneurial spirit within their teams.

Define, and dramatize, the vision. The Chinese abhor the abstract, nonquantifiable, and unclear. To ensure a sense of security, corporate leaders must explicitly outline long-term objectives. Everything in China is a means to an end. Without a magnificent destination, the journey—the process, the joy of collaboration and creative release—is pointless. Most individuals, incapable of defining themselves except by external acknowledgment, will lapse into anxiety-driven passivity. They will seek refuge in the harbor of hierarchy, opting for safe silence rather than proactive self-expression.

At JWT, everyone knows the definition of success: we transform passive exposure into active engagement, forging brand ideas that underpin long-term relationships with consumers. This vision requires vivid, unambiguous promulgation by the CEO. Whether participating in one-on-one discussions or group rally sessions, the chief executive articulates a common vocabulary to define success standards. JWT has banned such twentieth-century terminology as "TV commercial" and "360 degrees" (the latter refers to the use of more than television and print in a media plan), which have been replaced by "filmic expression," "ideacentric," and "connection plan." Manifestations of our common mission are displayed on t-shirts, elevator doors, and backpacks; through public relations efforts and annual party skits; inside newcomer orientation material; and even on reception-area clocks.

Provide a training framework for creativity. Managers must overinvest in training and, more specifically, outline a step-by-step path toward creativity. The Chinese are capable of conceptual brilliance. But when required to take risky leaps within a hierarchy, they are stymied. Workers, even at senior levels, are more confident in logical than lateral thinking, particularly when answers can't be proven. At JWT we have articulated five inviolable steps of engagement planning, though they may seem basic to Western advertising executives:

- Identify a consumer insight, a fundamental motivation for behavior that springs from conflict in the heart. This conflict can be between or within human and cultural truths;
- Identify a unique brand offer, rooted in a product or brand truth, that addresses the insight;
- Fuse the unique brand offer and consumer insight into a brand idea, the long-term relationship between consumer and brand;
- Express the brand idea as "engagement ideas," creative platforms that encourage consumers to actively participate with the idea; and
- Develop a connection plan, a marriage of media and creative idea that leverages the former to increase the salience of the latter and vice versa.

Aspire to guru status. In China, masses must be led toward an unfamiliar promised land that exists at the intersection of stability and opportunity. The credibility of bosses therefore must be beyond reproach. In Confucian China, a civilization in which individual identity is tantamount to societal recognition, connoisseurship must be acknowledged in public, by other industry role models. CEOs worth their salt have published a book proclaiming a paradigm for glory. JWT's recruiting efforts have been enhanced by company leaders' television appearances and think pieces in magazines.

Ensure consistent, unified management. Opacity is a defining feature of China's business landscape. Enemies lurk in the shadows. In large state-owned enterprises, promotions of executives are floated as trial balloons in mass media. Opposition, always anonymous, can come from any quarter, often derailing elevation. This happened to a friend of mine, a high-ranking cadre at Shanghai Media Group. To this date, he still has no idea why he fell from favor and who—or which faction—resisted his rise.

Nontransparency is fundamentally counterproductive and Chinese employees do not like it. Conventional Chinese leadership is characterized by two unfortunate traits. First, corporate dictators, struggling to maintain a position atop pinnacles of power, issue unclear instructions that require nervous, even oracular, interpretation. Second, they divide and conquer, encouraging rival power factions at lower levels of the organization. Survival is rooted in the obeisance of minions who, unable to see the big picture and unwilling to advance an untested agenda, are locked into submission. JWT China, on the other hand, has a culturally balanced leadership team, and is aligned in terms of product, ethical, and management issues. To minimize political maneuvering, there is a no-holds-barred approach to challenging convention and zero tolerance for operationally independent silos, cliques, and camps.

Stable management is also patriarchal. The Chinese, reticent when it comes to the unknown, crave the safety of family. Corporate leaders should position themselves as tough-but-loving parents, dispensing discipline and guidance in equal measure. Similarly, the company should encourage employee-to-employee bonds—through online social network groups, annual trips, movie nights, seasonal parties, four o'clock fruit, and birthday celebrations.

Create an environment of dangerous silence. In China, fear of losing face stifles self-expression, particularly in front of superiors. During creative reviews and client meetings, there are frequent silences. Genuine individualism remains relegated to the counterculture, a tiny group disconnected from the mainstream.

To combat lowered eyes and shy smiles, management must explicitly foster a seemingly paradoxical atmosphere wherein self-expression is safe and silence is dangerous. Performance evaluations must reward conceptual adventurism rather than process management. Hierarchical advancement must be fueled by the courage to persuade, a willingness to articulate the abstract, an eagerness to put an idea on the table and have it shot to pieces. Those who fail to offer points of view must be called to task, shamed by their lack of boldness. Experimentation and learning that frames debate must be applauded. Managers must listen, probe, and identify nuggets of inspiration. Raises should not occur across the board; they should be meritocratic. The greatest rewards should be reserved for the laterally bold, conceptually vigorous, and intellectually broad.

Provide frequent positive reinforcement. Although meritocratic values are critical, if young Chinese do not have tangible sense of advancement, they will retreat. Raises, however modest, should be given every year for the deserving unless bosses hope to trigger resignations. Promotions for the deserving should take place at least every eighteen months. Within most advertising agencies' client management department, there are no fewer than nine seniority designations. The creative unit boasts almost as many. A few years ago, China's largest foreign media company streamlined seniority grades from nine to three, in accordance with global corporate imperatives. Emotional turmoil ensued, turnover spiked, and the managing director was fired.

Offer amateur psychotherapy. Managers must coach, listen, advise, cajole, and encourage. They must be prepared to spend 25 percent of their time as counselors. The Confucian combination of restrictive regimentation (face, hierarchy, rules, obedience, conservatism) and long-range ambition (drive, status projection, careerism) is a spiky brew. Employees want to shine, but they are afraid to let it out. They want applause but fear the stage. The new generation, sans professional role models, is ill equipped to navigate the crosscurrents of these contradictions. Furthermore, they lack insight into their own motivations and do not possess the vocabulary to express anxiety. The simple question, "How do you feel?" can prompt tears. Offices should be furnished with comfy couches and stocked with tissues.

Innovation will never spontaneously combust in China. To unleash creativity, managers must forge an environment in which conceptual exploration is encouraged and rewarded.

9

WINNING DESIGNS IN CHINA: STANDING OUT TO FIT IN

The Chinese consumer is becoming increasingly modern and internationalized. However, while egos and ambitions are huge, the new generation is not becoming individualistic in the Western sense; that is, people do not define themselves as independent of society. The middle class, those who can afford nonessential items, is torn between two impulses. The first is projection of status, which leads to a desire to be noticed, aggressive self-expression, and experimentation with new modes of style and design. The second is protection, a fear of sticking out too obviously or challenging existing hierarchies and social restrictions.

The Chinese saying "the leading goose gets shot down" is as true today as it was yesterday. People want to be acknowledged by society as special, but they cannot afford to be too ahead of the curve. Western-style individualism is enticing, but reaching for it comes with the risk of social alienation.

Across a broad swathe of categories, the conflict between standing out and fitting in manifests itself in design and product preference. There are, however, two caveats. First, willingness to accept a less conservative expression of identity is greater within younger age groups, who are more accepting of Western style, and across primary cities (Shanghai, Beijing, Guangzhou, and Shenzhen). Second, it is possible to push the curve, to encourage Chinese to experiment with more audacious new fashion, but this must be done gingerly, without crossing an invisible line of overt rebellion. Brashly grabbing attention is a no-no, irrespective of age, education, or economic background.

Here are a few design principles that ensure standing out while fitting in.

Make the design elegantly grand. Status counts. Face, the currency of forward advancement, is fundamental in Chinese society. Big is in. Two-door cars sell less well than four-door sedans for both practical ("it's large enough for my family") and aspirational ("people will notice me") reasons. Backseat leg room must be ample enough for VIPs who are expected to employ chauffeurs. Lobby foyers and other public spaces will always be designed to impress, not charm. But, increasingly, mass with gravitational pull must be lightened with streamlined refinement. Giorgio Armani, applauded for classy understatement, is doing well in China. Gold-trimmed rococo interiors, ten years ago the mark of continental sophistication, are now off-putting. Instead, "Shanghai chic"— large spaces, long lines, simple shapes, and uncluttered rooms—is the taste of the upwardly mobile. Public spaces must impress but, increasingly, without crossing the red line into ostentation.

Avoid signaling aggressive intent. The business landscape is a battlefield, but the Chinese know the best offense is savvy defense. Chinese society— competitive to its core, morally relativistic, and disoriented by a first-generation ethos of capitalism—is saddled with a massive trust deficit, both individually and institutionally. Trust facilitation is therefore the first step in establishing collaboration. Any signals of overly bold ambition—hot red sports cars, ready-to-pounce kinetic design—will be instantly rejected. Mercedes-Benz is still more appropriate "for my boss, not me." Vivienne Westwood, a rebellious fashion brand, will not achieve critical mass in China unlike, say, Dior or Chanel, both the quintessence of French elegance. The same goes for Versace and Dolce & Gabbana, niche luxury labels more popular among wealthy men's mistresses than their wives. Wives prefer the elegance of Prada, Chanel, or Burberry. Seattle grunge, with its ripped jeans and coarse fabric, never caught on. Hip hop, on the other hand, boasts urban playfulness and rhythmic funkiness. It will be cool for years.

Sparkle, don't glare. If you want to capture attention, whisper. China chic is monochromatic with a flash of color, a gaze punctuated by a wink. Mont Blanc, perhaps the most successful men's luxury brand, is a masterpiece of sotto voce dazzle. During focus groups, respondents speak of graceful craftsmanship and smooth writing. In one-on-one discussions, however, it's the six-pointed white star that mesmerizes. It enables a man to grab attention just by slipping a pen in his pocket. Diamonds have surged in popularity at the expense of gold— the former sparkles, the latter glares. Ford's aggressive Fiesta commercial positions the car as "born bold, born sexy" but softens the advertising with actors' costumes that are not too titillating.

Ensure instant brand recognition. According to Rahda Chadha and Paul Husband, authors of *The Cult of the Luxury Brand: Inside Asia's Love Affair with Luxury*, putting logos on bags was the single most important factor in spreading luxury mania in Asia. This is because brand selection is a tool for "showing you know." Andrew Wu, head of luxury group LVMH China, says, "The Chinese believe there's no point in paying a lot of money for a brand if no one knows what you own." Visual identity is therefore a critical element of design appeal. Successful brands possess distinctive visual cues. Consider Louis Vuitton's LV logo, Bottega Veneta's leather cross-weave, Coach's uniquely shaped strap, and Chloe's add-on locket. However, visual symbols must be prominent but not gaudy. Gucci's shiny, in-your-face "double G" belt buckle is popular only among the newest nouveau rich; more sophisticated types, particularly in coastal cities, prefer the eye-catching understatement of Tiffany's silver jewelry inside pale blue boxes or Cartier's classic watch face accented by a narrow strip of gold.

Project substance. Brands should help a go-getter stand out without suggesting superficiality. Substance cues are therefore key in generating product appeal. This can be done by integrating a streamlined, high-tech beauty in design templates. Apple's iPhone, iPad, and iMac sublimely fused substance and style. Innovation streams—that is, a cascade of new designs—also convey substance beneath the sparkle. Every make of automobile must roll out several models per year. Mobile phones should showcase cutting-edge features, even if some of them are only for image-building purposes. Before Nokia sold off the division that manufactured the jewel-encrusted Vertu phone, for example, the model generated limited sales but loads of powerful PR. Pioneering concepts signal hefty research-and-development budgets—product intelligence—and justify price premiums.

Chinese consumers are drawn to product designs that enable individuals to simultaneously stand out and fit in. Although the balance should be expressed differently depending on category dynamics and segment-specific motivations, it is a must.

10

DIGITAL CHINA: LIBERATED CONSUMERS, CONSTRICTED CORPORATIONS

China's technologically liberated consumers are more than ready for a digital commercial revolution. But manufacturers and their communications partners—advertising agencies, both digital and traditional, as well as media companies—are letting them down by not approaching the sector strategically.

LIBERATION FOR EVERYMAN

It is difficult to overstate the impact of the Internet on China. Shielded by online anonymity, free-wheeling surfers broadcast accomplishments, weigh in on current events, download porn, hook up for sex, release rage through violent video games, criticize the government (gingerly), and plug in to virtual communities. The "Great Firewall" extinguishes hints of collective protest, but overall, Chinese people have more opportunities to explore the world and are freer to express views than at any time in history.

For bargain-crazy consumers, the rise of e-tailers presages an era of commercial nirvana. According to the government-run China Internet Network Information Center, in 2010, 40 million Chinese booked hotel rooms, airline tickets, and holiday tours on travel websites. Online activity accounted for only 2 percent of total 2009 retail spending, up from 1 percent in 2008; however, rates in coastal cities are already much higher. Aquarius Asia, a digital consulting firm, estimates that approximately one-third—or 142 million—of Chinese Internet users shop online, emboldened by the emergence of services like Alipay, e-commerce behemoth Alibaba's version of PayPal. Online auction websites such as Taobao—also part of the Alibaba stable—have emboldened shoppers to ruthlessly compare prices, realigning the balance of power between buyer and seller.

BRAND CONVENTIONALITY

But most *brands*, unfortunately, have not harnessed the power of the digital revolution. Few have exploited online tools to lift profit margins. As a rule, cyberspace has been carpet-bombed with cheap ploys that offer zero message consistency or insight into the emotional drivers of Internet users. Of course, there are exceptions. Pepsi's "Get on the Can" challenge provided ego-driven youth a platform to shine, literally, by emblazoning faces on beverage packages. McDonald's "Meet Me at McDonald's" effort, perhaps one of the most effective social network campaigns of 2010, harnessed the power of online affiliation to (a) deepen engagement with the company's "I'm Loving It" brand idea, (b) create digital buzz, and (c) drive traffic to its restaurants. VANCL, a youth fashion brand, provided trendsetters with a digital platform to "define your own style" by modeling—and selling—their favorite articles on their own online store. Nokia's "Reborn" viral and Ovi app campaign connected surfers to Bruce Lee, an icon of Chinese masculinity. Most of the time, however, China's digital landscape resembles a real world bazaar: noisy and clanging, promotion happy, discount driven, with the vast majority of online advertising slapped onto highly trafficked portals.

REQUIRED: A NEW BRAND-BUILDING VISION

The communications industry must raise its game to harness the energy released by China's digital big bang.

The brand idea—still sacred. Without the unifying power of the brand idea, conceptual chaos erupts. For decades, advertisers' responsibility has been to forge brand ideas that evolve, but do not fundamentally change, over time. They are rooted in the fundamental motivations of consumers. Through sports shoes, we buck societal convention to "Just Do It" on the basketball court; through engagement rings, we demonstrate enduring passion because "A [De Beers] Diamond Is Forever."

Brand engagement occurs over the airwaves, through the latest iPhone app, or by means of an online loyalty program. And the brand idea, the long-term relationship between consumer and product, is at the center of it all. The industry must acknowledge that new technological experiences are never, in and of themselves, ideas. Instead, they allow consumers to *engage* with ideas in new ways. Marketing efforts are often digitally "clever"—headlines such as "P&G Turns Virtual Makeover App into Max Factor Contest," "Budweiser Lime Launch Ties into Tudou's First Drama Series," "Unilever Links Hot Steam with Warm Wishes in Lipton Contest" abound—but rarely reinforce an enduring brand idea.

From passive consumption to active participation. The fundamental role of the brand will not change as a result of China's digital evolution. Indeed, as brand options multiply and media costs skyrocket, the need to minimize consumer disorientation is more urgent than ever. However, the one-to-one nature of digital expression provides opportunities to deepen and broaden involvement. Creative ideas can become engagement ideas, transforming passive exposure into active participation. Rather than produce work that interrupts, advertising agencies should develop content that people want to spend time with. De Beers's "Love World," a microsite where young men express commitment by creating a virtual world of omnipresent love, is the shape of things to come. So is Nike Plus, a high-tech manifestation of the "Just Do It" spirit that enables runners to compete with athletes anytime and anywhere on the planet. Axe's "sexy wake-up call," an app that brings the product's "masculine irresistibility" into the bedroom, demonstrates technology's power to reinforce a core brand proposition.

Consumption of communications through digital devices—mobile phones, tablets, computers, and so on—is revolutionary because manufacturers no longer broadcast messages. Through a bewildering array of channels, engagement is one to one, between marketer and users or between users themselves. Content is played with, commented on, expanded upon, competed with, and exchanged within brand communities. Corporations need to accept that their ability to control messaging—how a product is positioned, how brands are commented on publicly—will never be the same. (A caveat: Broadcast media will never be eclipsed as the primary means of defining propositions. The thirty-second television commercial, passively received, is an irreplaceable, albeit expensive, weapon in forging conceptual order.)

THE COMMUNICATIONS INDUSTRY: CHANGE REQUIRED

The digital engagement imperative presents four fundamental, and interrelated, challenges.

Real-time measurement. Advertising agencies must hone their ability to measure the effectiveness of digital engagement. Broadcast media efficiency is a question of reach and frequency; digital creative success, on the other hand, is measured through time spent (or "stickiness") interacting with a campaign, viral spread, click-through rates, conversion to purchase, and return on investment. Any strategic planning department worth its salt must maintain a robust analytics practice.

Continuous engagement. Creative agencies must move away from only executing campaigns—discrete television and print bursts that announce product news—toward continuous engagement planning. In an era of technological liberation, there are infinite ways to connect consumers with brands and brand communities. Operations must be restructured to facilitate rapid creative response to real and virtual world developments. This means recruiting the likes of bloggers, videographers, online performance artists, and app developers to fashion engagement ideas, and also "story managers" to maximize the buzz generated. Strategic partnerships should be struck with innovators. Agencies should operate like newsrooms do, focused on the big story but flexible enough to quickly modify a campaign as consumers react to creative stimulus.

Partnerships with online opinion leaders. In China, digital word of mouth—that is, comments regarding a product or service that circulate over the Internet—is extremely important, even more so than in other countries. The Chinese are still relatively inexperienced consumers with limited income, so they are actively seeking information to reduce the risk of wasting money on substandard items. In addition, the new generation is wants to be cool, so brands that boast online buzz are embraced. Marketers should tap into the agenda-setting power of popular bloggers and microbloggers such as fashion guru Han Houhou or trendsetter Yao Chen, an actress with a Sina Weibo following of almost 13 million fans.

These e-fluencers want to demonstrate product expertise. However, according to Dynamic Logic, a division of Millward Brown that specializes in measuring the effectiveness of online communications, brands are still low on the pecking order among social network topics. Communications agencies could fill this gap by establishing partnerships with leading online voices to develop exclusive branded content for opinion leaders to share with fans. Converse, for example, sponsored an online shoe design competition for fashion bloggers. Nokia invited music opinion leaders to interact directly with pop singers before and after their online music concert. Muji, the Japanese household goods retailer, developed a platform for bloggers interested in interior design to "show off your Muji style."

Digital mainstreaming. Digital is not a department or specialization, nor is it a discrete profit center. It is a new medium, incredibly potent, just as television was in the 1950s. And creativity remains at the center of the digital ecosystem. Global agencies must integrate digital savvy—genuine technological experimentation—into each account and creative group. Certain disciplines—such as analytics, technology optimization, digital production, and project management—should reside within a centralized "experience department," but digital adventurism must permeate the entire organization.

Media innovation. The "revenue war" between media companies and advertising agencies must end. Media shops will always excel in negotiating low rates with vendors based on volume. They also boast the administrative prowess to plan media across time and geography. But the process-driven culture of traditional media companies is incompatible with ideacentric creativity. As the digital universe expands, ideas must increasingly "live through" media, an acknowledgment that ideas, and how consumers experience them, are inseparable. Advertising agencies need the freedom to establish partnerships with, and derive revenue from, digital media owners. Development of innovative digital solutions must be a strategic imperative of all communications experts.

CHINESE ENTERPRISES: VAST OPPORTUNITY, STRUCTURAL LIMITATIONS

Through online car clubs, digital baby-care communities, and a hundred million microblogs, the Chinese have embraced social networks on a scale Westerns firms find difficult to fathom. But these burgeoning communities intersect with brands only tangentially. China is a reassurance-driven market in which the importance of personal recommendations is paramount. It is time to establish common cause with digital influencers to transform online communities into virtual brand villages; translate affiliation with social networks into sustained dialog with individuals; monetize one-on-one interaction through online loyalty and customer relationship management programs; and elevate the long-term profit contribution of discrete customers.

The evolution process will be complex and time consuming; digital development in China is currently constipated for several reasons.

Primitive suppliers. Suppliers are, by and large, unsophisticated. The only large digital agencies in China are online media agents; the majority place low-end banner ads and television commercials on mass-reach websites or portals. These companies, many corrupted by rampant kickbacks, treat creative as an add-on "design service." Revenue is based on page views, not click-throughs. Depth of engagement—that is, time spent with a digital idea—is still an abstruse concept. While investment in analytic tools has grown, few are sophisticated enough to measure or track returns.

Limited talent. Digital conceptual craftsmanship—the expression of brand ideas through digital media—is undeveloped. Most creative leaders remain tethered to the safety of traditional broadcast advertising. Senior digital talent is largely imported from abroad. The challenge of inculcating a passion for new technology while remaining faithful to brand-building fundamentals is immense. This is particularly true in conservative China, a country that prizes concrete predictability and shies away from the untested—that is, anything that does not guarantee fixed return.

Chronic short-termism. Chinese enterprises, like their agency brethren, are not structured to embrace the potential of digital brand building. Digital spending accounts for only 7 percent of total media activity, while e-commerce is immature even given the prevalence of online shopping. According to Aquarius Asia, the top one hundred manufacturers of consumer goods in China are giving away a large share of their online potential. Three out of four major companies do not efficiently use tools like search engine marketing or search engine optimization to reach their target groups.

China is a market that reveres scale and volume. Its largest companies are structured, and managed, to drive low-margin sales. Although some enterprises have made tentative steps up value ladders, few have embraced brand equity as the lynchpin of sustainable price premiums. Shoddy corporate governance precludes CEOs from maximizing long-term shareholder return. Panicky marketing executives defer to omnipotent sales barons who enforce short-term promotional pushes; only the most enlightened leaders reject the belief that low price is a competitive weapon. The existence of independent fiefdoms—departmental warlordism—militates against transcategory collaboration for data collection, database management, and cross selling. Customer relationship management—that is, maximizing individual customer profit contribution over time—is still an alien concept. Business culture therefore remains antithetical to bold experimentation across digital domains.

Chinese consumers outpace Chinese corporations and agencies in exploring the new digital ecosystem. There are fundamental structural and cultural barriers that impede ideacentric, media-neutral advertising. Given the potential for digital engagement to redefine the relationship between consumers and brands, new media will transform the commercial and communications landscape. But, as always, progress will be agonizingly incremental.

11

E-COMMERCE IN CHINA: PATRIARCHAL BENEVOLENCE

The growth of China's consumer e-commerce sector is breathtaking, doubling year on year. Online shopping is more than a trend; it is a phenomenon. But it took a while to get there. It was not until two fundamental Chinese business concepts were addressed—the benefits and reassurance of scale, and low price as the ultimate competitive weapon—that online shopping crossed the inflection point.

The early days were not promising. Counterfeit goods were rampant and credit card penetration was low. Chinese buyers, a kick-the-tire cohort if there ever was one, were—and to a certain extent still are—suspicious of virtual transactions. These barriers have either faded away—practically everyone earning more than RMB5,000 per month owns at least one credit or debit card—or been structurally addressed by auction sites like Taobao, online booksellers like Dangdang, and specialty electronics sites like Newegg. These domestic players are avoiding the errors of their early international counterparts. eBay infamously crashed and burned on the mainland, even after it purchased online book retailer Eachnet in 2006. eBay transplanted a Western model to China and found itself outflanked by domestic competitors—its promise of the "excitement of victory" in online auctions fell flat, and the policy of charging registration fees was incredibly unpopular.

Taobao, by far the largest e-commerce generalist, currently rules the roost and will not be displaced any time soon. Statistics boggle the mind: More than 800 million products are available, with 48,000 items sold every *minute*. The site boasts more than 370 million registered users, and on good days turnover exceeds $300 million. Average individual expenditure, however, is less than $5.

The platform, a unit of Alibaba Group best known for its business-to-business network, has succeeded through low prices, an army of 100,000 couriers, user-friendly payment schemes that reduce postpurchase anxiety, and unrivaled breadth of manufacturer partnerships.

The scale imperative. In China, bigger is better because it elicits trust. Haier, the country's largest appliance manufacturer, is not particularly innovative, but consumers are drawn to its size, which suggests reliability. The company's efforts are underpinned by an expansive retail and distribution network deployed as a one-of-a-kind, national, twenty-four-hour service operation. During the past ten years, brands such as Yili and Mengniu have morphed from local dairy brands to national titans, thanks to both top-down government support and bottom-up consumer food safety concerns. Even luxury goods must project authority before craftsmanship—Louis Vuitton, Mercedes, and BMW succeeded, first and foremost, because of their global clout. In China, no one invests in status brands unless everyone recognizes them.

Taobao's scale is hugely beneficial. It satisfies consumers' demand for variety and their desire to compare endless product options. In this sense, size is liberating, delivering a new-age thrill of discovery. Scale also pulls the vast majority of business-to-consumer online retailers into the orbit of Taobao, the host of countless virtual stores. Furthermore, size translates into negotiating clout with partners. Suppliers must accept generous no-questions-asked money-back guarantees if product performance is a problem.

The satisfaction of bargaining. Cash-strapped Chinese are notoriously frugal. They are unwilling to pay an extra penny unless marketers can justify the price premium. Although face is lost when begging for a discount, mainlanders love a good bargain. It signals the ultimate aspirational personality trait—that is, resourcefulness. VIP, VVIP, and Platinum VIP cards—awarded to loyal customers who qualify for discounts—are still ubiquitous, a price of entry for any retail establishment. In China, smart shoppers know how to translate loyalty into both ego acknowledgment and price discounts.

Simply put, e-commerce makes people feel smart. In several ways, Taobao's scale has been deployed to transform the online shopping world into a wonderland of bargains. An endless array of merchandise, combined with algorithmically sophisticated search functions, facilitates comprehensive comparison pricing. There are no registration or transaction fees, and delivery charges, although not specified by Taobao, are extremely inexpensive; the price of courier service from Hangzhou to Shanghai, a journey of nearly two hours by car, is RMB5 (less than $1). Frequent limited-time-only promotions, sponsored by individual brands but hosted by Taobao, create brief windows of opportunity for savvy shoppers to grab discounts.

Taobao has shifted the balance of influence from manufacturers to hundreds of millions of Chinese consumers, each of whom has a voice in determining influential quality rankings by the awarding of "crowns" (the equivalent of stars).

Imperial control of information. In today's digital universe, data is power. Taobao, as well as other large vertically integrated e-commerce platforms, owns the transactional information—conversion and promotion hit rates, top-selling items, and so on—retailers depend on to gauge effectiveness of online activities. These data, jealously guarded, are then sold to manufacturers and research houses at a steep price. Just as the Communist Party exists as an ultimate arbiter of knowledge, information in the e-commerce universe is controlled and managed by digital giants who, in turn, exist by the grace of the omnipotent Ministry of Commerce.

Even social network traffic flows, instrumental in leading shoppers to specific websites, are influenced by centralized entities. Cost-per-sale "unions" (partisan groups of netizens) are paid to seed messages among thousands of bloggers and opinion leaders. They, in turn, drive traffic to specific e-commerce destinations. In return, the unions are entitled to approximately 20 percent of a retailer's click-through revenue.

E-COMMERCE AND GOVERNMENT

China's e-commerce scene is, like the Internet itself, a paradoxical combination of people power and top-down management. The government, working through companies happy to comply with state regulations, has imposed a framework that grants infinitely more transparency than existed before the digital revolution, bringing consumerist harmony to peasants and city dwellers alike. At the same time, the party has the final word on what is, and is not, allowed into the public domain. Patriarchal responsiveness, which most Chinese consider benevolent but is ultimately autocratic, portends a gradual evolution of China's traditional model of economic and political management. Revolution—a consumer-led free-for-all—is not in the cards.

12

ILLEGAL DVDs: WHY PIRACY IS HERE TO STAY

The *shanzhai* phenomenon—the imitation and piracy of brands—has become a national point of pride. Any country without intellectual property (IP) enforcement mechanisms has knockoffs, but the gusto with which Chinese infringe on IP agreements both frustrates and impresses. Nothing is off limits. Every luxury brand—from Coach to Fendi to Rolex to Omega—has battled with high-quality counterfeits for decades. Retail is no longer safe. Mickey Mouse and Hello Kitty have evil twins, while McDonald's and Starbucks look-alikes proliferate. When three fake Apple Stores opened in Kunming, a city in China's southwest, microblog posts raved that flawless execution was a testament to Chinese ingenuity. Knockoff baigoogledu.com displays the results of Google and Baidu—the most popular search engines in America and China, respectively—side by side. Fake iPhones have double SIM card slots. Unauthorized "Apple skin" covers turn an iPod Touch into a mobile phone.

THE CULTURAL CONTEXT

Disregard for intellectual property rights is deeply rooted in Chinese culture and will not disappear any time soon. A famous maxim of unknown origin states, "To steal a book is an elegant offense." Why elegant? Historically, unauthorized dissemination of imperial texts was a "noble crime" because, even though the texts were contraband, their distribution propagated traditional definitions of morality and hence strong central control. In an email exchange, Kristin Stapleton, professor of Chinese history at the State University of New York at Buffalo, noted, "The culture of the literati in imperial eras de-emphasized

Image 12.1 Microsoft's "Real is Better" campaign for Windows is one of the first efforts to tackle the issue of counterfeit products head-on. This ad dramatizes the risk of using fakes. The headline, a play on words, states, "Never Any Praise vs. Nonstop Praise." (Courtesy Da Mu Studio and Microsoft Corporation)

original creation, largely because of the backward-looking nature of Confucian thought." Imperial information, an expression of heaven's mandate, was sacred.

IP protection will always be an uphill struggle. Individual rights remain a theoretical notion at best. Chinese civilization exists courtesy of top-down command. Even the education system militates against broad-based embrace of IP protection.

Furthermore, the Chinese revere the concrete, the here and now. Unless IP infringement is broadly seen as an immediate threat to economic success, or advanced as a vital state interest, few will rally to its cause. To date, it is happening only in a few industries in which China hopes to develop a competitive advantage, such as software engineering and green energy.

Some companies are making appeals to the public to indirectly encourage the government to enforce existing regulations. Microsoft, in its groundbreaking "Real Is Better" campaign, capitalizes on the growth of online financial transactions by dramatizing the personal risks of using pirated Windows. Many consumers think illegal software is the smart choice because it's essentially free. Computer sales people have incentive to reinforce this perception because they increase margins by replacing genuine with fake products at the point of purchase. Wei Qing, the head of Microsoft's Windows business group, says, "We want to create a new religion, a new standard of civility in China. It will take a long time." Research suggests that preliminary efforts have helped increase preferences for genuine.

Chinese intellectually grasp the link between IP and innovation, but the threat does not yet hit home. Lax IP enforcement has not impeded China's crawl up the value chain thus far. New technologies will find their way into the country through joint venture agreements with foreign investors, indigenous development under the aegis of the state, and theft. The government knows current practices can't be legally justified—World Trade Organization (WTO) regulations are explicit—but it is unable or unwilling to confront the problem.

PIRATED MOVIES: THE CHUTZPAH!

The unabashed proliferation of illegal DVDs and music is probably the most striking feature of the *shanzhai* landscape. They are flagrant, out in the open, on every corner of every city. The international community is applying pressure—notably through the WTO—and China has responded by emphasizing its desire to elicit change and instigating intermittent crackdowns. For a while, pirated movie websites were prohibited from streamlining American and European films and television shows and, during the Shanghai World Expo,

Image 12.2 Illegal DVD stores are everywhere, close to the street, down hidden alleys. The government has no incentive to clamp down, except when senior American leaders visit. (Courtesy ImagineChina)

foreign titles were moved to the back of shops, sometimes behind hidden doors. Nevertheless, little can be achieved so long as the government is not prepared to clamp down on suppliers of pirated DVDs.

Needed: A new business model. On the Western front, no one has advanced a business model that generates incremental revenue for producers and offers prices low enough to compete with a product available cheaply (for about $1) in illegal shops or free through the Internet. Theoretically, this shouldn't be too difficult. Because of the poor quality standards of bootlegged disks and the slow download time on unlawful websites, Chinese consumers would be willing to pay, say, $2.50 for a high-quality DVD and perhaps a bit less for the virtual version. True, China margins would be lower than in the West, but, at this point, any return is better than no return at all.

A recent deal struck between Baidu, China's largest search engine, and One-Stop China, a joint venture involving Universal Music, Warner Music, and Sony, could be a hint of things to come. Baidu will effectively pay a licensing fee to the joint venture, supported through advertising revenues, for the rights to stream catalog songs and new releases. It will compensate music owners on a per-play and per-download basis for all tracks delivered through its MP3 search function. This untested model, an acknowledgment that a bit of revenue is better than nothing, could inspire other Western producers to establish unconventional partnerships with Internet portals and other sites that enjoy heavy traffic. Sohu.com already pays for streaming rights to *The Big Bang Theory, Mad Men,* and *Gossip Girl.*

Censorship forever. Government censorship policies further complicate matters because they increase the demand for contraband content. Even if the party liberalizes distribution restrictions per WTO regulations, censors will sanction only a narrow range of content in legal channels, both digital and brick-and-mortar. These neutered commercial entities struggle to compete with illegal brethren, an array of individually owned outlets, many stocked with thousands of titles, organized in category-specific formats similar to what one finds in an American video shop. (There is even a well-known hierarchy of copy quality—the lowest is DVD-5, then DVD-9, then DVD-Blu-ray.)

This begs the question of Chinese censorship and what is, and is not, allowed. As in dynastic times, anything inconsistent with the government's role of promoting a harmonious society will be prohibited. The natural hierarchy of the *wu lun,* five key relationship dyads that dictate human intercourse—between father and son, husband and wife, older brother and younger brother, friend and friend, and ruler and ruled—must be maintained. Notably, groups must never seek to become alternative centers of authority and challenge the party, and explicit or extramarital sexuality is always banned. The latter is driven by both the sensitivities of a genuinely conservative population and the government's patriarchal responsibility to protect the moral standing of the masses.

See no evil: Pragmatic release. It is important to note that the party has an interest in turning a blind eye to illegal content. Its "don't ask, don't tell" commercial policy tolerates a thousand points of sinful light. Ultraviolent video games are pervasive in Internet bars; illegal DVD shops sell anything and everything; and the digital universe is chock-a-block with porn—straight, gay, and everything in between. Prostitution rings are openly advertised in cyberspace.

So long as it remains in power, the government will never liberalize censorship rules or entertainment distribution. But it will not crack down, either. In Western eyes, this is profoundly hypocritical. To the Chinese, though, it is pragmatic. In China's high-context, morally relativistic universe, understatement—that is, knowing when to turn a blind eye to transgression—is both a skill of advancement and contributor to social order. The government realizes that the people, torn between Confucian regimentation and upwardly mobile ambition, are emotionally repressed and therefore crave release. So long as the channels through which this is delivered remain narrow and pose no threat to centralized authority, they will be accommodated. The 2009 Green Dam Youth Escort initiative, a quickly aborted attempt to control access to unpalatable Internet sites, elicited howls of indignation. Any efforts to clamp down on Western entertainment would be equally explosive, given the watered-down menu available through legitimate channels.

Is this so bad? Certainly, to foreign content providers, it is indefensible. That said, illicit entertainment has, in unquantifiable yet important ways, enhanced the relationship between Chinese and Western people. The Chinese love pop culture—*Desperate Housewives*, *24*, *Prison Break*, *Lost*, *Ugly Betty*, Michael Jackson, Mariah Carey, and all things hip hop. Western values of self-expression and individual opportunity are projected daily onto millions of television and computer screens. They are the most powerful antidotes to a new generation's increasingly sharp-edged Chinese nationalism.

In this sense, Western entertainment executives are potent cultural ambassadors, despite their forced pro bono contributions to global harmony. Unfortunately, they may never make a buck off it.

13

THE BUSINESS OF ADVERTISING IN CHINA: INCREMENTAL PROGRESS, NO BREAKTHROUGH

One of the most effective ways to impress China's glorious opportunities upon colleagues from abroad is go for a meal at a restaurant on the Bund in Shanghai. Overlooking the Huangpu River, the location offers a jaw-dropping view of both the stately architecture of the city's colonial heyday and a new, soaring skyline. The scene triggers a Pavlovian response from hungry ad execs, globalists raring to capitalize on an emerging giant's growth potential.

JWT is optimistic about China's ability to evolve into a civilized brand-scape, but we are also pragmatic. The Olympics did not herald an inflection point; progress will continue to be incremental, sometimes excruciatingly so. China remains a tough nut to crack, and expectations must be realistic.

CAUSES FOR CONCERN

Talent crisis. The fact that foreigners—including expatriate Chinese from Hong Kong, Taiwan, Malaysia, and Singapore—are still reasonably represented at the higher levels of the industry is a disappointment. Of course, there will always be a need for individuals with an international outlook to serve clients with operations outside the mainland. But advertising, as an industry, has had difficulty developing local talent. It's neither a salary problem nor a lack of intent on the part of agencies; the biggest challenge is that advertising is not fundamentally respected as a career path for many locals. An ad person's key strength is the ability to articulate the abstract and lead clients to embrace what can't be proven. The largely conceptual task doesn't appeal to many Chinese, who tend to take refuge in the concrete. There are too many talented thirty-five-year-olds who abandon the industry for a more respectable career. The ones who stick with it, and who have the capacity to inspire, are worth their weight in gold.

Vicious competition. There are too many agencies—more than 100,000 of all shapes and sizes. This surfeit leads to cutthroat competition, low fees, and plummeting profits. Client relationships with advertising agents are a promiscuous series of affairs in which short-term contracts are awarded to the lowest bidder. In fourteen years, I haven't seen a single local advertising agency become a viable competitor to multinational shops—even though most multinationals are hobbled by underinvestment and a severe talent shortage. Local agencies have not evolved to address the long-term brand-building needs of large corporations, multinational or domestic. The agencies' limitations are common to many industries in China, both manufacturing and services. There has been a chronic underinvestment in mid- and senior-level managers capable of abstract conceptualization, leaders who have the courage to challenge clients. For every million dollars in revenue, there are usually forty to fifty low-paid and under-trained employees, compared with fifteen relatively skilled staff in international shops. This means, for local shops, competitive strength is a question of quick turnaround and low price. Relationships with clients are reactive, not strategic, and significant profit is derived from media kickbacks.

Misleading size. The real China advertising market isn't that big. Reported figures highlight an ad spend well above $120 billion, but the figure is grossly inflated because all advertisers enjoy hefty discounts, anywhere from 25 percent to 70 percent off book rates. Furthermore, the accessible client base—local and multinational companies that will pay a premium to achieve deep brand equity—accounts for no more than 20 percent of industry revenue. Although this market accounts for an increasingly large slice of the pie (and is served exclusively by multinational agencies), the potential of China is still relatively constrained by Western standards and will remain so for years to come.

Shallow Chinese brands. Any market's potential ultimately hinges on the strength of its local brands, but the majority of state-owned enterprises are not structured to build equity. As discussed in chapter 3, there are few Chinese labels actively preferred by mainland consumers. While exceptions exist in the luxury cigarette and liquor categories, most are regarded, at best, as reliable commodities. This is because senior management is not market driven, and politically tethered corporate governance does not reward long-term shareholder growth; hierarchy impedes the flow of ideas between market-savvy young guns and CEOs, most of them imperial, self-protective Communist Party apparatchiks;

marketing is subordinate to sales—the latter controls budgets, while the former churns out promotional ads; and there is a lack of understanding of how to measure the success and depth of brands.

CAUSES FOR OPTIMISM

Deregulation. The legal barriers to acquisition and diversification, while still complex, are falling, making it easier for traditional advertising agencies to evolve into full-service communications groups. The JWT China Group, for example, generates almost 50 percent of its revenue from nontraditional services, including field marketing, trade consulting, branding and identity design, and customer relationship management. As recently as five years ago, the company's offering was primarily traditional advertising—that is, work placed on television or in magazines or newspapers. The digital revolution has dramatically opened consumers' minds to new products and services. From home decoration to automobiles, broad Internet penetration has accelerated consumers' knowledge, resulting in stunningly rapid adoption curves across a swathe of categories. HSBC, for example, is using customer relationship management to educate mainlanders about financial management and, at the same time, sell HSBC Premier accounts.

Microeconomic fundamentals. Chinese enterprises must reform or die. The most daunting structural challenge is production overcapacity, a legacy of the country's decomposing command economy. From air conditioners to autos and computers to apparel, supply far outstrips demand. To survive, companies have no choice but to end the vicious cycle of plummeting prices and surging red ink. They must build consumer loyalty, forge a sustained price premium by cultivating brand equity, and reinvest profits in future growth. In the past couple years, even state-owned enterprises such as Yili Group, one of the country's largest dairy companies, and telecom carrier China Unicom have begun to incrementally restructure and implement technocratic brand-building templates. While none has evolved into a true market-driven entity, progress is undeniable and bodes well for the future. More than 45 percent of JWT's revenue is from local clients, up from nothing ten years ago.

Deepening (pragmatic) partnerships. All local clients have certain things in common. They are hierarchical and the big boss wields absolute control, so maintaining close relationships—building trust, rooted in a combination of value-added expertise and empathy—with the CEO, or founder, is absolutely critical. Nevertheless, there are differences. Large state-owned enterprises tend to be much more Byzantine in terms of decision making, with one eye focused on the market and the other on political imperatives. Smaller private enterprises are more entrepreneurial, more apt to take risks and decide things relatively quickly. They also tend to be more receptive to unsafe creativity. The joy of working with local companies, despite the operational and relationship management challenges, is that they are genuinely passionate about their brands. Their ambitions are huge. They also have a natural appreciation of the ins and outs of both the Chinese market and the Chinese consumer, leading to bolder experimentation, assuming the stars are aligned in terms of clear objectives and open communication. From an ad agency's perspective, it's very much high-risk, high-return. Consequently, work done for local clients such as fashion retailer Metersbonwe or even COFCO, China's largest food conglomerate, is just as rewarding as that done for the largest multinationals like Ford or Nokia or Microsoft.

The pitch made to local business leaders is simple and hardheaded: Robust brand equity—that is, active consumer loyalty to a brand—leads to premium prices and a high price-to-earnings ratio. Popular brands are emotional propositions, ones that fuse functional and emotional appeal. Most leaders need convincing that when function and emotion are aligned, they are mutually reinforcing, and there is no need to choose between tactical and thematic campaigns, between nuts-and-bolts and evocative messages. Grasping how global brand-building concepts translate into a framework that leads to long-term propositions and justifies price premiums involves a certain amount of reorientation.

The analytical robustness of any recommendation has to be empirically bulletproof. Once business leaders endorse the logical thought flow, from underlying business problem to creative solution, minds open, and decision makers are able to put themselves more easily in consumers' shoes.

Consumer motivations. Chinese consumers—there are currently more than 125 million individuals with middle-class purchasing power—are a potent force. They are also the most brand-friendly people in the world. The hearts of Chinese people are conflicted between Confucian demands to both conform to the mandates of a hierarchical social structure and climb a narrow ladder of success. The pull between ambition and regimentation yields a coexistence of huge egos and weak self-esteem. Individual identities are repressed. In this fear-based, ultra-aggressive context, brands are instrumental identity surrogates. Consumers hungrily latch onto them as status projectors, particularly publicly displayed labels.

Brands are also embraced because they alleviate the disorientation of an overwhelmed new consumer set. Fifteen years ago, there was only one way to place a call: the public phone. Today there are more than three hundred models of mobile devices to choose from. Strong brands are, if nothing else, appreciated as efficient organizing concepts.

PART THREE

THE NEW, OLD CHINESE CONSUMER

14

BARBIE, STARBUCKS, AND COFCO: AN INTRODUCTION TO CHINESE CONSUMERISM

Although Mattel still insists it has big plans for the doll-cum-fashion-icon in China, Barbie's splashy debut was an embarrassing fizzle. In 2009, her corporate Svengalis opened a multistory glass shrine to our lily-white princess of American self-driven individualism. Nine months later, the flagship store closed. Planted at the epicenter of Shanghai's fashion district on Huaihai Road, its aisles overflowed with a plethora of outfits and accessories. Barbie swept onto the mainland projecting a colorful, modern, and international lifestyle. Theoretically, she should have entranced a new generation of Chinese adolescents, girls who dream big. The "Barbie ideal" is aspirational, at least among the optimistic middle class. But Barbie is white. She remains the quintessence of scrubbed-clean California. In the words of my fourteen-year-old next-door neighbor, "Barbie is so 'obvious.' She means nothing to me." Hello Kitty, meanwhile, never goes out of style. Her porcelain skin, round face, and invisible mouth are perennially popular. Her commercial appeal springs from a fusion of cuteness and understatement, two distinctly Chinese characteristics.

Starbucks thrives. In one of the great Houdini acts of marketing, Starbucks has profitably opened more than five-hundred coffee shops in a land that does not like coffee. The chain plans to operate 1,500 stores by 2015. How in heaven's name did Starbucks accomplish this in China's tea culture? First, Howard Schultz, the company's CEO, had the foresight to delegate major strategic decisions to Maxim Caterers, Starbucks's Hong Kong–based joint venture partner and fast-food operator. (In 2011, Starbucks started buying back shares

Image 14.1 Hello Kitty, although Japanese, is the epitome of Chinese feminine understated resourcefulness. Her facial expressions are muted, and she doesn't even have a mouth. She sells like gangbusters. Barbie didn't stand a chance. (Courtesy JWT)

Image 14.2 Starbucks in China is not an urban oasis of relaxation. The brand has achieved success as a gathering place for new-generation professionals, folks willing pay four dollars for a cup of coffee emblazoned with a premium logo. (Courtesy Frank Xu)

with the intention of eventually becoming sole owner.) Second, from the out-set, Starbucks did not try to persuade mainlanders to love expensive coffee. The "perfect blend" was deployed to reinforce international clout and quality standards, both fundamental in reinforcing a premium image. But Starbucks brilliantly established its stores as upscale public destinations. Isolated plush chairs were replaced with long tables large enough to seat professional groups eager to project new-generation affiliation in a public context and willing to pay for the privilege. Extensive tea options were brought in, sandwich and snack menus were broadened, and logo-emblazoned accessories—mugs, travel cups, even knapsacks—were introduced. And a successful office delivery ser-vice was introduced. Today, any commercial building without a Starbucks is grade B. Unilever, meanwhile, struggles to convert tea drinkers from green to black. Neither Nestlé nor Kraft has made inroads with roasted and ground cof-fee. Three-in-ones, presweetened instant coffee packets, sometimes called the candy of coffee, dominate cupboards.

COFCO stands up. COFCO—Chinese National Cereals, Oils and Foodstuffs Corporation—is China's largest food manufacturer, the holding company of brands that stretch across several categories, from cooking oil and noodles to chocolate and ham. A prototypical *yangqi*—a state-owned enterprise managed directly by the central government—COFCO was founded in 1949 as a foodstuff importer and exporter, but until recently Chinese consumers were not aware of the company, only its individual brands. After the 2009 tainted-milk scandal (dangerous levels of melamine were discovered in milk and infant formula, raising concerns about food safety and political corruption) COFCO turned crisis into opportunity. Led by its chair, Ning Gaoning, the company standardized production across all product lines and announced the news with a campaign heralding *quan chanye lian*, or complete chain management opti-mization. To Westerners, dry stuff indeed. But nervous locals welcomed the move and corporate brand awareness rose from 3 percent to 64 percent. Sales increased across major product lines. COFCO, heretofore the epitome of tech-nocratic facelessness, emerged as "a friend of the masses."

These minicases illustrate that China's consumers still march to a different beat. They are increasingly modern and international, but they are not becom-ing Western. They are motivated by a timeless need to project status, the weapon of advancement. But they are also plagued by anxiety about a world in which corruption rules and material interests are still legally unprotected.

Unifying conflict. The pervasive Confucian conflict, directly or indirectly, affects all marketing strategy. This tension between upward mobility and fear-based conformism shows up everywhere. Brands that help consumers simulta-neously stand out and fit in have the greatest appeal. Diamonds, for example, are popular because their sparkle is conspicuous but, at the same time, elegant and understated. The same goes for Mont Blanc's six-point-star logo. Furthermore, consumers are willing to pay a premium for any product that delivers a public payoff and, hence face. That's why Nike running shoes, infinitely cooler than domestic competitors, command a 250 percent price markup relative to cost of goods.

This unifying theme needs to be interpreted for different socioeconomic tiers. In lower-tier markets, definitions of success are more short term, more inextricably linked to the home. We also tend to emphasize protection because consumers who are not middle class—those who have benefited less from waves of economic reform—are less convinced that the world is safe. Likewise, brands are less familiar in tier-three, -four, and -five cities, so communications must be simpler and more direct than in primary markets, and the role of in-store experience and reassurance is vital.

Pragmatic advancement. Products need to be positioned as a means to an end, with clear return on investment. Communications must also dramatize public consumption in order to justify a price premium.

All benefits in China are externalized; egos are huge and everyone, from professionals on down, demands societal acknowledgment for contributions to and success within society. Luxury goods are tools for career development. (Disney's chain of English-language schools has succeeded spectacularly.) In the West, goods are often appreciated for their intrinsic quality. (Sometimes, this difference can be quite subtle. Europeans go to spas to relax. Chinese go to recharge batteries.) There is no cynicism toward brands. Furthermore, in a constricted mass-media environment and a society with a narrow definition of success, brands are the most powerful badges of identity. They are, by far, the freest platforms of expression and, as a result, beloved.

Rampant mistrust. The Chinese are suspicious shoppers because China's economic and industrial landscape remains uncivil, with limited protection of individual physical and economic interests. As a rule, they do not trust local manufacturers or take quality for granted. Reassurance in terms of product quality and affordability is critical:

- Consumers cotton to megabrands and conglomerates, entities such as Procter & Gamble or COFCO, whose swagger signals reliability. (Consumers would accept a Procter & Gamble infant formula, despite the company's lack of experience in this category.)
- Given comparable price, international brands are preferred to domestic ones, even in "Chinese" areas such as food, beverages, and over-the-counter pharmaceuticals.

- E-commerce volumes did not achieve critical mass until online retailers offered delayed payment schemes, risk-free money-back guarantees, and no transaction fees.

The following chapters will further explore the consistent yet shape-shifting undercurrents of the Chinese consumer, both status driven and self-protective, including the constants and variables of China's rapidly expanding middle class; ambivalent Tiger Moms and brands' roles in resolving the tension between ensuring both childhood delight and academic excellence; the psychological contours of the country's vast digital domain; the hypercompetitive auto market, an arena in which ego and anxiety collide; the dynamics of China's rising luxury segment; the creeping optimism of still-jittery consumers in lower-tier cities; and the crosscurrents of food consumption, at home versus in public.

15

THE NEW MIDDLE CLASS: CONSTANTS AND VARIABLES

China's middle class, a modern force with timeless cultural imperatives, will reshape the world. To harness its spending power, marketers must realize that becoming modern and international is not tantamount to becoming Western—Chinese consumers exhibit a unique combination of motivations and conflicts.

The middle classes as a demographic only really came about at the turn of the twenty-first century. Although Deng Xiaoping's 1992 Southern Tour effectively legitimized private wealth—and gave his economic reforms a much-needed fillip—the impact on people's lives was not really felt until the late 1990s. The sheer scale and magnitude of this transformation marks a spectacular inflection point for China—yet nobody has really come up with a suitable definition of the middle class.

Many analysts consider household earnings of RMB5,000 per month (about $1,400 on an adjusted purchasing-power parity [PPP] basis) is considered the lower edges of the middle class. The core middle class starts from RMB20,000 a month ($5,700 on an adjusted PPP basis). There are about 125 million people in this category—basically, anyone who is not struggling for day-to-day survival. According to Euromonitor International, a London-based market research firm, the middle class in China is defined as households with an annual income between RMB60,000 and RMB500,000; it estimates there will be more than 700 million people in this category by 2020. It is certainly a fallacy that this class exists in the primary cities only; it is to be found in every urban area in China, as can be seen in the growth of car ownership across all cities.

WHAT THE MIDDLE CLASS WANTS

Broadly speaking, the Chinese middle classes believe that with the right competitive tools, they will find an opportunity to transform their lives, in contrast to a blue-collar laborer, who sees his social and economic status as more or less fixed. It's the difference between basic needs of survival and physical safety and a need to satisfy social status requirements. The middle class engages with society to get recognition for financial success. It's important to note, though, that this is not about arrival, it's about being on the right journey—they see theirs as a continuous struggle upward, and there is an acute awareness that all could be lost in the blink of an eye. There is a need to demonstrate how high you have climbed but also to protect that ascent. Insecurity abounds. Civic institutions are unreliable; there is no political representation; wealth is not protected institutionally; the safety net, particularly health insurance, is incomplete. People say that all they want is to be happy and to be in control of their destiny, but at the same time they understand that this ideal is not truly practical. The political and bureaucratic system is too firmly entrenched to buck.

More subtly, on an emotional level, there is a sense that there are certain essential rites of passage to middle-class status, such as homes, diamond rings, education, and car ownership. But these items are expensive, and disposable incomes remain low—so how does one decide what to buy? Above all, the middle class seeks to create something sustainable, reducing the chances of falling off the middle-class pedestal. This pressure weighs particularly heavily on men, who are the ultimate providers for their clan and often do not feel in control. A man's ability to fulfill this role determines whether or not he is regarded as an upstanding member of society. Individuals are incredibly conservative; they seek society's endorsement in order to know that they have mastered the rules and climbed the predefined hierarchy.

ORDER vs. CHAOS

Every strand of Chinese thinking reinforces the supremacy of stability and order; the country is unique for its conflict between ambition and conformity, from abiding by the hierarchy to pulling yourself up the hierarchy. Wound into this is an extraordinarily ambivalent relationship with the state. The central government is seen as the means for people to advance and to create order from chaos. While there is a general frustration with corruption and the slow pace of reform, and widespread demand for institutional reform that protects the interests of society, no one wants rebellion. They want a continuation of the status quo, with the state as the lynchpin. Strong government is necessary to assuage the classic middle-class fear that things could fall apart at any moment.

Reform is happening, but it is a slow race between what the state will allow and what the people will tolerate. With average annual per capita incomes still comparatively low and urbanization far from complete, it will be decades before the basic current structures of power reach a critical contradiction. But those at the top of the socioeconomic pyramid are already hedging their bets. This is why so many of China's wealthiest citizens are busy securing foreign passports as insurance against future instability. Nearly half of Chinese with assets worth more than 10 million yuan, or $1.6 million, are considering moving abroad, according to a 2011 survey by the Bank of China and the Hurun Report, a compilation of the PRC's richest individuals. The US and Canada, countries perceived to offer robust rule of law, are the most popular destinations. The main reasons given are better education and asset security, and a less polluted environment.

EVOLUTION OF MIDDLE-CLASS
CONSUMPTION PATTERNS

Historically, the Chinese are incredibly price sensitive when it comes to products for the home. These items will not be exposed to societal scrutiny—the home is rarely visited by outsiders—and given the need for conspicuous consumption it makes sense for cost savings to start here. You don't see people spending money on expensive bedspreads. That said, comfort is important, and both the willingness to indulge and consumer education on product quality are growing, albeit relatively slowly and from a low base. This is a typical symptom of an evolving middle class.

Evolution means not only the range of goods that appear to consumers is changing but also the value placed on quality services—be it banking or health care. There is a dearth of good service in China, and there seems to be an ever-widening gap between what's available and what is in demand. The time is ripe for foreign companies, with more knowledge and experience than their domestic counterparts, to enter the market. This begs two questions. First, will the government recognize the need for foreign competition in the sector and allow liberalization? Second, how will foreign companies decide to play aspirations of individualism and the reality of social conformity?

PROMOTING SOCIAL ADVANCEMENT

While China's middle class is becoming more modern and international, it is not becoming more Western. A brand's success is rooted in an appreciation of people's fundamental motivations—and in China this means that a premium-priced product must be a tool for social advancement. And the range of product categories perceived to achieve this objective has expanded significantly.

DeBeers. In the fifteen years since DeBeers entered the market, the penetration of diamond engagement rings has risen from 8 percent to 80 percent. The company achieved this by understanding that marriage is perceived differently among Chinese than Westerners. While the latter like to believe that passion and romance last forever, the former see commitment as persistent, not love as such. De Beers gave the Chinese man a tool to demonstrate his reliability.

SK-II. Upper mid-tier skin-care products such as P&G's SKII are achieving critical mass. The desire of middle-class women to leverage youthful beauty as a professional competitive advantage has resulted in the reduction of the white space between extremely expensive luxury brands such as Estée Lauder and Dior and local mass-market products.

Siemens. Most Chinese consumers are still loath to purchase expensive foreign appliances because they are used only at home and the quality of local brands is acceptable. However, products that have high visibility or can be displayed have made great strides. Siemens, despite an average price premium of 40 percent versus Haier, is the second largest refrigerator brand after Haier.

The bottom line is that the product is a means to an end. The Chinese have no excuse for buying luxury goods, given their level of income, but luxury is so externalized it enables inconspicuously conspicuous consumption—that is, the ability to show off without being seen to do so. It is all about convincing consumers that the product will help them climb the social ladder. If there is a craftsmanship to selling products in China, it's communicating how a product will help the owner solidify status while avoiding clichés.

THE JOURNEY OF SUCCESS

Clichés can be avoided if marketers acknowledge that China's middle class is not a monolithic socioeconomic slab. Yes, all aspiring professionals—in China, career and class identity are inextricably linked—are torn between impulses to, on one hand, boldly project status and, on the other, remain understated. Across all income levels, achievement must be underpinned by substance, lest suspicions of superficiality arise. Every member of China's new middle class is on an arduous journey to success, a climb, up different tiers and income levels, to the top of Mount Glory. But there are differences. Ten years ago, practically every-one was a neophyte. Today, the middle- and upper-middle, as well as wealthy classes have all achieved critical mass. The strategies of brands targeted to each must shift accordingly.

Acceptance. Young college graduates, earning RMB4,000 to RMB5,000 per month, are unproven, in search of acceptance. They need acknowledgment of their potential, not admiration for their achievement. Sail, one of the least expensive vehicles sold by General Motors, celebrates a "new world, opening its doors for you." But the "new man's" initial excitement is quickly replaced by a fear of elimination. Wrigley's Double Mint chewing gum asks, "Are you really ready?" and presents fresh breath as a shield against coworker alienation. For individuals just out of the starting gate, brands can sharpen their basic survival skills—to pounce on opportunity or demonstrate their potential. Rejoice sham-poo links dandruff-free hair to having the confidence to approach the boss when a chance to translate English arises. Ariel detergent links clean, white shirts with an ability to "rise and shine at the office."

Recognition. Once strivers are in mid-career, they must be recognized for both their past achievements and their capacity for further advancement. Products play an active role in their winning the game by demonstrating their advanced survival skills. In one ad, Sony Handycam associates digital trans-mission capabilities with resourcefulness by, somewhat ironically, enabling a vacationing professional to delay returning to work. Technology brands from Motorola to NEC to Hewlett Packard are productivity weapons, competitive advantages deployed on the business battlefield. As people scale their work hier-archies, it also becomes increasingly important to them to sharpen their internal tools—for example, a "heart both focused and wild" (Kia Motors), "determina-tion to face the future" (China Mobile's Go Tone network), a "combination of calmness and the will to go the distance" (Buick Regal), and "breadth of vision, over time and place" (Sapphire Cove, a real estate complex).

During the middle stages of advancement, a happy family is an important fac-tor, a necessary-but-not-sufficient prerequisite to being taken seriously as an adult constructively engaged with society. That's why many automobile ads targeted to business people feature parents with their (only) child and Epson commercial printers dramatize color accuracy by depicting a father educating his daughter.

Admiration and iconization. Toward the top of the hierarchy, the *laoban*, or boss, requires unanimous respect and deference. Given the ubiquity of rival factions and impatient upstarts, power is conditional. Authority, therefore, must be self-evident—hence premium Ballantine scotch's tagline, "When suc-cess speaks for itself, there is no need to show off," or BMW's call to "Reflect your inner leadership spirit."

In China, iconic stature is the best defense against corporate maneuvering. Icons are paragons of wisdom, masters of the system. They are revered because they both lead and teach. This is why the most premium products often base their appeal in "shared mastery" and "artistic connoisseurship," potent demonstrations of internalized confidence. The late Chen Yifei, China's most esteemed contemporary painter, equated depth of creative vision with the digital pixilation of LG's flat-screen televisions. And Chen Xiyang, a famous conductor, intones, "True masterpieces are tried and tested over time, just like Zun Zai Lai premium yellow wine."

The middle class is on a perilous journey of advancement, both material and societal. In this context, brands should enable strivers to achieve surer footing every step of the way.

16

CHINA'S LOWER-TIER CITIES: BRIGHTER EYES, BIGGER MARKETS

During the past decade, in tandem with the central government's campaign to rebalance investment between coastal and inland cities, a new mass-market consumer class has emerged. A huge income gap still exists between urban and rural residents, and the consumer spending share of GDP is at historic lows—it has gone down by seven percentage points over the last decade to 36 percent; in the US it is 70 percent. But purchasing power in second- to fourth-tier cities is increasing by about 10 percent per year. This raises the question of what motivates lower-tier consumers. The tension between self-protection and ego gratification afflicts both lower-income and coastal consumers, but the former are easily the more cautious.

DEFINING AN EVOLVING LOWER-TIER MARKET

A growing middle class. Mass-market and lower-tier consumers are not the same. Practically every medium-sized city—provincial, capital, or otherwise—has a nucleus of individuals with a household income in excess of RMB5,000 per month—which is often defined as the lower threshold of the middle class. These people's buying motivations—protection at home and bold status projection in the public arena—are essentially the same everywhere. The challenges in targeting the inland middle class are operational, not attitudinal. Companies must transform inefficient, multilayered sales and distribution channels into more centralized, cost-effective networks that reduce kickbacks, lower intermediary fees, and monitor inventory flows.

And wealthier mass-market consumers. There has long been a sizeable mass market in coastal capitals. But the emergence of a new mass market in lower-tier cities is a relatively recent phenomenon. It is important to note that there is no formal definition of city tiers. Shanghai, Beijing, Guangzhou, and Shenzhen are generally classified as first-tier because of their size and per capita income. These four metropolises represent 9 percent of China's total population. Prefecture- or county-level capitals are generally classed in the third tier. But the breakdown between, say, tier two and tier three cities is not precise. Property broker Knight Frank defines second-tier cities as having populations of more than three million and a minimum average annual per capita income of US$2,000. Using that definition, there are about sixty cities that are second tier.

Despite increasing raw material and real estate costs that are driven by global commodity shortages and mainland property speculation, domestic and multinational companies are investing heavily to capitalize on the growth and rising incomes of markets:

- It is rumored Apple will introduce a cheaper version of the iPhone with a retail price of less than RMB1,000.
- Both Anta and Lining, the largest local sports shoe and apparel manufacturers, operate more than 9,000 retail outlets, mostly in cities in the second, third, and fourth tiers.
- Metersbonwe, the largest youth fashion brand, now manages more than 3,000 stores and has enjoyed compounded growth of almost 50 percent since the middle of the past decade. Its blue jeans cost RMB200, double or triple the price of unbranded competitors.
- In tier-two and tier-three cities, international apparel brands (the Gap, Zara, and H&M) are filling in the white space between luxury fashion brands and generic, low-end merchandise. In Xiamen, a medium-sized city in southern Fujian province, there are already four Uniqlo stores, and their prices are marginally higher than in the chain's Japanese home market.
- Ford has expanded its inland sales network; by the end of 2012, it will manage five hundred distributors, up from only two hundred at the beginning of 2011. (Low-priced local auto brands such as BYD are almost exclusively sold in lower-tier areas.)
- Anheuser-Busch InBev has acquired several provincial breweries. Harbin, originally a northern regional brand, is expanding nationally, at price points significantly higher than local competitors'.

- Lenovo has pinned global growth prospects on penetrating the hinterland. The company has dramatically deepened its sales and distribution network, right down to the rural fringe.

MASS-MARKET MOTIVATIONS

So the inland mass market is alive and kicking. But what motivates the people driving growth?

Glimmers of new optimism. Despite continued stress and anger triggered by corrupt bureaucrats and an inadequate social safety net, things are getting better. Lower-tier consumers are distinctly more optimistic than ten years ago. Incomes are rising: the average migrant construction worker in Shanghai earns approximately RMB4,000 per month, double the amount five years ago and more than the entry-level salary for college graduates. And because of the growth of inland cities, decent jobs can be found closer to home. The synaptic gaps of infrastructural, industrial, and distribution networks are gradually closing.

Marketers have begun tap into this budding optimism. Anta's tagline—*yong bu zhi bu,* or move forward, eternally—encourages youth to tame their "dragons in the heart" through courage and perseverance. The company's 2011

Image 16.1 A tide of rising incomes means hope for the future. Despite diffused anxiety, optimism—the urge to surge—persists, at all ages and income levels. (Courtesy ImagineChina)

Image 16.2 In lower-tier cities, the basketball court is a temple of self-expression. The increasingly optimistic dreams—and frustrations—of lower-tier young male consumers were captured in Anta's 2011 "Basketball Is Life" campaign. (Courtesy Zhu Jinjing, director of JQK Production, and Anta)

"Basketball Is Life" campaign encourages young men to "at last" go for it, to play with the same drive, on and off the court. Women's aerobics, heretofore an activity for urban elites, is catching on in smaller cities as a way of "releasing joy." Denizen, Levi's mass sub-brand, encourages young people to have the courage to "fit out, start up," and step out of comfort zones. "Let's Gap Together," a striking campaign that juxtaposes Chinese and Western creativity, invites youngsters to embrace the world. Samsonite's mass premium American Tourister luggage brand exhorts a new generation that is "ready for discovery" to "take on the world." Chris Leong, the former chair of Nokia China, asserts lower-tier consumers are asking for more. "The roads are paved! Tier-four consumers are not bumpkins. They want games and entertainment. They know they can have a joyful life." Nokia's Angry Birds promotion was a smashing success.

Protection still trumps projection. Although optimistic, most lower-tier consumers still live in relatively acute economic conditions, and this will remain the case for decades. Average income is just over $100 per month. Random taxes are still imposed, despite frequent crackdowns by central government anti-corruption authorities, on everything from school fees to textbooks.

Economic distress creates distinct needs—a diffused anxiety and protective impulses—that brands must not ignore. Overall, mass-market consumers still look for different benefits from the middle class. While the latter are hope driven, poorer consumers remain relatively fear driven. They want to gain face with family and friends but are avid savers, leery of abandoning tradition and motivated by protective messages.

The schism between projective and protective values can be seen across a broad spectrum of products, particularly for everyday items. Leading lower-tier paint brands stress nontoxicity, not aesthetic expression. Wang Da Shan, a low-priced infant formula, achieved an 8 percent market share by focusing exclusively on resistance to disease, whereas leading premium brands such as Nestlé, Wyeth, and Heinz link immunity to academic performance or mental agility.

Even adult categories such as female hygiene must alter their message when broadening appeal beyond the urban middle class. At the premium end, liberation and removing barriers for success are common. However, third- and fourth-tier markets require a reassurance sell. Procter & Gamble's Whisper sanitary napkin tailors its absorption benefit differently for high- and low-income targets: "Stand up!" for middle-class consumers versus "Helps you protect your family" for lower-class consumers. Success is often defined in terms of strengthened familial bonds or admiration from the community. Ponds, a skin-care brand, links youthful skin to a romantic, stable marriage. Nokia has targeted migrant workers with the message that "friendships can grow stronger over time."

Image 16.3   In-store reassurance is critical for China's new consumers, particularly in lower-tier markets. "Promoter girls" are charged with placing products in shoppers' hands so they can examine them closely. (Courtesy Always)

It is important to note that in-store reassurance is also critical. According to the research agency Millward Brown, consumers in the third, fourth, and fifth tiers are more likely to change their preference based on information presented at the point of purchase. The agency suggests relying on in-store promoters, road shows, and sampling activities, which give inexperienced shoppers a chance to squeeze the merchandise before committing to purchase.

A FEW LOWER-TIER STRATEGIC IMPERATIVES

In addition to relevant positioning, success in the mass market requires omnipresence, value beyond price, skillful portfolio management, and direct, easy-to-digest communications.

Bigger is better. Lower-income consumers, relatively inexperienced in navigating the brand landscape, prefer the safety and security of big brands. In emerging markets, once market leadership is established, a virtuous cycle is born. Size helps by reducing the risk of losing face that can occur when seen using the wrong brand; providing surrogate indicators of quality in a country where mass-market consumers do not take basic safety for granted; and generating channel power—scale is a weapon in securing the loyalty of disjointed middlemen or centralizing promotional budgets.

Brands that boast deep penetration of the distribution channel include Lenovo, China Mobile, China Unicom, and many local appliance manufacturers such as Changhong and TCL televisions. On the multinational front, many Procter & Gamble products, including Rejoice and Head & Shoulders shampoos and Whisper sanitary napkins, are ubiquitous, as are Nokia, General Motors, and Nestlé.

Value beyond price. Low price is a necessary ingredient in achieving broad penetration, but inexpensive is not good enough. "Frugal innovation"— providing more value for less money for more people—must be relentlessly pursued. Successful brands should offer additional benefits lest they descend into a never-ending spiral of commoditized price and low loyalty:

- Nokia's success is driven by the wide availability of cheap phones, and the same is true for appliance brands. However, affordability alone is not enough to secure long-term loyalty and sustainable margins, hence Nokia's expected launch of a phone operating system that offers easier connectivity to the Internet but is not a smart phone.
- The Chevrolet Sail has redefined quality expectations of low-cost cars. It is the first purely foreign auto brand priced under RMB60,000 and has sold more than 260,000 vehicles, mostly outside primary cities.
- Canon's new product development is heavily skewed toward entry-level digital cameras. Across lower-tier markets, the company has broken the digital single lens affordability barrier.
- Procter & Gamble's Olay has scored with a natural antiwrinkle line to address lower-tier consumers' fear of chemicals.
- In partnership with GlaxoSmithKline, domestic bandage manufacturer Yunnan Baiyao has hit a home run with bandages that contain traditional Chinese ingredients, stealing 40 percent of Band-Aid's pan-China market share.
- Lenovo has pioneered development of the affordable laptop. It launched the low-end IdeaPad line and doubled the number of laptop models priced under RMB8,000.
- Hisense, a local brand, captured almost 20 percent of the liquid crystal display (LCD) television market with a low-cost flat-screen line that foreign and domestic competitors have been unable to match.

Portfolio management. Once relegated to niche status while local players met the needs of a price-sensitive mass market, most multinational brands now build image with premium products and generate scale with cheaper ones. For example, there is Rejoice Soft for high-end consumers and Rejoice Oil Free for the mass market. These tactical and thematic messages must still be harmonized with a unified brand idea. Rejoice shampoo uses "confidence from softness" across all price tiers but interprets confidence differently across different segments and price points—on one end, as a catalyst to family harmony; on the other, career progression.

Direct messaging. Above all, the golden rule of mass marketing—simple sells—is inviolable. Message comprehension is the largest barrier to purchase, particularly in lower-tier cities. This is why KK beer, a mass-market brand owned by Anheuser-Busch InBev, establishes its freshness proposition by showing a fish leaping out of a tank, and why Sunlight detergent demonstrates stain removal by holding a white collar to the sun. These concepts are creative yet direct. "Creative demonstrations," such as Rejoice's comb dropping through soft hair, work well. So do slice-of-life ads that dramatize product efficacy in the context of everyday situations.

17

CHINA'S BOOMING LUXURY MARKET: GOLD MINE OR LANDMINE?

The largest luxury manufacturers are salivating at the prospect of striking it rich in the world's fastest-growing market. Trend lines dazzle. China is now the second-largest consumer of luxury items; it boasts more millionaires than Japan. In Beijing, Shanghai, and Guangzhou, more than 80 percent of recent newlyweds earning more than $800 per month have bought a diamond engagement ring; automobile purchases—twenty million passenger cars are sold every year—have skyrocketed. The new generation is seduced by flash; the CEO and founder of Metersbonwe, China's largest youth fashion brand, possesses more than forty Mont Blanc pens.

The luxury segmentation in China is quite diverse, with CEOs sitting on top of the pile but never secure in their position; new consumers of luxury goods who see them as a means of moving forward; independent women seeking to reinforce their status and success; youth, the broadest part of the pyramid; and established wealth, the narrowest part. In each case, consumption is rooted in subtly exerting power and control—these people want to move up through the hierarchy, but their ambitions can't be too blatant. According to Taylor Nelson Sofres, a market research company, 64 percent of Chinese think luxury brands denote success, and only 1 percent believes they denote superficiality.

Image 17.1   In China, luxury consumption is an investment, a tool, a means of advancing up a narrowly defined hierarchy of success. Luxury goods are wielded as weapons on the business battlefield, not enjoyed for intrinsic beauty or craftsmanship. (Courtesy ImagineChina)

ALL THAT GLITTERS...

However, China's luxury landscape is loaded with challenges. Any weekday visitor to Plaza 66, Shanghai's most exclusive shopping mall, will wonder, "Where are all the people?" For many brands, profit is elusive, and volumes are weak. Cadillac drove ashore confidently but recently stalled. The Passat is struggling to escape from Volkswagen's heritage as "the taxi company." Hugo Boss is lost in the "mass premium" jungle, no longer a head turner.

Contrary to conventional wisdom, knockoffs are not the big threat. Any image-conscious mainlander who can afford the real deal would not be caught dead with a fake. The three major problems are as follows.

The ambitious new middle class is strapped for cash. Spending is constrained in China. Even in coastal cities, per capita income is an eighth of that in America. A yearly income of $25,000 is almost a king's ransom. Many status-mad thirtysomethings buy Gucci key chains, not Prada handbags. And the role import tariffs play should not be underestimated. For example, China imposes levies of 50 percent and 30 percent on cosmetics and luxury watches, respectively. According to a China Ministry of Commerce study, Chinese prices for twenty luxury brands of watches, suitcases, clothes, liquor, and consumer electronics are 45 percent higher than in Hong Kong, 51 percent higher than in the United States, and 72 percent higher than in France. As a result, many Chinese luxury consumers make their purchases overseas—and many brands use their retail presence in China primarily for image-building purposes. It was rumored in 2010 that the government is considering a tariff reduction, but no formal announcement followed.

Premium products are largely undifferentiated. Many Chinese still do not know the difference between a Mercedes and a BMW. In less than ten years, the brand universe has gone from darkness to big bang, and it remains an untamed wilderness in which familiar markers are few and far between. Luxury junkies are loyal to no one; they reach for the latest fix and then switch promiscuously. Huaihai Road in Shanghai is plastered with blond ice goddesses that neither provoke nor intrigue. It is worth noting that very few brands have a local marketing arm. These brands are religions to their creative directors in Paris or New York, and so the degree of localization is far less than what is required. It is wrong to assume that creative and marketing programs can just be imported from abroad.

Luxury brands are tarnished by association with the wrong type of customer. There are two Chinas today. The first is rising, dynamic, upwardly mobile, young, and optimistic. It has burst from the shackles of a decaying command economy. The second is falling, a land of hulking state-owned enterprises, a profit-free zone in which Rolexes are doled out as bonuses. It's a land of rigid hierarchy, corruption, and shiny $2,000 suits that would make gangsters blush. Any brand tainted by association with old China is on the way out.

TIPS FOR SUCCESS

Is every luxury product doomed? No. Some brands—Mont Blanc, Cartier, Louis Vuitton, and Zegna—are doing well in terms of both volume and margin. They have tailored their efforts to address the realities of the marketplace in the following ways:

- Constant innovation to satisfy a passion for new. In China, mobile phone users buy new smart phone models every six months; in the United States, it's every two years. Alfred Dunhill is the classic case of a brand paying the price for its perceived failure to innovate.

- An extensive line of accessories ranging from mobile phone straps to coin purses. These items boast cachet but do not require significant cash outlays. They appeal to a huge, penny-pinched youth segment as well as business people who frequently exchange gifts to signal trustworthiness.
- Skillful portfolio management that balances high-end image (Zegna, Armani) and affordable scale (Zegna Sport, Armani Exchange).
- Design that addresses the need to show off, albeit in an understated manner (Mont Blanc's subtly obvious white star, Cartier's classic gold-framed watch face). As consumer sophistication increases, branding must become more discreet (Louis Vuitton's premium bags sans LV logo, custom-made items for the most exclusive customers).
- Consistent communications that position luxury as substance, a publicly displayed tool of advancement, not a private indulgence (Martell's no-nonsense connoisseurship vs. Hennessy's "Heart of Cognac").
- Education programs that teach how to wield a brand for maximum impact. Everybody is eager to learn, whether it's about a product's history (for example, Burberry's classic British heritage, Patek Philippe's "Across the Generations" campaign), process and technique (Breitling and Bentley's "Celebration of Perfection"), ingredients and provenance (Johnny Walker Blue taste tests), or even about the luxury lifestyle more broadly (BMW's lifestyle stores). Some companies even bring brand extensions into the children's bedroom (the Louis Vuitton teddy bear).

Chinese consumers have limited purchasing power, lack experience navigating the brand terrain, and are divided between twenty-first-century strivers and Paleolithic central planners. However, given the country's incontestable dynamism, the best and brightest brands can glitter like gold.

18

CAR-CRAZY CHINA: WHERE EGO AND ANXIETY COLLIDE

Ten years ago, the only automobiles on the streets of China's coastal cities were nondescript black sedans and shoddy Volkswagen Jetta taxis. Today, the country's highways are overflowing with cars of every shape, size, and color. While foreign brands still dominate the market—with many produced on the mainland—local manufacturers are coming on strong, particularly in lower-tier markets. Approximately 20 million passenger cars are sold nationwide every year. In Beijing, one household in three has an automobile.

Auto ownership, perhaps not unexpectedly but still remarkably, has become a rite of passage into the ranks of the middle class. Although a home mortgage is still the key to landing a wife, Chinese men face a new imperative: you can't say you've made it unless you have a car. (Women influence husbands' selection of automobile brands. However, few cars are targeted directly at women, an obvious opportunity for the future, given the increasing disposable income of professional women.)

China: Not car friendly? The ardor of China's love affair with cars was not statistically ordained. In many respects, the country is not car-friendly. Ultra-aggressive drivers are a menace, and 100 percent import tariffs are prohibitive. By developed market standards, incomes are pinched; buyers spend approximately 120 percent of their declared yearly income on a first vehicle, versus ratios of 30 to 40 percent in the West. In tier-one cities, plate fees cost an additional US$5,000. Cars are not a necessity; in a land of single children, there are no soccer moms. The subway and public transportation system is increasingly

Image 18.1   Autos have emerged as a required badge of middle-class arrival. Ego affirmation explains frequent over-the-top vehicle personalization. (Courtesy JWT [top photograph]; ImagineChina [bottom photograph])

robust; Shanghai's metro is now the most expansive in the world. And maintaining a car is a hassle—parking spaces are few and far between, highways are choked with traffic, and even car washes are rare. But people still buy.

Status is king. Of course, convenience is a key factor. More professionals, driven by rising real estate prices, are buying homes far from city centers, so automobiles can be practical for them. If the need was purely functional, drivers would buy the cheaper local brands, but the spectacular growth in sales of premium marques points to something else: an unquenchable thirst for status. China's conflict between upward ambition and hierarchical regimentation mandates that members of the new elite proclaim their position on a ladder of success. Cars are ideal status projectors, given their large out-of-pocket expense and inherent conspicuousness.

The need to project authority explains why auto benefits are externalized; cars are positioned, directly or indirectly, as vessels of professional progression. Mazda's "Zoom Zoom!" campaign has been adulterated to incorporate public admiration cues. Even BMW, known in the West as a "driving machine," has fused Western internal satisfaction with a quintessentially Chinese "more room to grow" payoff. Audi 8 appeals to men who are masters of the commercial landscape or connoisseurs of true quality. Even lower-priced cars resort to identity affirmation or social standing reinforcement. Ford Fiesta appeals to post-1980s types who were "born bold, born sexy." Mid-tier Volkswagen Passat employs spokesman Jiang Wen, an iconic film director, who declares, "The powerful can change a generation."

The instinct to project status also accounts for some of the market's more peculiar characteristics. Cars here are huge. SUVs such as Honda's CRV, BMW's X3 and X5, and Audi's Q5 and Q7 are popular despite the high price and lack of interest in off-road adventurism. Roomy backseats are a must for aspiring CEOs who must, one day, hire a chauffeur. Online car clubs—sites on which legions of men wax poetic about "mechanical second wives"—pervade cyberspace.

Buyer anxiety. While cars and identity are inextricable, marketers must avoid monomaniacal status-driven sells. Middle-class buying instincts are polarized between bold ego magnification and insecure protection. For every renminbi invested in advancement, two are put aside for rainy days. Disposable income is constrained, in absolute terms, by low wages. Sky-high savings rates are reinforced by a tattered social safety net, insufficient health care, real estate prices that are worryingly high relative to income, an overregulated financial-services market that precludes rational return, and a political system in which economic interests remain neither protected nor represented. The outlay required for a car is, to say the least, a risky proposition.

HOW TO REASSURE

Auto manufacturers must root brands in projective and protective benefits. The dealership experience, in particular, is critical in addressing both needs. Regarding the former, the sales force must treat prospective customers as visiting royalty. Premiums should be offered as testaments of appreciation; vintage red wines and Mont Blanc pens show respect. Wives and children who accompany fathers to showrooms must be pampered.

Status fixation, however, is often trumped by anxiety. To mitigate last-minute jitters, marketers must make buyers feel secure. Here are a few ways of closing the deal:

Present the brand as global leader with unmatched scale. Brands with long heritage buttress perceptions of scale, as do frequent mid-cycle innovations and product upgrades. Model names should be stretched across price tiers to add brand heft, although care must be taken to avoid image degradation of premium lines, usually through skillful deployment of sub-brands. Buick's efforts in this respect have been masterful, as have Audi's.

Focus on fuel efficiency and safety standards. Ford's Mondeo Eco-Boost hits the sweet spot by seamlessly fusing engine power with impressive mileage claims. Dealership agents should be guardian angels, obsessed with family safety. On-site brochures must highlight antiskid brake systems, airbags that protect against whiplash, and any features linked to control of the road.

Provide ironclad service guarantees. Throughout an extended warranty period (and beyond), dealerships should promise a 48-hour turnaround on repairs. Supply chains and inventories must be reconfigured to minimize shortage of parts; all parts must be available within 24 hours. More ambitiously, in geographies requiring long travel to service centers, assistance should be sent to the driver.

For China's ambitious middle class, big cars and big egos go hand in hand. However, given the insecurity of the skittish new elite, brands must both project status and protect interests, both physical and economic. This pivot requires flexibility and focus.

19

CHINA'S SENIOR MARKET: GRAY TODAY, GOLDEN TOMORROW

Within the next several years, China's gray market—people aged fifty and older—will be the most potent spending demographic on the planet. By 2025, there will be more than 500 million mature Chinese consumers (36 percent of the country's population), up from 300 million (21 percent) today. Their average annual per capita spending power will exceed $4,100, two-and-a-half times the 2006 figure.

Yet this potential bonanza has been ignored by most marketers. According to China's National Seniors Bureau, only 10 percent of products and services bought by senior citizens are actually targeted to them. Why? First, their current incomes pale in comparison to those of younger, middle-class cohorts, who mostly reside in China's coastal cities. Second, mature consumers are assumed, often erroneously, to be ultraconservative culturally, caring little about brands and the aspirations they embody. As Chen Yimu, a 62-year-old Internet user, makes perfectly clear, such apathy will fade: "We want to look pretty. But there are no fashion brands for seniors. When will our turn come?"

Mainland gray can be golden. Marketers, however, must realize that, as incomes rise, China will become more modern, more international but not more Western. Goods must be positioned in accordance with cultural imperatives. Brands must resolve a fundamental and uniquely Chinese conflict—between fear of an ever-changing modern world and titillation by newfound freedoms and broadened horizons—especially among the elderly. Those that do will be rewarded with deep loyalty and robust price premiums.

DISPLACEMENT vs. OPTIMISM

On one hand, the over-fifty generation suffers from a sense of displacement. Spanning civil war and the Cultural Revolution, the era in which they came to maturity was politically and economically insecure, with success or acknowledgment contingent on sacrifice. They were conditioned to believe that absolute loyalty to authority—son to father, young to old, ruled to ruler—was the gravitational force that would pull new China out of 150 years of imperial and republican chaos. Their worldview is characterized by Confucian faith that age is tantamount to wisdom, that obedience by and respect from the younger generation are the fruit of elders' long, hard struggle through sixty years of nation building.

The forces unleashed by economic reform—mandatory retirement, mobility that increases the physical distance between parents and adult children, and a conflict between traditional collectivism and newfangled ego affirmation—threaten this sense of entitlement. The over-fifty cohort, anxious and self-protective, questions its own relevance.

That said, hope springs eternal. Driven by rising incomes, digital technology, and connections with the outside world, sunset days can blossom into rainbow years. The mature market is also beguiled by the promise of new friends, burgeoning fitness and travel options, online self-expression, and the revolutionary concept that fun need not be guilty pleasure. Brands must mitigate the anxiety of displacement by becoming guiding lights into a new world of opportunity.

POSSIBILITIES OF ME

Brands must pivot from fear-based messaging and unleash new opportunities for the individual.

Justifying the treat. Brands should provide permission to bite into forbidden fruits by positioning old-fashioned values as the source of future happiness or self-indulgence as a reward for enduring deprivation. Older Chinese are ruthless savers so AIA insurance skillfully asserts that, after years of hardship, freedom from worry is a worthy financial goal. Burberry's "real quality never goes out of fashion" and Dove's celebration of "real beauty" can be focused into mature-targeted campaign platforms.

Making olden golden. Brands must explicitly acknowledge the wisdom of people older than fifty and generate admiration of "elder masters." Shide wine elegantly links the clarity of white alcohol with the "acumen of ancient sages." In one droll HSBC ad, a silver-haired father wields a credit card to restore family harmony while paying for an expensive meal. Even Nike, during the lead up to the 2008 Olympics, featured a guru in TV ads to personify an ageless "Just Do It" spirit. By airing senior-relevant copy, these brands suggest an unusual, if suboptimally harnessed, insight into the minds of mature Chinese individuals.

Attaining "forever young." Brands promoting health benefits should move beyond worry-based protection (for example, supplementing calcium deficiency to guard against weak bones) to embrace life-enhancing liberation. Furthermore, clichés of lively grandmas and grandpas have passed their sell-by date. New Balance elegantly targets for its running shoes elders who crave "new roads and a new life." Vitality benefits can also be dramatized by using the young generation as a playful foil. In Japan, Pocari Sweat, a sports drink, fueled the victory of spry old men over SMAP, a local boy band, on the basketball court.

REINFORCEMENT OF WE

To attract Chinese consumers, brands can forge new constructs of social intercourse.

Tightening family bonding. In order to strengthen the over-fifty market's sense of belonging, brands can bridge the gap between new and traditional ways of life by facilitating intergenerational communication. Historically, nondifferentiated gifting has been the most prevalent means of encouraging offspring to fulfill their Confucian obligation to parents. Recently, however, a few products have begun to address the widening generation gap with a bit more nuance. Ericsson reminds sons that real caring is conveyed through on-going dialog with fathers. China Mobile has gone beyond "connecting people" by opening "lines of love" between daughters and mothers. Savvy brands also acknowledge grandparents' interest in their grandchildren and the idea that joy and responsibility should be shared. Nestlé's Taitaile, a flavor enhancer, explicitly endorses—and facilitates—a mother-in-law's dominion over the kitchen and hence the entire family's nutritional well-being.

Building new communities. In an era of sweeping change and social disorientation, brands should be platforms for social bonding. Which property tycoon will break ground by building a luxury village for seniors? When will De Beers throw diamond anniversary parties for couples whose love lasts forever? Chat rooms, blogs, and social networking sites for the elderly have begun to spring up everywhere—digital technology already facilitates the fortification of old and new acquaintances. Few marketers, however, have capitalized on this sociological paradigm shift. Who will be the first to sponsor online "silver dating"? Brands should also tap the collective sense of national pride, giving the seniors who helped mold the new China a megaphone through which they can, together, cheer for it.

China's market of mature consumers will be gigantic, but it is being ignored by most marketers. As spending power mushrooms, brands must tap into the tension between fear of displacement and excitement for new beginnings. Those that do will emerge as guiding lights on a vast new commercial horizon—and reap significant profits.

20

CHINA'S AMBIVALENT TIGER MOMS: WHEN IN ROME . . .

There is a lot of truth in Amy Chua's self-congratulatory *Battle Hymn of the Tiger Mother*. Chinese moms, today and in the past, will stop at practically nothing to ensure their children are armed with the weapons required to obliterate barriers to future financial success. That said, contemporary mothers, flooded with information that promotes a more liberal model of modern parenting, are conflicted: on one hand, they exert tremendous pressure on their kids to excel academically; on the other, they feel guilty for imposing so much stress on cherished dumplings.

There is increasing awareness that a monomaniacal focus on grades can, in the long run, put young adults at a disadvantage. They know, in an interconnected world that prizes creative problem solving above rote memorization, the smartest kid in the class may not, ultimately, win big.

From McDonald's to Disney, the most successful kid-tested, mom-approved brands offer new tools to resolve the tension between a timeless fixation on academic triumph and a new-generation embrace of childhood liberation.

EAST vs. WEST: POLARIZED CHILD-REARING TRADITIONS

In the West, concurrent with the rise of the middle class, children have been freed from the shackles of Victorian regimentation. Americans, with their sacrosanct belief in the power of self-determined individualism, encourage sons and daughters to discover themselves, freely and joyfully. Until the parental umbilical cord is severed, around the age of eighteen, everything from *ABC Afterschool Specials* to elementary school music and art classes teaches us to discover what makes each of us special. Richard York, former chair of HSBC, posits, only slightly tongue-in-cheek, that the US financial crisis was triggered by the view that "every child had a right to a big bedroom," each one a dreamscape of self-indulgence. Selective universities base admission on intangible assets such as leadership potential and self-possession, cultivated in high schools boasting an endless array of extracurricular activities.

In China, self-actualization is a dangerous game: the individual has never been, and will never be, the basic productive unit of society. Identities are inextricably linked to the clan and nation, twin poles of obligation. Childhood has *traditionally* been defined by obedient acquiescence. The *Standards for Being a Good Student and Child*, guidelines propagated by ancient sages, extols ultraconformism as the only viable path to adolescence: "Be filial to your parents. Respect your brothers. Be trustworthy, honest and kind. Draw near to people with good virtues. Whatever time you have left should be devoted to studies and learning." Few kids overtly challenge parents. Rebellion, expressed in digital chat rooms and violent video games, virtually never occurs at the dinner table.

CHANGES AFOOT

Despite ancient cultural imperatives, China is not static. Several contemporary influences buck traditional definitions of proper child rearing:

The one-child policy. China's draconian birth-control policy, still strictly enforced among urban dwellers, has produced a generation of plump, mouthy, prepubescent kids. Historically, parents' weapon against future uncertainty was an army of strapping boys—the odds were that at least one would be able to provide security for their parents in their old age. Today, parental hopes, pride, and anxiety are invested in a single child. (Despite a national birth ratio skewed to boys, the traditional strong preference for boys is weakening, particularly in major cities.) These little emperors rule the roost. Safeguard soap's Lunar New Year television and digital campaigns highlight twelve-hour germ-fighting action that "protects your adorable king." Products targeted to children, from infant formula to educational toys, command huge price premiums. Computers, costing at least a month's income, penetrate every living room. Pizza Huts are filled with overweight eight-year-olds who sass hapless parents desperate not to provoke a scene. No, today's indulged youth are far from submissive. They are both seen and heard.

For the parents of pampered singletons, "fun" is no longer a dirty word. Rising incomes, especially in primary cities, underpin the growth of non-essential, hedonistic product categories. The single child is the center of a familial universe, the apple of every eye, and his bedroom rivals set pieces from *Babes in*

Toyland. Large flat-screen televisions, hooked up to DVD players and Nintendo and Wii game consoles, are no longer unattainable luxuries. As municipal officials pull out all the stops to make Shanghai a global tourist destination, locals are buzzing about the imminent arrival of Disneyland. The Western ideal of childhood as a wonderland of discovery now has many adherents in China.

International media that promote alternative values. The ubiquity of Western media as part of China's increased engagement with the outside world has popularized the aspiration of self-driven adulthood, one largely incompatible with Confucian obligation-driven childhood. Today, the most popular foreign television series—from *Desperate Housewives* and *Lost* to *The Big Bang Theory* and *Friends*—share a distinct dynamic: all idealize irreverent individualism within a mutually supportive group context. Local mass media have glorified Western *and* Chinese icons of individualism, including Warren Buffett, Bill Gates, Steve Jobs, Kobe Bryant, Alibaba's founder Jack Ma, and blogger-activist Han Han, each of whom, directly or indirectly, roots success in challenge and mediocrity in subservience.

China's progressively multifaceted relationships with foreign universities and enterprises also bolster belief in creativity as a competitive weapon. Every year, US colleges admit more than 100,000 mainlanders into classrooms in which high grades and active in-class participation, a radical concept back home, are inextricably linked. Likewise, an army of—admittedly, elite—childbearing twenty- and thirty-year-olds have been recruited by US and European Fortune 500 companies, each of which promulgates proactive innovation as required for forward advancement and greater financial reward.

Economic growth fueled by entrepreneurialism and the availability of higher education. During the past five years, the Chinese government has relentlessly extolled an innovative spirit as the lynchpin of twenty-first-century prosperity, on both national and individual levels. Parents question whether their children are equipped, emotionally and intellectually, to compete in a modern global economy, which leads the parents to challenge conventional child-rearing practices. Many claim they want to be friends with their kids, rather than one-dimensional authority figures. They encourage questioning and exploration and go to great lengths to cultivate inquiring, nonconformist minds. While China's system inches forward at a snail's pace, parental attitudes and aspirations have changed dramatically.

It is often said that China's higher education standards are too regimented and its university courses lack academic rigor, but economic growth has in part been driven by wider availability of advanced degrees. In 2000, approximately 1.5 million university graduates entered the labor force. Ten years on, it was six million. Career paths have also burgeoned. As recently as the early 1990s, the government allocated graduates to either the bureaucracy or state-owned enterprises. While positions within the party or large state-owned enterprises are still prized for stability and proximity to the corridors of power, cherished jobs are also with multinational corporations such as Microsoft, Procter & Gamble, Morgan Stanley, and McKinsey. It is understood these companies value initiative and independent thinking, characteristics at odds with traditional childhood obedience.

THE MORE THINGS CHANGE...

Despite the profound impact of globalization and China's new capitalistic ethos, the country's underlying social structure has remained remarkably intact. Social mores and hence economic growth are still rooted in top-down, mandated paths to success, inevitably involving technocratic mastery of facts and figures, as well as Confucian intergenerational obligation that keeps rebellious, even challenging, impulses in check.

Confucian doctrine may be taught briefly only in the classroom, but the gravitational pull of traditionalism is felt everywhere. China's education system, meritocratic yet illiberal, is a manifestation of a to-be-seen-but-not-heard ethos. Its primary role is to advance the interests of the nation, as defined by the

Image 20.1 Despite the government's professed desire to cultivate creativity, China's education system revolves around mastery of received wisdom, even in high school and at university. Teachers are never challenged by students. (Courtesy ImagineChina)

Communist Party. Ninety percent of today's business and government leaders received engineering degrees at elite universities; they are beneficiaries of a highly centralized system that brooks no dissent and has no interest in doing so.

So it's not surprising that pedagogical practices have not evolved since the Cultural Revolution. While Western teachers are extolled for engaging students, Chinese teachers regard subservience as an adaptive strength. (Pupils rarely question, let alone challenge, their instructors.) The *gao kao*, the nation's all-or-nothing university entrance exam, rewards regurgitation of facts, not critical reasoning or originality. Individuals' ranking vis-à-vis peers is compiled starting in kindergarten, and, although public posting has become less common in recent years, any student can know how she, or any student, measures up by asking the teacher. Children do not compose essays, outlets of self-expression in Europe and America, until the seventh grade. Beyond soccer, school-sponsored after-school activities do not exist.

Students are not the only ones who fear teachers. Parents do, too. Even iron-fisted executives tremble during parent-teacher conferences in fear of being blamed for their children's substandard marks. One colleague complained to me, "She will do anything to improve her class's test scores. She thinks she is my boss!" In a land where conformist instincts are deeply ingrained, embrace of convention—that is, achieving "perfect normalcy"—is tantamount to childhood success.

STUDY: STILL THE ONLY PATH FORWARD

Children, despite three decades of high-calorie diets and plush toys, are still compelled to express commitment to their parents through study. The pressure to conform to success markers is awesome. An oft-quoted ancient proverb, as true today as it was 1,500 years ago: "Those who work with strength are ruled. Those who work with their minds manage others. Those who excel in scholarship become officials." The Chinese character for "teach" (*jiao*) has the character for "good child" (*xiao*) embedded within it, suggesting that the act of learning is the most concrete manifestation of filial piety.

Parents lord the academic accomplishments of other children over their kids; when a student falls behind her peers, the extended family—mom, dad, four grandparents, aunts, and uncles—loses face. Most elementary school pupils work with outside tutors to improve their grades; less-than-perfect scores can result in being grounded. In focus groups, parents worry about six-year-old hypochondriacs whose symptoms recur on Sunday evenings.

Yes, it has become trendy to subscribe to modern parenting. Mothers wax poetic about newfangled childhood and its promised delights. But, in the end,

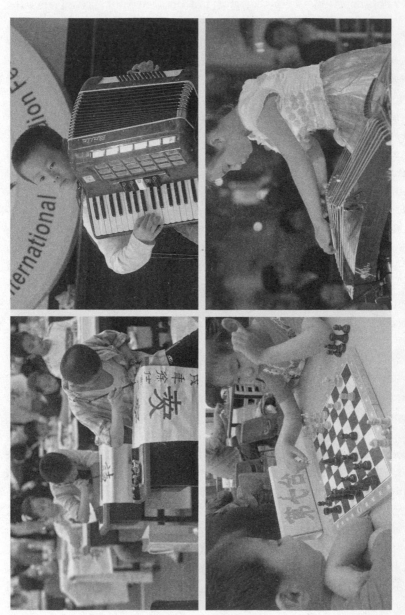

Image 20.2 In China, even childhood is a rat race. The competition for academic achievement is intense. Hobbies, particularly playing instruments, have little to do with self-fulfillment. They are means of cultivating the discipline required to excel in school and, later in life, on the business battlefield. (Courtesy ImagineChina)

only grades count. Every infant formula is positioned as a brainpower booster. Dumex focuses on "memory as a weapon." Enfantbon strengthens information retention *and* creativity. Wyeth claims its balanced formula produces "multi-dimensional intelligence." Baby-crawling competitions and cram courses for toddlers presage a dog-eat-dog climb up narrow academic and professional hierarchies. Parents ruefully acknowledge that, short of emigrating to the West, their children have no choice but to play by China's hard-nosed rules. The system, a manifestation of timeless cultural priorities, is entrenched.

What's the natural result of a monomaniacal focus on academic achievement? Stress and guilt. According to a study conducted by the China Teen Research Center, 75 percent of children aged thirteen to fifteen spend more than eight hours studying every weekend; 65 percent feel stressed or very stressed about academic performance; and 66 percent take courses during summer and winter holidays. Parents are equally anxious. Research piloted by the China Institute of Education and Learning found that 50 percent of mothers "care about nothing other than their child's studies," but 83 percent "worry about reducing the burden of heavy daily workloads." One mother expressed ambivalence: "I know he is unhappy. I know he should enjoy life. But this is China. What can I do?"

The tension between parents' determination to prepare children for the rat race and their more humane impulse to cut slack is palpable. Their angst is underscored by the growing realization that China's memorization-driven pedagogy is ill suited for emerging economic sectors, particularly services and positions requiring leadership or creativity.

BRANDS TO THE RESCUE: HAPPY ACHIEVEMENT

The ambivalence of parents is fundamental; hence the profusion of brands that aim to reconcile achievement with delight. Five key themes have emerged:

Eliminating the struggle between "good for you" and enjoyment. Chinese mothers are drawn to brands promising "stealthy learning"—that is, intellectual development masked as fun. Disney will succeed both as an educational franchise—its English learning centers are going like gangbusters—and theme park. McDonald's restaurants, temples of childhood delight in the West, have morphed into scholastic playgrounds in China: Happy Meals include collectible Snoopy figurines wearing costumes from around the world, while the McDonald's website, hosted by Professor Ronald, offers Happy Courses for multiplication and "*chengyu* fun" (that is, classical four-character Chinese phrases, the usage of which is a sign of a keen mind). Smarties's "colorful creativity" platform encourages kids to "sweeten imagination" by arranging candy pellets into art pieces. Skippy peanut butter combines "delicious peanut taste" and "intelligent sandwich preparation."

Transforming protection-based safety into joy. Parents stop at nothing to protect investment in their child. That is why some of China's most powerful brands have safety propositions. Procter & Gamble's Safeguard soap, for example, has maintained a 25 percent market share for more than twenty years by focusing on "germ kill." China Mobile offers "safety check" and "school time management"—short-message services for parents who demand "anytime, anywhere" communications with teachers. China's millennial generation is swaddled. In the words of an eight-year-old, "I have a wonderful time when I'm on my own but my mother worries. Sometimes I feel like I'm in jail." In the past few years, progressive brands have begun to address the tension between safety-driven regimentation and discovery. Safeguard has elevated its aforementioned germ-killing functionality into a richer "freedom to learn" angle. Omo detergent skillfully links "powerful grime removal" with worry-free exploration, while Zhonghua toothpaste connects "twelve levels of 'germacheck'" with a "new world of culinary adventure."

Surreptitiously honing competitive instincts. The competitive hurdles young children confront on a daily basis are omnipresent. Playtime must deliver more than mindless release; it should also whet the drive to win on the battlefield of elementary school advancement. Computer games are hawked as balance, reaction, and alertness enhancers. Transformer toys, board games, and musical instruments exist as means to victorious ends. Quaker Oats sharpened conventional nutrition claims with "endless energy," the X factor of Chinese ping-pong champions. In 2008, McDonald's created an Olympic cheering squad for little ones to compete for a trip to the Beijing Games where they could meet national champions. Parents also applauded the chain's soccer skills camps.

Increasing both IQ and EQ. Intellectual skill is a necessity for success but is insufficient on its own. Parents embrace anything that promotes EQ—emotional quotient, or civilized sensitivity—and IQ balance. China's EQ push has been further reinforced by the party's promotion of a harmonious society and underscored by an anachronistic propaganda campaign about "eight shames" and "eight glories." Spitting and throwing trash on the ground are out. Sacrificed bus seats and Lei Feng, the People's Liberation Army soldier-cum-Cultural Revolution martyr, are in. Consequently, Dumex milk powder features a "Golden Wise nutritional system" and a boy smart enough to divide cake with varying numbers of friends. Dada's Little Warrior, Wrigley's popular chewing gum, tells youngsters to be "Super Good Kids" who "love to help, discover and create, protect the environment and build team spirit."

The plot of the iconic early twentieth-century author Lu Xun's short story, *Kong Yiji*, is evidence that excessive focus on academic excellence is nothing new. The fate of the eponymous character, a lifelong student who fails to pass the Imperial Exams and winds up an impoverished object of ridicule, demonstrates that bookworms meet bitter ends. Children today win by fusing empathy and smarts into the ultimate adaptive trait: resourcefulness. Street-wise kids are cool, providing they do not cross the red line of parental disrespect. Kjelden's, a butter biscuit brand, depicts lovable yet shrewd tykes who hatch a "great cookie heist" in grandma's kitchen. Leading up to the 2008 Olympics, Coca-Cola aired a hugely popular commercial featuring Yao Ming, slayer of trash-talking NBA barbarians. Tricked into forfeiting a bottle of Coke to a savvy seven-year-old, a humbled Yao realizes he has met his match. And the nation cheered.

Releasing stress. Brands can also cultivate affinity by rewarding victory and providing vehicles for anxiety release. KFC celebrates Children's Day with a special gift pack. Pizza Hut lets parents acknowledge children's academic performance with "triumph feasts." McDonald's promotes itself as a respite from the rigors of music, chess, and swimming lessons. Brand-sponsored online avatars, ones that can be created on sites such as Coke's iGame Central, offer kids a release. So do Danone's "unveil your inner Superman" cookies and Tang juice's "slay the evil ogre" programs.

Chinese parents have no choice but to put their children on a path to success, where academic achievement is preparation for a lifetime of bloodthirsty competition. Moms and dads are torn between China's classic tough love approach to child rearing and new-generation appreciation of childhood delight and self-discovery. Brands play an important role in resolving this conflict.

21

YOUNG DIGITAL LIVES: A PARALLEL UNIVERSE OF AMBITIOUS RELEASE

Everyone knows the new generation of young Chinese is consumed by all things digital. The country boasts 500 million Internet users (150 million of whom have access to high-speed broadband services), 250 million microbloggers, and 800 million mobile phone users. Chinese digital mania begs the question of how people engage with new media—what emotional urges are released, how self-expression is manifested—and whether these drivers are fundamentally different from those of Westerners.

EAST vs. WEST

Chinese youth are a unique cohort. On one hand, they are tremendously ambitious. They have grown up in an economic environment in which the need for success—always defined in terms of professional and monetary achievement—is reinforced at every turn, by parents, grandparents, and teachers. On the other hand, China remains a profoundly rule-based, regimented society. Restrictions to self-expression, both implicit and explicit, are omnipresent. Students, always in uniform, do not dare to question teachers. Pedagogy focuses on drills and memorization. With no marching bands, choirs, debate clubs, or swim teams, there is little US-style subculture tribalism. And media are 100 percent state-controlled, offering a very narrow range of content or platforms for uncensored self-expression. The government's 2012 restrictions on "overly entertaining" television shows—programs deemed provocative because they allow audience members to vote for real-life contestants who may not personify party-sanctioned values—will only exacerbate the bland political correctness of broadcast media.

Adding fuel to the fire is the alluring-yet-forbidden fruit of Western individualism, enticingly conveyed by glossy fashion magazines and illegal DVDs, not to mention iconic US and European brands such as Nike and Apple.

THE INTERNET AND CONFLICT RESOLUTION

The tension between projection of ego and alienation avoidance—a contemporary game changer versus timeless cultural imperatives—is a powerful dilemma for most Chinese. It results in a paradoxical coexistence of infectious optimism and strict limitations on free thought.

Given this conflict, digital liberation is manna from heaven, despite the snooping of 50,000 net police and government efforts to make users register their real identities with the authorities before assuming online pen names. The anonymity of new media is a blank canvas of self-expression. A recent IAC/JWT survey of young digital mavens found that while a large minority of Americans agree that they live some of their life online (42 percent for both sexes), more than double the percentage of Chinese youth feel similarly (86 percent). The gap between the samples is even wider when respondents are asked whether they

Image 21.1 Karaoke is one of the few offline (and socially acceptable) platforms for emotional release. Online options, on the other hand, abound. They are anonymous and therefore safe. (Courtesy ImagineChina)

Image 21.2   It is difficult to overstate the impact the Internet has had on China's new generation, even in lower-tier cities. Net cafes, often the size of football fields, are everywhere. (Courtesy ImagineChina)

have a parallel online life; only 13 percent of Americans agree they do compared to nearly five times as many Chinese (61 percent).

Is the online world a channel for repressed citizens to spew venom at corrupt officials and "anti-China" CNN? Yes, but it also represents the chance to have a second life. It is a fantasy-driven virtual journey, albeit one that mirrors real-world aspirations of standing out while fitting in. Furthermore, in cyberspace, dreams can be instantly gratified, a stark contrast to the molasses-like progression mandated by offline hierarchical codes.

MARKETERS AND EGO AMPLIFICATION

Marketers can tap into the power of digital liberation by ensuring their communication campaigns address this thirst for bold ego affirmation. Motifs include *release,* or liberation from the restrictions of a regimented social structure; *acceptance,* or fitting in without sacrificing individual identity; *acknowledgment,* or generating talent recognition without progressing through real-world restrictions; and *transcendence,* or allowing the demands of society to fade away while rediscovering one's pure self.

Release. Video games are perhaps the most ubiquitous means of primal release. Almost 50 percent of global *World of Warcraft* players are young

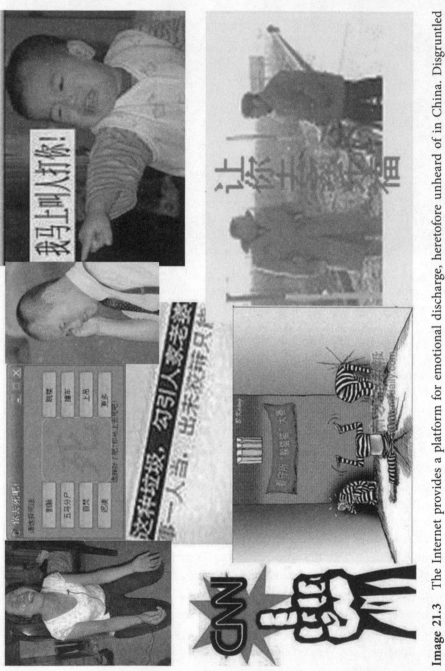

Image 21.3 The Internet provides a platform for emotional discharge, heretofore unheard of in China. Disgruntled farmers, angry babies, and grieving parents let it out in cyberspace. (Courtesy JWT)

Chinese men. The omnipresence, even addictive power, of violent video games gives free rein to depravity and obliterates reality-based norms. As one avid fan put it, "Online, I can be gay. I can be king of darkness. I can be whoever I want to be. No one can judge me."

Release doesn't have to be dangerous. Mindless fun can be compelling too, as evidenced by the pervasive *shanzhai* phenomenon, lighthearted copy-cat ads that poke fun at established brands ("Just Don't It"), celebrities (a tone-deaf Jay Chou, one of Taiwan's most popular singers), or cultural icons (puppies painted like pandas). The most potent liberation occurs when inner feelings, difficult to articulate face to face, are conveyed across a digital comfort zone, sometimes in a larger-than-life manner. De Beers's "Love World" site, for example, enables men to create a planet of "love monuments" and deposit them safely into girl-friends' email boxes.

Acceptance. China's young generation grew up in sheltered, protective households. Parents monitored every move and stressed the importance of conventional achievement. As a result, Chinese youth are not confident in their cool. They crave peer acceptance. A quote from Man Zhou, a celebrated software hacker, is typical: "At first, I thought I had limitless choices in life, but then I realized I needed to grow up and adapt to society. Maybe it's different in America, but in China, our culture forces us to become just another square person."

The digital world liberates "the real me," hence the popularity of social networking sites. According to Synovate, 72 and 78 percent of Chinese use the Internet to, respectively, "chat with people you know or have lost contact with" and "meet and chat with new people," almost double the rates of Japan, the United States, and France. A desire to seek out and connect with like-minded people explains the success of Ford's "Excitement Challenge," which generated 600 million clicks on Ford.com as individuals shared experiences while transforming themselves from "boring to bold." Nike's online and offline "Nine Gates, Nine Tribes Tournament" linked team affiliation to lifestyle and personality preferences. Beijing was taken by storm.

Acknowledgment. Chinese egos are huge, but blatant status projection is frowned upon, given values of saving face and understatement. The Internet therefore provides a platform to shine. Millions of admirers can, almost instantly, applaud uniqueness. Chun Xu, an online novelist, became a big name within a year. Li Yuchun, also known as Supergirl, morphed from an odd-looking wannabe pop star to national icon in three months. Her victory in a massively popular televised singing competition was fueled by 400 million short-message service votes and a multitude of fan sites. (Thanks to the whiff of democracy inherent in viewer voting, the government has since banned audience participation shows.) Within weeks, the Dorm Room Boys, two twenty-year-old students, became lip-syncing sensations, securing Motorola and Pepsi contracts in the process.

For modern Chinese, narcissism is more alluring than Buddhism. Virtual stars such as web movie director He Ge and sports blogger Li Chenpeng are proof that, online, it takes only a moment to become larger than life. Pepsi's "Get on the Can" competition attracted enormous attention, as did Pringles's "My Own World Record," Nokia's "Who Has the Best (Dance) Moves?" and Colgate's "Star Search."

Transcendence. Young Chinese are fundamentally optimistic about the future, but they need an occasional break. Pervasive conformity, not to mention a belief that society corrupts, fuels their desire to cleanse their souls. Because of its broad reach, anyone on the Internet can achieve moral or omnipotent transcendence. One example of the latter was a Chengdu student who gained acclaim by helping the People's Liberation Army locate a helicopter landing platform during the 2008 Sichuan earthquake. Cisco's "For the Children," a web-based educational assistance network, allowed even small potatoes—as ordinary Chinese often refer to themselves—to perform acts of supreme benevolence for underprivileged rural kids.

Real world success is a long and twisted journey, but in the digital universe, laws of gravity do not apply. Giant leaps to liberation are not only possible but commonplace. Marketers can harness the power of the Internet to forge enduring bonds with grateful, avid technology mavens.

22

THE CHINESE AND FOOD: SURVIVAL AND SUCCESS

China's relationship with food is a window into basic instincts. The country's cuisine is a manifestation of a civilization that has never taken survival for granted. An understanding of what and how Chinese want to eat is a quick way to know China. With the ever-popular dim sum of Guangdong province literally meaning "touch the heart," it's fair to say that food is a window into the Han soul.

In most categories, local brands, including Mengniu and Yili (both dairy companies) and COFCO (everything from chocolate to pork), rule the roost. Although Chinese cravings differ from those of Westerners—noodles, not burgers, are comfort food—it is a myth that people reject foreign food brands simply because they are foreign. Western marketers were slow to enter China and made mistakes. Kellogg, for example, launched cold cereal, an alien category, at prohibitively high prices. Since then, many have made significant progress. From Kraft and Nestlé to Dove and Coca-Cola, brands have tailored products to suit Chinese tastes. Recent successes—Lipton milk tea, Danone fortified calcium biscuits, Pizza Hut's seafood lover's pizza—are testaments to the power of empathetic insight. Yum! Corporation's KFC menu localization has been particularly impressive. Hot wings and chicken burgers are the biggest sellers, but the menu also includes products like Beijing Chicken Rolls, Golden Butterfly Shrimp, Four Seasons Fresh Vegetable Salads, Fragrant Mushroom Rice, and Tomato Egg Drop Soup.

The following are a few basic principles of marketing food in China.

Delicious balance. Chinese cuisine is tremendously varied—Shanghai food is sweet and oily, while Sichuan dishes are hot and spicy—but the balance of yin (cooling) and yang (heating) is important everywhere. From stir-fried beef with broccoli to sweet and sour pork, dishes should be harmonious. Yin foods, not necessarily low in temperature, include toast, bean sprouts, cabbage, carrots, cucumber, duck, tofu, watercress, and water. Yang foods include bamboo, beef, chicken, eggs, ginger, glutinous rice, mushrooms, and sesame oil. China will never be a coffee culture because Chinese believe beverages should be cooling, but Nestlé three-in-one coffee is a hit because sweetness balances bitterness. Illness is perceived to spring from yin and yang imbalance. "Heat patterns" (for example, headaches, bleeding) are remedied with cooling foods, while excessive yin (for example, runny noses, night sweats) are cured with heating foods. Chinese are less lactose intolerant than commonly assumed, but dairy products, including ice cream, are perceived to be damp. Even today, milk sales increase if the product includes something dry, like bits of wheat.

Safety: Never assumed. Counterintuitively, international brands are preferred to local brands, assuming compatibility with local taste and acceptable price. This is because Chinese never take safety for granted. Before the 2009 tainted milk scandal, local dairy brands were known for purity. But dairy manufacturers, in cahoots with local officials, abused this trust by adulterating products with illegal ingredients. That's why all leading brands of infant formula are foreign, despite price premiums of up to 400 percent. That's also why endorsements from central government organizations—such as national dental and medical associations—are highly sought-after for any item that goes inside the body, from toothpaste to orange juice.

Protection is king. Chinese fear invasive elements, hence the appeal of germ-killing products in many categories, including soap (Safeguard), toothpaste (Colgate, Crest, Zhonghua), mouthwash (Listerine), air conditioners (Midea), and even dishwashers (Little Swan). It is therefore not surprising that foods that promote immunity are embraced. Infant formula, again, is a case in point. Every brand must demonstrate resistance to disease before moving on to performance benefits. Physical transformation, on the other hand, has less appeal. "Bigger, stronger, taller" babies are not objects of admiration; every mother wants her child to be perfectly normal. Emotion protection is important, too. Breakfasts are warm and soft, nourishing hugs moms give families before they dive into a cold world—the Chinese don't crunch before noon, so cold cereal will always be niche. Special K would be most effectively positioned as a woman's energy bar.

Advancement always. Once physical safety is a given, food becomes a weapon in the game of life. First, most nutritional benefits are associated with academic excellence. Energy is closely linked to intelligence or, more specifically, concentration and quick-witted resourcefulness. Calcium strengthens both bones and brains. In a dog-eat-dog society, a sharp mind, not a buff physique, is the difference between success and failure. Second, convenient foods are means to an end. They provide the fuel needed to start every day with a kick, so every indulgent food must also be good for you, a sugar-coated pill. Third, transformative benefits have growing appeal for the mature market. Dietary supplements, particularly in first-tier cities, should help the older person perform on the basketball court and at the office. Osteoporosis scaremongering no longer works.

In the hypercompetitive business world, the comfort of food lubricates trust and transactional gain. Partnerships are tested in Chinese restaurants at round tables in private rooms. Dishes are meticulously choreographed. Proper seating is paramount, with the guest of honor placed directly opposite the door, flanked by the hosts. Serving oneself prematurely is a big faux pas. Leaving before the fruit comes is even worse.

Familiarity at home. A glance through any city's expat guide gives the impression that Chinese are culinary adventurers. Shanghai's restaurant scene rivals that of any American or European city. Spanish, tapas, Japanese, Western brunches, Asian-French fusion, Johnny Walker parties, glamour clubs, wine bars…the list is endless. But, deep down, the Chinese are restrained about foreign food or new tastes. Inside the home, a refuge from the outside kaleidoscope, they are loath to experiment. Pizza Hut will receive delivery orders for office parties but rarely for consumption at home. Despite Starbucks, roast and ground coffee is not purchased in supermarkets. Italian restaurants are ubiquitous in all major cities, but few Chinese enjoy pasta with the family. In public, anything goes. People pay a premium to project internationalism, hence Häagen-Dazs's success as an ice cream parlor—a small scoop costs almost US$6—but failure as an overpriced in-home treat. With professional acquaintances or romantic dates, the world is a stage.

PART FOUR

CHINESE SOCIETY

23

FAMILY AND COUNTRY AND ME: AN INTRODUCTION TO CHINESE SOCIETY

Josephine Pan is a strikingly modern, attractive, perceptive woman. She is a business director at JWT, the company I lead. Her fashion sense is refined, fun, and creative. She independently manages several of the company's largest accounts, both global (e.g., Johnson & Johnson) and local (e.g., Metersbonwe, the nation's largest youth fashion brand). Her savoir faire makes her the emcee of choice at Lunar New Year banquets. She has traveled extensively throughout Europe and the United States. But, at thirty-eight, Josephine remains unmarried. When asked why, she states with a matter-of-fact tone of resignation, "My father never approved of any of my boyfriends." She recently purchased an apartment adjoining her parents' unit.

Simon Yu is a study in contrasts, a quintessentially Chinese fusion of surface gentility and buried rage. Now twenty-five, he obtained a master's degree in visual design in London. He also participated in the Cannes advertising festival's "Young Lions" cyber competition. (His entry, an aggressive "save the planet" banner, railed against "empty words.") At six feet four inches, Simon towers above his peers. Talented and trendy, his dream job is to lead MTV's animated content unit. Fiercely nationalistic, he is also painfully shy. He softly decries "foreigners who think we eat dogs and don't understand why we're special." But his deepest anger is reserved for the government. An active microblogger, Simon tweets fast and furiously. A typical entry: "The government has no balls. Impotent men can't have children. How can we succeed as a country?"

Zheng Chen, the son of a company driver, is a high-achieving twenty-one-year-old college senior. He aced China's meritocratic college entrance exam, scoring a very rare 530 points. Passionate about math, Zheng attends a prestigious university and was selected chair of his student council during his sophomore year. He has already landed a full-time job after graduation at Ernst & Young, a "Big Four" accounting firm. Self-possessed, he attributes his achievements to an ability to "figure out what's important" and "not put too much pressure on myself." When asked what drives him, Zheng answered, "I don't want to '*gufu*,' or let my parents down. I want them to be proud of me in front of their friends." Regarding his own goals, he simply says, "I want to matter. I want to be admired by society. Most importantly, I want a life free from worry, for me and my parents."

Josephine, Simon, and Zheng Chen reinforce a key reality of contemporary Chinese society, one Westerners have difficulty grasping: The individual is not, and never will be, the fundamental unit of society. Individual identities are displaced onto the clan and nation. This quote from Confucius, frequently trotted out in government-controlled media, says it all: "To put the world right in order, we must first put the nation in order; to put the nation in order, we must first put the family in order; to put the family in order, we must first cultivate our personal life; we must first set our hearts right."

Family first. It is difficult to overstate the primacy of the clan, driven by a profound sense of mutual obligation, obedience to natural hierarchical order, and protective bulwark against contemporary economic realities. Every young adult forfeits a chunk of income, no matter how constrained, to his or her parents as a demonstration of respect. Failure to return to one's hometown during important festivals, particularly Lunar New Year celebrations, is a sign of decadence. Consigning elderly parents to nursing homes, though a more frequent phenomenon than it was a decade ago, is worse still. Boyfriends and girlfriends are not introduced to parents unless a marriage proposal is in the cards; "casual romance" is an oxymoron and rarely happens. Every date is an assessment of marriage material.

China's little emperors (single children) are overindulged, sassy, and plump (17 percent of all Chinese kids are now overweight). But few challenge the fundamental responsibility of childhood: academic performance. Relatives gather outside school gates after not only the national college entrance examinations but also elementary school calligraphy tests. The Chinese family remains pan-nuclear—that is, four (grandparents) plus two (parents) plus one (child). Extended family relations are elaborate and hierarchical. Mother's brother and father's brother have different ranks, as do maternal and paternal first cousins. Older brother is superior to middle brother, as is older sister to younger sister.

Mothers-in-law continue to hold great sway in matters ranging from infant formula selection to education strategy.

The blurring of individual and familial identities is reinforced by contemporary economic uncertainty. Aggregation of finances remains a protective bulwark against the realities of modern China—health care, even in cities, is patchy and expensive, lubricated by bribes and kickbacks, while housing prices are sky high. According to hedge fund sponsor Pivot Capital, in 2011, the average home-to-income ratio—that is, the price of a home in relation to yearly salary—in Beijing was 27:1. Ratios have reached 15:1 in other major cities and about 10:1 in smaller regional urban areas. At the peak of its housing bubble, the U.S. ratio was less than 5:1.

Country second. Chinese nationalism is a double-edged sword. Productively harnessed, it enables 1.3 billion souls to confront practically any challenge, from devastating earthquakes to Herculean industrialization. It fuels a unifying drive for national greatness. On the other hand, when the national dignity is compromised or, as propaganda organs often put it, the "feelings of the Chinese people are hurt," all hell breaks loose. Latent paranoia rises to the surface, and conflict resolution becomes almost impossible.

It would be a mistake, however, to assume that China's prickly nationalism springs solely from *recitative* party propaganda. The timeless coexistence of Confucian ego—that is, a yearning for acknowledged achievement—and repressed ambition is also important. Every Chinese suppresses dreams of scaling the heights of fame, but paths to the mountaintop are few and far between, limited by pervasive hierarchy and webs of impenetrable *guanxi*, or relationships bound by mutual obligation. This tension has been exacerbated by the emergence of a new generation of capitalistic mandarins who inspire jealousy in the masses. Luckily, the "urge to surge" finds a convenient release on the national canvas. "China is great. So I am, too!" When the party pulls out all stops for patriotic events such as the 2008 Beijing Olympics, there is no cynicism.

Ambivalence toward government. China's conception of itself as a civilization rather than a nation-state explains why its inherent nationalism does not automatically translate into support for the Chinese Communist Party. The renewed popularity in 2011 of revolution-era Maoist "red songs," encouraged by Bo Xilai, the former party chief of Chongqing, is misleading. The relationship between the masses and the party is ambivalent and codependent. (Mr. Bo was purged from power in March 2012. His demagogic populism raised the specter of cult-driven factionalism that led to chaos during the Cultural Revolution.)

Citizens are impatient with fat-cat cadres who wrap themselves in the twin banners of stability and harmony, and enraged by local and provincial leaders who steal land from peasants or enterprises that disregard safety and environmental concerns. The rise of digital media has further shortened fuses and been occasionally instrumental in forcing the government to change course. One example: In 2011, authorities ordered a Dalian petrochemical plant to be shut down after thousands of netizens demonstrated, both online and in the streets, following a toxic spill scare. But representative—as opposed to *responsive*—government remains an abstraction. Faith in the party's ability to gradually reform itself without upsetting the apple cart is still essential to economic development. Unless China's growth paradigm implodes, the strong arm of the party will continue to reassure.

Anti-individualism. Egos are huge in China. Everyone protects, and advances, his own interests. The Internet has emerged as a largely anonymous open microphone for self-expression. But no one rebels. The seeds of civil society have never been planted. Beijing's trendy 798 Space, with its avant-garde artists and writers, is an alien colony, not part of a new creative zeitgeist.

Underdeveloped civility. Top-down, anti-individualistic government precludes the emergence of civil society. The party, unwilling to cede a scintilla of control over affairs of state, must oversee everything. Few trust the operational independence of charities, despite the emergence of a nascent community spirit after the 2008 Sichuan earthquake. Wards of the state, they are prone to the same corrupting influences as any party organ. The 2011 Red Cross scandal, an outrage that transfixed the country, only reinforced misgivings: Under the name "Guo Meimei Baby," a twenty-year-old boasted on her microblog that her title was "Red Cross commercial general manager," a claim verified by Internet portal Sina. She also posted photos of her jet-set life, including an orange Lamborghini she drove in the south (her "little bull") and a white Maserati she kept in Beijing (her "little horse").

The chapters that follow will illustrate the enduring, family-oriented, anti-individualistic structure of Chinese society through the prism of daily life, including my personal experience living in a traditional neighborhood; a day at the zoo; the rhythm of weddings and funerals; evolving sexual mores; the rise of Christmas in China; and the obstacles preventing the emergence of a civil society in the context of the 2008 Sichuan earthquake and the tainted milk scandal.

24

CODEPENDENCE: CHINA'S MIDDLE CLASS AND COMMUNIST PARTY

The motivations of China's emerging middle class are full of contradic-tions; consequently, so are its attitudes toward, and expectations of, the Communist Party. Despite their ambivalence toward the central government, the burgeoning incomes of the bourgeoisie will not trigger abrupt change; there is too much codependence between rulers and ruled. The former craves control; the latter craves stability. The result is ultraslow political evolution.

Middle-class insecurity. China's consumers, while boldly ambitious and desperate to climb the hierarchy of success, are insecure. Their wealth is new and incomes are still limited. Nothing comes easily, especially with skyrocket-ing real estate prices and hefty tariffs on hallmarks of middle-class consump-tion such as cars and luxury items. And, of course, most economic interests are not protected by institutionalized, enforceable law.

High-income individuals are dependent on the party's continuation of a pro-growth agenda, over which they exert little direct control. Corruption is rampant, and the system is biased in favor of state-owned enterprises. Entrepreneurs have limited access to investment capital. More broadly, they exist in a competitive dog-eat-dog arena in which universities pump out more than six million fresh graduates every year, while guarantees of cradle-to-grave subsistence have been removed. The middle class is forced to conform to narrowly defined standards of success, all mandated by the power structure.

Most Westerners, nurtured with a high degree of faith in representative democracy as a bulwark against fraud and excesses of the state, might expect

Image 24.1 The Chinese are impressed by the government's regular demonstrations of top-down control. The epic military parade in honor of new China's sixtieth anniversary was greeted with cheers, not cynicism. (Courtesy ImagineChina)

economically empowered Chinese to push for significant political reform. They see anger as the natural response to the lack of impartial civic institutions to defend these newly won gains.

Sublime order. But the Chinese are, first and foremost, reliant on the Communist Party to maintain order. It must stabilize the platform on which continued economic progress rests. The middle class recognizes rulers' imperfections but would never trade away strong central control if they foresaw the slightest risk of chaos. Because they define government's primary role as the advancement of national interests rather than protection of individual rights, they applaud the skill of technocratic cadres. In Chinese eyes, these are mandarins who have connected the country with the outside world, promulgated a long-term development strategy, and built a national infrastructure from scratch. Government has funneled capital into industries such as telecom and autos, which provide well-paying white- and blue-collar jobs. China's economic miracle is appreciated by its beneficiaries as a top-down phenomenon.

This belief in the prowess of the party as a unifying force is why quintessentially Chinese imperial displays—such as 2009's operatic, testosterone-fueled Sixtieth National Day parade—are met with little resistance, despite staggering cost and questionable quantifiable return. It also explains why very few educated Chinese protest indiscriminate use of the death penalty, except in the most egregious cases, even though due process does not exist. (A refrain one often hears on the street is "China has too many people.")

Growing ambivalence. While the middle class accepts Beijing's autocratic inclinations, there is growing ambivalence. Individuals still look toward the central government to maintain order, a critical factor in protecting hard-earned (and easily lost) economic gains. But they also expect the party to become more responsive to the people as they pursue traditional hallmarks of middle-income identity. By most measures, this is not happening. Property rights are still an abstraction; the health-care system is overly bureaucratic and corrupt, serving those with the deepest pockets rather than the greatest need; and investment vehicles, to say nothing of shareholder rights, are few and far between.

The government, attuned to escalating middle-class demands, knows it must evolve into something more responsive and flexible. It knows it must listen more—hence the party's schizophrenic attitude toward the Internet, gauging public opinion with one hand and gagging digital dissent with the other. But a dynastic impulse to frame the debate, reinforced by a cultural aversion to turmoil or rebellion, ensures that structural reform will be slow and ruthlessly incremental, and therefore imperceptible to foreign eyes.

Stagnating services. Given growing incomes, the gap between the needs of sophisticated middle-class consumers and the government's inability to provide for them will first become apparent in service industries. Despite nominal adherence to World Trade Organization timetables, even this sector—most conspicuously, health care and financial services—will remain highly regulated for many years to come.

Well-off individuals will not be free to invest or care for family members as they wish. Quality standards within state-owned providers will remain mediocre. Bureaucratic infighting will trump consumer choice. Surgeons will still be bribed by patients' relatives to ensure adequate care. Medical equipment will still be manned by inadequately trained and poorly compensated staff. Local banks, while dependable for low-end transactions, will offer no investment alternatives beyond basic savings and high-risk, opaque mutual funds. The needs of young urban professionals planning for retirement or a child's overseas education will remain unmet.

Why will the service sector fail to liberalize con brio, despite the avowed imperative of stimulating consumer spending? Yet again, in a bid to retain control of what the party labels strategic interests, social and political stability outweighs the development of institutions—in this case, a transparently regulated private sector—that protect individuals.

An eye toward progress. Still, middle-class citizens regard the state as the lynchpin of society. For all their desire for institutional reform, they would rather continue with the status quo than revolt against it. Despite party failings, they also see the enormous progress that has—bit by bit—been made over past decades. In a spring 2010 survey by the Pew Research Center's Global Attitudes Project, 87 percent of Chinese said they were satisfied with the way things were going in their country. They were equally enthusiastic about the future of their economy. Nearly nine in ten (87 percent) expected the economic situation in China to improve during the next twelve months. So things are getting better, enabled by a "modernization framework" designed by party autocrats who, when push comes to shove, still rule with an iron fist. Personal freedoms have expanded exponentially. Lifestyle options have multiplied stunningly in a short time. Career options have blossomed.

The Chinese people have only just begun their journey toward a middle-class higher ground. The government has decades, not years, to morph into something it currently is not: a modern, noncorrupt, self-correcting entity. The question, however, is: Does it have the confidence in itself, and the wisdom of its subjects, to begin its own gradual metamorphosis?

It's far from a sure thing.

25

THE LONG, LONG MARCH: CIVIL SOCIETY IN CHINA

Chinese society exudes an engaging combination of ambition and warmth. On a human level, Westerners could learn a lot from the fidelity Chinese children exhibit toward their parents and grandparents. And only the coldest heart could fail to be charmed by the spicy, funny street scenes, filled with pajama-clad adults, the buzz of lively debates, or the click-clack of mahjong tiles.

Most Americans are cultural and moral absolutists. Our nation has been shaped by geographic isolation and exceptionalism, a faith in our position as "a shining city upon a hill." Many feel that if behavior is American—or at least Western—it is civilized. This, of course, is a useless standard. Culture is relative, as are value systems. Both are shaped by distinct topographical, environmental, and economic circumstances. And any suggestion that Chinese, or any other, culture is uncivilized is patently ridiculous.

Indeed, the Chinese are culturally disposed to respect benevolence. Mencius, Confucius's immediate successor, whose works were part of neo-Confucian orthodoxy from the twelfth century on, regarded a Good Samaritan ethic—the Chinese call it *ren*—as a fundamental part of human nature, albeit one that requires cultivation in a "favorable environment." He wrote, "If people witness a child about to fall down a well, they would experience a feeling of fear and sorrow instantaneously without an exception. This feeling is generated not because they want to gain friendship with the child's parents, nor because they look for the praise of their neighbors and friends, nor because they don't like to hear the child's scream of seeking help....Without a mind directed by compassion, one is not human."

Modern China, however, often fails to live up to Mencius's ideals.

MAINLAND SOCIETY: SORRY, NOT YET CIVIL

Any properly functioning society is regulated by laws and institutions that apply to all individuals. The Chinese government understands this; hence its constant harping on the importance of the rule of law and the need for a harmonious society in which the gap between rich and poor is narrowed. Based on this definition, it is fair to say that China is, indeed, not yet civil. There are few, if any, institutions designed to guarantee the basic interests of individuals. The state has no internal checks and balances, and throughout Chinese history, it has existed on a plane quite above daily life. Statutes are composed with intentional ambiguity so they may be interpreted in different ways in different circumstances, safeguarding the authority of the Communist Party.

It is hazardous to make moral judgments from our Western perch, but how do we then track the country's progress toward civility? Let's say progress depends on protecting the economic and human interests of all citizens, individuals who are becoming inextricably linked with sustainable, rational economic growth. Such an ideological and bureaucratic sea change would manifest itself in many ways, large and small.

Fewer preventable deaths. It seems that every month there's another round of hand-wringing over the unnecessary loss of lives in coal shafts and unguarded schools or as a result of consuming toxic food. Poor safety precautions are usually to blame, and these are the fault of a system in which the central government is unable to ensure local authorities and corporations meet promulgated standards. Institutional accountability does not exist. The only way to bring errant officials in line is fear.

Amnesty International: Less frequent use of capital punishment. It is estimated that there are about 10,000 executions in China every year, and the public supports this policy as essential to maintaining order. The burden of proof is an alien concept. Rulings on guilt or innocence are carried out indiscriminately, often by local officials pressured to fill punishment quotas. Rampant death sentences are both acknowledged and assailed by Beijing, but, to date, the only attempt to rein in the death penalty has been an edict banning local governments from making the final decision.

Courts less biased toward local commercial interests. The judiciary exists to safeguard the interests of the state. Although plenty of statutes have been drafted regarding intellectual property and consumer rights, laws do not bite. When a case is taken to court, it will be dead in the water unless tried in a disinterested jurisdiction. Property rights, let alone rural land reform, are not yet ironclad because eminent domain abuses exist on an epic scale. Rule of law is still more a checklist concept than an ethos.

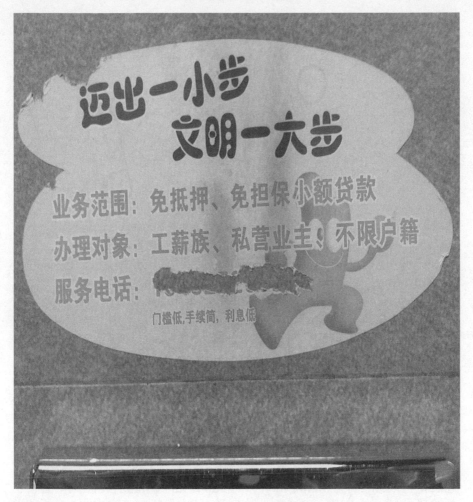

Image 25.1 Despite progress, the development of China as a civil society has a long way to go. At urinals, Shanghai Expo's mascot, Haibao, tells men, "One small step forward is a giant leap for civility." (Courtesy Tom Doctoroff)

Better-maintained public bathrooms. It is churlish to complain about unhygienic bathrooms in China given the dramatic leaps in quality in recent years. But what strikes most visitors is not the absolute level of bathroom conditions but the discrepancy between public and private spaces. While restaurants, office buildings, and theaters are richly decorated, lavatories are still fashioned with cardboard stalls, paper-thin walls, and substandard piping. Organizations do not invest in private spaces as they do public ones because the needs of individuals are subordinated to those of the group.

Chinese brands that succeed in the West. No local Chinese brand is anywhere near achieving leadership in market share in either Europe or America.

To do so, products must offer added value to sophisticated consumers while commanding a price premium. Breakthroughs are impossible without functioning marketing departments—empowered with budget control—that balance long-term intangible asset value and short-term revenue. The vast majority of local enterprises, on the other hand, are excessively sales driven.

Most of the brands that have made real progress—even within China—are from small or mid-sized companies, usually in the food and beverage or personal care categories. Larger players—notably household appliances, cars, mobile phones, and banking—have failed to take off because of poor corporate governance that leads to structural deficiencies and chronic short-term thinking. The absence of an impartial board of directors charged with ensuring long-term shareholder growth remains a huge hurdle, one erected by a government that prioritizes maintaining order over the protection of individual economic interests.

Acknowledgment of and explanations for Communist Party leadership transitions. The party will never brook alternative power centers, nor is there incentive to do so; despite many illusions to the contrary, there is no bottom-up push for representative democracy. But opaque factionalism still dominates the political scene. For steady growth and rational resource allocation to occur, a less corrupt, law-based government must emerge. This will require a far greater degree of public accountability (as opposed to murky, backroom brokering) than currently exists. The Chinese recognize the reality of "intra-party democracy"—it means building up systems and institutions for rational administration as well as less secretive leadership transitions.

Eased regulations for private hospitals and foreign banks. Since the start of the twenty-first century, China has witnessed an explosion in consumer choice. A plethora of luxury fashion, automobile, and fashion brands are lapped up by an ever-expanding middle class. However, despite nominal adherence to World Trade Organization timetables, the service sector—most conspicuously, health care and financial services—remains highly regulated, and needs stay unmet. Why has the service sector failed to liberalize, despite the avowed imperative of stimulating consumer spending and minimizing export reliance? Why are foreign banks unable to issue credit cards or offer mutual funds and other investment vehicles to mainland customers? Why does the state fail to promote the economic and medical needs of a cash-flush middle class? Yet again, in a bid to retain control of what the government labels strategic interests, social and political stability outweighs the development of institutions that protect individuals.

Improved traffic, airline, elevator, and sports etiquette. Airline scheduling is more secretive than Politburo meetings. In a bid to have everyone ready when the air traffic gods have spoken, the authorities do not deign to announce delays until passengers have been herded onto planes like sheep. Crossing the street in Shanghai can still be a death trek, only marginally safer than five years ago; the concept of pedestrian right of way remains, to most, a theoretical abstraction. Taxi drivers can be kamikaze pilots, accelerating and decelerating like hyperactive children on lithium. In lifts, personal space simply does not exist, let alone queues. Resonant belches waft to the ceiling, and cacophonous conversation pierces eardrums. So-called friendship matches between domestic and foreign basketball teams descend into hooliganism. Civil society, even in the lead up to the Olympics and China's much-vaunted debut on the world stage, did not exist, despite an attempt to implement it by fiat.

Equal access to banking capital for private companies. Misallocation of resources is, by far, the most pressing economic problem in China. Vibrant, resourceful small and medium-sized enterprises are starved for commercial loans, while bloated, state-owned dinosaurs are flush with cash. Both central and local governments have one eye fixed on social stability (that is, minimizing layoffs) and the other on profit, leading to irrational decision making. The heavy hand of the state trumps individual shareholder interests, leaving entrepreneurs hungry for impartially allocated credit.

THE SICHUAN EARTHQUAKE AFTERMATH: FORGING A NEW CIVIL SOCIETY?

In May 2008, three months before the Beijing Olympics, China was hit with its largest natural disaster in thirty years. Yinchuan, a town northwest of Sichuan province, was the focal point of a magnitude 7.9 earthquake, strong enough to make buildings sway more than 900 miles away in Beijing. Nearly 70,000 people were killed, 375,000 more were injured, and at least 4.8 million lost their homes.

Many Western pundits questioned whether this misfortune—which rounded off a five-month period of freak snowstorms, train wrecks, and ethnic unrest in Tibet—would break the spirit of the Chinese in the run-up to the Games. There is no question that the uprising in Tibet, and the anti-Chinese protests that followed from Paris to San Francisco, put a black mark next to the Olympics, which were intended to showcase national pride. But the response to the earthquake also brought out an admirable resilience and unity of spirit in the Chinese. It showcased the expression of genuine empathy—not China's hallmark—for the victims.

Chinese DNA: Valor in adversity. National determination, particularly when the chips are down, has always been the country's greatest resource. Ming emperors called on millions to rebuild the Great Wall when the dynasty was threatened by nomadic incursion from the north. During the 1930s, the Communist and Nationalist parties, enemies even today, put aside their differences to resist Japanese invasion.

China believes that unity is tantamount to survival. And the central government's patriarchal legitimacy hinges on maintaining order and stability. After the quake, the authorities seamlessly assumed control. Relief efforts, despite gargantuan logistical hurdles, were impressive by any standard. The outpouring of national grief was meticulously choreographed: three days of national mourning and a concurrent ban on any entertainment programs. Media coverage was a blend of managed transparency—every day, the death toll climbed by a few thousand—and propagandistic tales of inspiring heroism. Even the slogan of the Olympic torch relay was changed, from the celebratory "Light the passion, spread the dream" to the more subdued-yet-resolute "Spread the holy flame, contribute caring love."

Was the government entirely sincere? From the famine unleashed by the Great Leap Forward to the persecution of millions during the Cultural Revolution and 1989 Tiananmen massacre, the Communist Party was responsible for some of the greatest tragedies of the twentieth century. It's hard not to imagine that a hypocritical, self-aggrandizing Beijing to some extent played the emotions of its citizenry to further shore up its own power.

But even to foreigners who had lived in China for more than a decade, the genuine, bottom-up concern for the well-being of victims and their families was surprising and moving. When a group of my Chinese friends and I gathered to watch a memorial television program, quiet tears were shed, not the manufactured Sturm und Drang that often characterize official mourning in China.

At JWT, employees spontaneously organized a charity drive to rebuild a school in one of the shattered villages. A group of digital media technology researchers from Shanghai Jiao Tong University, working with a Sichuan technician, sent out a television signal so refugees in tents could have some entertainment. The Shanghai Hope Project Office said it was prepared to accept five hundred orphans from the quake-stricken areas. And, in the first two days after the quake, China's Red Cross received about $26 million in donations, mostly from individuals.

Critical factors: Internet and information. Was this evidence of a new spirit of generosity, one presaging the emergence of a truly civil society? Not quite. A ruthlessly competitive, money-hungry mind-set still characterizes many middle-class Chinese. However, the country and its people *are* making progress on the empathy front. In this case, it was heightened by two new influences. First, the Internet fuels both emotions and cash drives—tales of agony and triumph told by real people rather than propaganda mouthpieces spread through cyberspace, inspiring millions to give to a far-away cause. Second, the flow of information from the government was, relatively speaking, factual and fast. Premier Wen Jiabao's immediate, ubiquitously broadcast trek through quake wreckage convinced the nation that the disaster was worthy of a national rallying cry. A fresh, non-Orwellian style was embraced by millions, a lesson the government, we must hope, will not forget.

Facilitated by modern technology and a less defensive government, China's tradition of surmounting adversity was leveraged on an epic scale. In the process, the country emerged stronger, more confident, and less prickly. Could anyone not be touched by a nation resolved to overcome woe and stand up again?

Opportunity and inspiration really *are* borne of crisis.

CHINA'S DAIRY SCANDAL: TWO STEPS BACK

China's posttragedy civility didn't last long. In September 2008, the tainted goods scandals that have undermined confidence at home and eroded the country's reputation overseas for years returned to the headlines—larger and more dramatic than ever before. It emerged that six infants had died and 300,000 were ill with kidney damage from consuming milk or formula containing excessive amounts of melamine.

Like most other tainted goods scandals, this one was rooted in corruption and corner cutting, as parties within the dairy supply chain put their financial interests ahead of consumer safety. The bulk of China's milk ultimately comes from small-scale farmers who pass the raw product on to agents, who in turn sell it to dairy companies. Lacking the vertical integration of Western dairy industries, the system is insecure, as demonstrated when certain groups and individuals added the melamine—which artificially boosts protein content—to substandard or watered-down milk in order to pass quality-control tests. It didn't help that when people along the supply chain did voice concerns, they appear to have been ignored or suppressed.

The company most at fault, Sanlu, was allowed to slide into bankruptcy, and its former general manager was sentenced to life in prison. Two milk collection agents received the death penalty.

International scorn, domestic PR disaster. Globally, this was just one more question mark regarding the safety of anything Chinese, a handicap to any local company seeking to establish a branded presence abroad. Children in the United States, Europe, and Japan may not drink Chinese milk, but they play with Chinese-made toys, which have had their own safety scandals. The cumulative impact has pushed the day Chinese brands are able to compete in

Image 25.2   In China, anything can be unsafe, even milk. In 2008, Sanlu Dairy knowingly contaminated its milk powder products with melamine, an illegal ingredient. Hundreds of thousands of children developed kidney stones, and six died. Some leaders were brought to justice, but the entire nation was disgusted by the clear evidence of corruption. (Courtesy ImagineChina)

developed markets—at a price premium—further into the future. Expansion into emerging markets has also suffered, at least in the short to medium term.

In China, the setback is even more severe. Reservations about the quality and reliability of local brands have always run deep; hence the popularity of international trademarks in practically every category, from soy sauce and paint to mobile phones and automobiles. Local brands' dominant market position in key categories such as beer, cigarettes, and appliances is largely driven by either price-value considerations or passive familiarity, rather than robust brand equity. Even value-added dairy items such as yogurt and ice cream have historically been vulnerable to multinational brands' inroads if the affordability issue can be addressed.

This trust setback is still critical in a variety of ways.

First, it is viewed as a national shame, a by-product of incestuous, co-dependent managers and officials—all Communist Party members—who feed from the same trough. It's an indictment of a system in which checks and balances do not exist. The government achieves much of its legitimacy by extolling its role as a patriarchal protector, consistent with Confucian imperatives, and guardian of public interest. Leading dairy companies such as Yili Group, Bright Dairy, and China Mengniu have benefited tremendously not only from capital investment but also active government promotion of dairy as an essential element of daily nutrition. In the context of their oft-repeated goal of forging a harmonious society, this scandal made policy makers look hypocritical and manipulative.

Second, Chinese hope for the future is invested in the child—the single child, precious and fragile. Because milk is digested, rather than merely touched, worn, or played with, the perceived threat to national well-being was immediate and shocking. People have since become even more vigilant in making buying decisions, not just for food products but for practically any commodity.

Third, Chinese manufacturers—and the government—now must work harder than ever to reestablish the tentative trust in local goods. In 2005, international brands controlled approximately 80 percent of the infant formula market; by 2007, domestic players Shengyuan, Yili, and Yashili were, respectively, the second-, third-, and fourth-largest brands. The scandal effectively undid much of the progress they had made. Propaganda drives, ranging from strident proclamations that guilty officials would be dealt with severely to ads featuring apparatchiks drinking milk in order to reassure the public, only went so far to repair perceptions.

A dreary impact. Three years later, China has largely picked itself up and moved on from the scandal, just as it did with other, similar episodes. Local brands' spending on advertising has continued to rise, partly because the public requires further quality reassurance in areas such as food, beverages, personal care, and pharmaceuticals (that is, products ingested by or applied to the body). Sadly, advertising messages have become even more prosaic and less rooted in emotional benefits, since basic reliability must be reestablished.

There has been no actual boycott of locally produced goods, however. In China, the ultimate *caveat emptor* market, the tolerance for substandard products has always been high. Furthermore, in many areas, the Chinese, even within the burgeoning—albeit penny-pinching—middle class, are constrained by limited options and limited incomes. In most categories, multinational companies price their goods two or three times higher than domestic competitors do. Some are now following the strategy employed by the likes of Procter & Gamble, introducing products at lower price tiers in order to grab a larger share of the mass premium segment, a price range that both multinational and local companies have historically ignored. But the range of products and price points currently available is not broad enough to support a mad rush toward international brands.

In the end, the losers in this sorry debacle have been Chinese consumers, who sometimes feel that the odds are stacked against them. Because of the scandal they feel even less safe, a huge psychological blow for people who prize stability as a precursor to progress. The government, it is hoped, will someday realize that its fundamental, institutionalized lack of accountability precludes the nation from evolving into a truly modern society, a goal cherished by both rulers and ruled.

26

LIFE IN SHANGHAI'S LANES: A COMMUNITY AFFAIR

It's a truism that you can't know China unless you connect with the lifestyles of the people. A few years ago, I put my money where my mouth is and bought a quintessentially Shanghai-style house in a traditional *lilong* (or *longtong*) in the center of the city's old French Concession. These lane houses, perhaps the most distinctive facet of Shanghai's architectural heritage, are a fusion of Chinese courtyards and Western row houses—tall and narrow residences, organized in a dense, gridlike pattern with east-west and north-south lanes. Most developments are tucked away from main thoroughfares, providing an intimate calm despite the urban hum just a few steps from one's abode. Residents are generally not well off. Rents are heavily subsidized by the government; on the open market, downtown real estate value rivals Hong Kong prices.

LILONG CHARM

Each unit houses several families, at least one per floor, so lilong life is intimate. Typical sights and sounds include laundry, including underwear, hung everywhere; staccato click-clacks of nightly mahjong competitions; pajama-clad men and women taking out the trash; hawkers roaming about, advertising their wares, usually through a megaphone, with chantlike monotony; makeshift appurtenances on balconies to provide extra space for anything from air conditioners to scraggly plants; the yips and yaps of small dogs, often poodles, socializing with other neighborhood pets; the twang of novice violinists; bicycles and mopeds and, increasingly, cars in front of every door; occasional altercations, usually about space infringement.

Image 26.1　Traditional Shanghai *lilong* life is cramped, increasingly geriatric, but loaded with smiles. Foreign "invaders" must work hard to achieve acceptance by suspicious neighbors. (Courtesy ImagineChina)

Lilong life, certainly not for everyone, has charm. But, with an open eye and mind, one can plumb the scene for insights about the fundamental motivations of Chinese people, even the structure of Chinese society.

Conflict resolution: A community affair. Lilongs are usually managed by an informal power structure, only loosely aligned with municipal government organs. Individual rights rarely trump collective harmony. My plans to enclose my roof garden and turn it into a sunroom came unstuck when a low-level district representative informed me that the neighbors did not want the original structure changed. In order to save face, the representative refused to tell me who had complained; what entity, if any, could hear an appeal; and the specifics of what, precisely, constituted structural alteration. Some time later, the entrance guard told me a few suspicious residents had banded together to send a message: as a foreigner, I was entitled to no special privilege, and my Western lifestyle should not disrupt the unity of the neighborhood.

Trust investment: A sunk cost. Trust facilitation requires active, skillful investment. Smiles and friendly chitchat go only so far. As construction started on the other renovations for my home, with buzz saws piercing the lane's daytime calm, I came bearing gifts: chrysanthemum tea, moon cakes, and baijiu, a strong Chinese spirit. To demonstrate my commitment, I visited neighbors during my office hours and wore business attire in order to convey respect. When the people next door claimed the noise pollution was dangerous to their health, compensation negotiations were conducted by intermediaries, and I ended up paying four families $250 each, the equivalent of one month's salary for the average Shanghainese. But at the same time it was important to stress the presence of a bottom line: three months in, I politely rejected a demand to pay for "lost rental income."

It's no surprise trust is not taken for granted in China. Just dealing with the construction company about renovations to my home was a dog-eat-dog battle of supremacy. Customer satisfaction is not the assumed priority it is in the West. Each party must protect its economic interests, because commercial practices have been neither institutionalized nor standardized.

It all starts with the contract. Terms are intentionally vague; deliverables are defined, but specifics, such as materials, component pricing, and timing, are not—which means the contractor has incentive to increase margins by skimping on quality. The owner must therefore double-check the value of everything, from waterproofing material and ventilation fans to drainage pipes and floor joists. Workers, mostly migrants from poor provinces, are poorly supervised, so daily visits are required to verify adherence to specs. It is standard for clients to withhold as much as 30 percent of payment to retain leverage over suppliers during the one-year guarantee period, lest repair requests fall on deaf ears. Threats of legal action elicit smirks because of the ineffective, often corrupt, judiciary.

Older vs. younger generations: A big gap. The older generation, buffeted by relentless upheaval during the past fifty years, is fundamentally more protective than the younger one. In Shanghai, approximately 20 percent of citizens are older than sixty. In my lane, the figure exceeds 50 percent as young people forsake the intimacy of lane life for the modern conveniences of new apartments. Unless I greet older cohabitants directly, eye contact is averted. Their suspicions regarding my intentions are thinly masked. On the day I moved in, one neighborhood godfather, a husky, loud-voiced eighty-year-old, was forthright in his questioning. Where's your wife? Why don't you live in an expat apartment building? What time do you leave for the office? When are you going to resell your property?

On the other hand, younger people, even of modest means, ask for tours of the house and greet me warmly whenever they see me. They are eager to practice English and exchange political views. They want to know what DVDs are good and which television shows and commercials I like. The new generation's broad worldview and incessant curiosity is not limited to the middle class. It penetrates all levels of society.

Joy in the corners: Happiness persists. The Chinese, despite limited means and honed self-protective instincts, are happy. The flip side of an insecurity-based worldview is an appreciation of minutiae. The con brio vigor of chess wars, muted by the buzz of gossip, is a delight. New Year fireworks elicit howls of laughter. The morning bun hawker derives satisfaction from each sale. Old men take pride in their pet turtles. Every door is surrounded by plants, a sign of emotional invest-ment in one's abode, no matter how modest. Weddings are a joyful community affair. Neighbors unfold lawn chairs to relax, often in pajamas, and watch the world go by.

27

A DAY AT THE SHANGHAI ZOO: FAMILIES IN ACTION

Expatriates in China fall into one of two general categories: China friendly and China unfriendly. People are either drawn to the country's warmth and ambition or repulsed by its shoddiness and lack of civility. Those in the latter camp should get back on the plane—the Chinese have a spider sense for arrogance. If they sense contempt, they discreetly go for the jugular.

There is no greater testing ground of one's ability to navigate the Chinese landscape than the Shanghai Zoo on a public holiday. Unlike the Beijing Olympics, or other events conceived to gain international face, a day at the zoo is strictly local; signage is (mostly) in Chinese. The zoo is also apolitical—there are no fuddy-duddy red banners exhorting harmony. Far from judgmental eyes, the Chinese let their hair down. With no dignity at risk, they are irrepressibly themselves, free to both shock and awe.

On the shock front, the crush of humanity induces anxiety. Competition for nose-against-the-glass views of popular exhibits—fish, auspicious symbols of prosperity, are big draws—is aggressive. The concept of personal space, let alone respect for toes, does not exist. There is much jostling, pushing, and poking. Parents allow children to relieve themselves on public lawns.

Furthermore, the whiff of bureaucratic corruption is everywhere. Kickback-fueled renovation bids result in third-rate "upgrades" to everything from panda cages to peacock gardens. Bumper car and Ferris wheel rides can charitably be described as creaky. Peeling paint, weed-infested gardens, cheap signage, and scum-filled alligator ponds are evidence of a brittle bureaucracy that prizes checklists and cut-rate construction, not quality or service. China's dynamic market economy is nowhere to be seen; every concession stand sells corn on the cob, sausages on a stick, and low-end ice cream. Souvenir stands hawk flimsy inflatable giraffes and nothing else.

Who's at the zoo? The masses. With nary an international fashion brand in sight, the tumult is fun. Families—from infants to their grandparents—love being together, and unrestrained laughter pierces the air. Children are lifted onto the shoulders of doting fathers with a combination of king-of-the-jungle pride and papa-bear affection. Boyfriends and girlfriends, wearing matching t-shirts, walk arm in arm.

Family values, a unifying force as China hurtles toward modernization, are on display. In a crowd of ordinary Chinese, the country's preoccupation with face disappears. Educational zeal is also in the air. Parents quiz their five-year-olds on the difference between orangutans and gorillas; every exhibit boasts placards overflowing with fun facts. Parents encourage their kids' embrace of the new.

Shanghai's facilities pale in comparison with those of such institutions as Singapore's Night Safari or even the Detroit Zoo. The conditions in which the animals live have a long way to go. But the zoo has made recent progress, especially against an international standards checklist. Animal exchanges occur between Shanghai and other foreign cities. Cages have been replaced with (scraggly) natural habitats. Viewing areas have been enlarged and walking paths broadened. Gardens have been landscaped. Trash receptacles are everywhere. Bathrooms, recently primeval, are cleaner and friendlier to the handicapped.

There are two Chinas, one falling and one rising. At the zoo, both are on display. Pessimists will shake their heads at stultifying bureaucracy, robotic service, and boorish civility. Optimists are reassured by the unquantifiable: relentless energy, a broad-based urge to surge underpinned by a thirst for knowledge, and cohesion of the clan.

28

CHRISTMAS IN CHINA: UNIVERSAL RELEASE, TRANSACTIONAL GAIN

Just because China has embraced Christmas does not mean the country is becoming Western. Appearances can be deceiving.

Christmas tunes play on radio stations. Every top-grade office building in Shanghai, Beijing, and Guangzhou is decked out with holiday displays. Seasonal music is piped into elevators far and wide, even in Communist Party buildings. Santa, Frosty the Snowman, and Rudolph are ubiquitous. Department stores never used to have Christmas sales. Now they all do.

The Chinese have not discovered Jesus. Evangelical Christianity may be spreading, particularly in the countryside, where adherents can be quite passionate, but most mainland Chinese know very little about the deeper meaning of Christmas. They cannot articulate the difference between Jews and Christians, let alone that between Catholics, who acknowledge the pope, and Protestants, who do not.

China's Jesus is, more often than not, interchangeable with Buddha. He is someone to turn to, particularly in periods of uncertainty or fear. The idea of having a relationship with Jesus through acceptance of his Golden Rule in exchange for salvation is a nuanced abstraction. It is not a powerful offer for today's pragmatic, ambitious, and worldly younger generations. In China, morality is relative; standards shift based on ever-morphing external circumstances. No matter what circumstance, embrace of Christian morality is absolute, Jesus's word—charity to others, including the weak, particularly strangers—is a prerequisite to salvation. The tenets of Occidental Christianity are poorly understood and, frankly, unattractive as a selling point for religion.

So why is Christmas hot? There are two reasons. First, Christmas is a win-win. It fuses fun, a universal release, with transactional gain. Second, and more subtly, Western holidays, particularly Christmas and Valentine's Day, are useful tools for reinforcing an individual's position within a Confucian context.

To the Han, Christmas is not Western. Instead, the holiday is international and modern and carries a whiff of status, the ultimate commodity in China. Santa is a symbol of progress; he represents the country's growing comfort with a new global order, one into which it is determined to assimilate, without sacrificing national interest. Individuals who make merry are making a statement. They are declaring themselves new-generation players, able to absorb new elements and apply them in a Chinese framework.

On an even deeper level, Christmas is an investment in the future. Men carry a heavy burden. In matters of the heart, women are demanding. Mothers-in-law will not approve of a prospective groom unless he can afford an apartment, an increasingly elusive requirement given skyrocketing real estate costs. Cars have become a must for couples intent on entering the ranks of the middle class. Chinese relationships are rooted in dependability, not romantic love. Of course, the desire for passion is universal, but love is not enough to seal the deal. Men must first and foremost prove themselves. They must establish their commitment in terms of emotional dedication and material potential. The Christmas gift is one more opportunity for young Chinese men to proclaim, "Darling, I would do anything for you." It has been embraced as a means of demonstrating steadfastness.

Chinese Christmas festivities are still rather newfangled. For fifteen years, however, Valentine's Day has been de rigeur. If a boyfriend does not give his girlfriend an expensive present, he will no longer have a girlfriend. The reason is obvious—Valentine's Day is all about showing one's love. This drive explains the phenomenal spread of engagement rings. Diamonds are a new cultural imperative; they have achieved 85 percent penetration in tier-one cities, up from less than 10 percent in 1995.

Chinese adoption of Christmas rituals does not imply Westernization. The holiday has been co-opted to advance a distinctly Chinese agenda: projection of status in a culture in which individual identity is inextricably linked to external validation.

29

RITUALISTIC OBSERVATION: THE DARK MATTER OF CHINESE CIVILIZATION

The most rudimentary Confucian imperative is that of *li,* or ritual, pre-cognitive subservience to a prescribed natural order that manifests itself in automatic behavior. No matter how modern, Chinese are instinctively obedient to Spring Festival rituals—attending family gatherings, and avoiding sweeping, washing hair, and using vulgar language. The tomb-sweeping festival, at which respects are paid to one's ancestors, *must* be observed.

CHINA'S COSMOLOGY

Everyone wonders what makes the universe tick; Westerners rely on empiricism—that is, scientific validation—to support the existence of relativity, quarks, dark matter, and so on. Chinese, however, are inductive, not deductive. Everything starts from faith in one imperative: the balance or harmony of yin (feminine) and yang (masculine), elements propelled by the circular flow of a vital life force, *qi.* From solar structure to heartbeat regularity to an individual's life path, *qi* affects everything.

Universal holism. Most premonotheistic societies adopt a cyclical view of time to explain the past and predict the future. The brilliance of the Chinese worldview is its analytic and diagnostic completeness. Perhaps impelled by the historical instability of the great Asian landmass—pandemonium from earthquakes, droughts, floods, and locusts broke out like clockwork—they have meticulously charted the nature of birth, death, time, fortune, disaster, rainfall, and everything else since their dawn of civilization. As early as 500 B.C.E., the elegantly elaborate equations in the *Book of Changes* were accepted as conventional wisdom. Furthermore, heaven and Earth were unified, making matters still more complex. The structure of family homes and city layouts mirrors the configuration of the stars; generational progression is syncopated with the flow of time itself. The essence of Chinese universal holism is rarely articulated— few college-educated individuals can discuss the *ba gua*, the intricate divination system that underpins the yin-yang balance in heaven and on Earth—but manifestations of it are everywhere and affect everything from wedding dates to license plates.

Logical superstition. We often think of the Chinese—given their predilection for lucky numbers, amulets, and feng shui—as superstitious, but to them it is all perfectly logical. Every so-called superstition preserves or extends natural order. Chinese health practices—from acupuncture to tai qi—maintain the body's alignment with *qi*. So do architectural beliefs; feng shui avoids interruption of *qi*. Gambling, fortune-telling, morphology, phrenology, and numerology are all addictive because they reveal future *qi*.

Chinese revere circular objects because they represent completeness, a harmony between yin and yang. The number eight, for example, is extremely lucky; it is a representation of infinite smoothness. Nines and threes are auspicious, too. Four is feared (the Chinese pronunciation of "four" is similar to that of "death," while the symbol itself also has a dangerous look, all angles and dead-ends). Lucky license plates, identity cards, and telephone numbers are auctioned off. Likewise, round faces are beautiful while high cheekbones, particularly ones that protrude outward, are very bad, even if they are perfectly symmetrical.

PASSAGES: WHEN CULTURAL DNA REVEALS ITSELF

Even if liberated by a gold MasterCard, most modern Chinese are traditional at heart and always ceremonially correct during important life junctures, particularly marriage and death.

Weddings. Despite the trappings of modernity, weddings are chock-a-block with ritual, primal expressions of China's worldview. Looks, however, can deceive. Chinese marriage celebrations are, at first glance, anything-goes affairs, eruptions of ostentation and status projection. In the past twenty years, gatherings have morphed from dusty administrative procedures to superficially Western, over-the-top materialistic spectacles. (The average price for a wedding party in Shanghai, flowers included, is approximately $25,000, more than three times the average annual per capita income.) Young couples of limited means

Image 29.1 Chinese weddings have become opulent. The average cost of a wedding party has risen to $25,000, more than twice the average annual per capita come. This wedding, complete with catwalk runway and spotlights, is a public coming-out party for an aspiring middle-class power couple. Still, traditional bows to fathers remain de rigeur. (Courtesy JWT)

find a way to dazzle with rented Mercedeses, abalone, shark fin soup, cham-
pagne flowing down a mountain of wine glasses, white wedding gowns with
ten-foot trains, celebrity performances, and audiovisual productions glorifying
the bride and groom's love.

But cultural imperatives, both intergenerational and communal, are never
far from the surface. Parents and grandparents are treated with reverence, with
expressions of appreciation from sons to fathers solemnly expressed on stage,
before any food is served. Great care is taken to minimize lost face. Every word
of every toast is meticulously scripted, and professionally trained emcees ensure
proceedings unfold according to plan. No matter how much money is spent on
the party, guests show up in casual attire, because society is family. Wedding
gifts are cash stuffed in red envelopes, not personal items selected from a bridal
registry. Money, in this case, is not strictly transactional—it is used to pay for a
party that lubricates interfamily bonding. A bride, no matter how successful at
work, assumes a role of feminine subservience on her wedding day: as the groom
circulates from table to table to make toasts, she trails him, lighting cigarettes.

Funerals. At Chinese funerals, the primal urge to seek solace from cosmological order becomes touchingly apparent. In 2009, the father of a close
Chinese colleague, my finance partner for more than a decade, passed away after
a struggle with diabetes. The funeral, which took place on what is considered
a lucky date in Shanghai, was characterized by clocklike precision, structured
ritual, and oceans of humanity—a combination that could perhaps occur only
in China, a land where large-scale mobilization meets transcendent release.

The ceremony started at 10:50 A.M. sharp in Ba Xian Ting, or Eight Spirits
Hall, a mammoth funeral home complex with at least a dozen rooms hosting
hundreds of families in a single day. When I asked the guard to point me in the
right direction, he quickly scanned a scrolled computerized printout, identified
the name, and sent me on my way. The room in which last respects were paid
was small, without seats, starkly modern yet festooned with six-foot memorial
wreaths neatly lined against the walls. The body, surrounded by flowers, was
placed on a glass-covered bier. Lovingly tended and beautifully presented, the
father rested beneath a large black-and-white photo, one from which his kind
eyes and beatific smile comfortingly beamed. Mourners, perhaps fifty of them,
were dressed respectfully, albeit in everyday attire. Few wore black, perhaps
because of limited means.

Western observers might deem the proceedings awkwardly regimented.
Indeed, all words and gestures reinforced the father's contribution to society
and fulfillment of obligation, with few personal stories and no moments of
levity. An emcee opened the proceedings by acknowledging leaders in attendance. The first person to speak was not a family member but, per protocol, a

representative of the deceased's employer, a state-owned enterprise from which he had retired more than fifteen years earlier. Her speech, scripted yet sincerely delivered, extolled the man's professional accomplishments, work ethic, and commitment to the harmony of the work unit. Her words were not brief. She meticulously covered the arc of an engineering career that spanned three decades, limning steps of labored ascension, a worker's climb from fresh graduate to acknowledged master of his domain.

After the forty-minute service, groups of four stepped toward the altar, bowed three times with crisp precision, and placed single yellow roses on the casket.

Despite the discipline, or perhaps because of it, the room brimmed with warmth. The father's elder son, forty years old and dressed in a black waistcoat tied with a white hemp sash, spoke on behalf of the family, recounting the story of a humble man born of peasant stock, a striver who elevated himself from humble beginnings by dint of hard work and a sharp mind. The son's tone was measured, but his voice broke at the end. "Don't worry, Dad," he said. "We will be good men. We will take care of Mom. We will never forget what you have taught us. We will raise our boys in a way that honors your memory." He quietly wept, quickly composed himself, and said a last good-bye. Mourners cried softly, too.

China is not an individualistic country and likely never will be. But, as this last tribute demonstrates, expressions of love and grace can be found everywhere.

A few tips. Foreigners should pay heed to this primeval, almost instinctive, layer of Chinese culture. Insensitivity to employees' family obligations will deeply alienate. Failure to consult feng shui masters during office relocation will trigger mutiny. On minor family holidays such as the tomb-sweeping festival, an empathetic boss should automatically release staff at 2 P.M.; the government, officially atheistic, looks askance.

Furthermore, the stars impact sales revenue in unexpected ways. Weddings, for example, are unlucky during rooster years—the Diamond Trading Company was caught off guard by a sudden plunge in engagement ring demand. Marketers also buy media based on whether purchasing a product is lucky or not at any given time. Big-ticket items—cars, appliances, and computers—should be bought only *after* Chinese New Year.

Above all, the Chinese believe every individual has his own date with destiny, an ineluctable fate. Foreigners must respect cosmological mandates.

30

SEX IN CHINA: PRUDENCE AND PRURIENCE

A police bust of a Nanjing swingers club left twenty-two people facing trial on charges of engaging in group sex, a crime that carries a maximum prison sentence of five years. The incident laid bare the tensions in contemporary Chinese society between a new reality of "liberated" behavior and traditional cultural imperatives. On one hand, the Chinese are having orgies. On the other, the price for fun may be jail.

Decadence all around. There is no doubt that sexual mores in China are dramatically more liberal now than fifteen or twenty years ago. Prostitution is everywhere; it's difficult to check into a three-star hotel without being accosted in the lobby by pimps or pleasure girls plying their trade. Every high-ranking cadre seems to sport a Gucci-clad *xiao laopo* (mistress, or "little wife"). Premarital sex is commonplace; ten years ago, most college students graduated as virgins, while today fewer than half do. Sex paraphernalia shops, usually managed by old ladies wearing white lab coats, are as ubiquitous as massage parlors, many of which offer "happy endings." Karaoke joints, both seedy and ornate, have become meat markets, where comely country girls are paraded for inspection between rounds of dice games and off-key musical stylings. Gay clubs have popped up in every city; "money boys" prowl dance floors in search of tricks. Online pornography, despite intermittent government crackdowns, blankets cyberspace, covering every possible predilection—and it's free.

Conservatism rules. And yet, in many ways, China's attitudes toward sex remain, by Western standards, prudish. Young women who have boyfriends during high school are considered bad. Mass advertising is tame, reflecting not only strict censorship guidelines, promulgated by the state, but also broad

Image 30.1 Every major city is chock-a-block with sex shops, patronized by old and young alike and often supervised by sweet grandmas. In China, romantic passion is not an end in itself. It is a means for sealing long-term stability. (Courtesy ImagineChina)

conservatism among the public at large. Underwear models are invariably Caucasian, because Chinese blanch when a fellow citizen strikes a degradingly erotic pose. Even urban fashionistas with dyed hair wince at dresses cut too low or risqué tattoos. While premarital sex is now the norm, there is very little hooking up. Modern women conform to traditional standards of seductive demureness; men are tight-lipped about their exploits, even after a beer or two. The vast majority of homosexuals still resign themselves to the inevitability of sham marriages.

Is today's jarring coexistence of prurience and prudery merely a transitional phenomenon on the road to complete sexual liberation? Or is something more timeless manifesting itself?

In the West, sexual love and marriage are inseparable. The root of a healthy union, regardless of whether it has been sanctioned by the state, is a romantic passion that deepens over time. When love withers, the union is considered, by society and individual, empty at the core—hence divorce rates in excess of 50 percent. Not so in China.

Sacred stability. In the PRC, where the clan, not the individual, is the basic building block of society, marriage is less a union of two souls than two

Image 30.2   A typical wedding portrait, airbrushed to heavenly perfection. Such images are designed to signal a fusion of idealized romance and commitment to family and friends. (Courtesy Lily Sun)

extended families. It is not truly consummated until a new generation is produced. Romantic love, desired and even useful as a bonding agent, is a secondary concern, a means to an end. Men demonstrate worthiness by proving their commitment: Valentine's Day, a platform on which devotion can be displayed, is almost as dear to the Chinese as Lunar New Year. Marriage is a protective union, a bulwark against the vicissitudes of a world in which individual rights do not exist, self-expression is often viewed as a threat to the established order, and institutions designed to protect individual interests are rare. In America, De Beers's slogan, "A Diamond Is Forever," glorifies eternal romance. In China, the same tagline connotes obligation, a familial covenant—rock solid, like the stone itself.

Pragmatism and release. The Chinese, supremely practical in most aspects of their lives, are less focused on sexual fulfillment than their Western counterparts. This is why, given the right professional opportunity, spouses are willing

Image 30.3   A typical over-the-top entrance for one of China's many public bathhouses. Prices are cheap. Daily city life is stressful, but ordinary folks have access to many relaxation spots. Massage parlors, both regular and with "happy endings," are on every corner. (Courtesy JWT)

to live in different cities or even on different continents. It also explains why, according to a 2001 study conducted by condom manufacturer Durex in more than one hundred countries, China ranked third to last in frequency of intercourse by married couples. America ranked first.

As a result, men in China have access to a much broader variety of sexual options than American or European men do. Sex is commercialized—and ritualized—here to an extraordinary degree. With a wink and a smile, prices of high- and low-end services—by the hour or overnight, from manual or oral stimulation to full penetration—are quoted as freely as a McDonald's menu board. Men joke about "above the line" (that is, of the head and heart) versus "below the line" needs, separate and unequal.

Wives often turn a blind eye to sexual activities outside the home so long as they pose no threat to cohesion. Levels of tolerance vary, of course, but women, more often than not, endure a husband's hour with a prostitute or a trip to the massage parlor so long as dedication to family is not in question. A mistress—a de facto threat to solidarity—is more likely to be a deal breaker but not necessarily so. According Xu Xinjin, the owner of a marital advice hotline, divorce because of extramarital affairs is still relatively uncommon. Many go on for years because no one wants to hurt the family's only child. Yes, the number of men—and women—tempted into dangerous liaisons is on the rise. But those who have them, particularly after a child is born, are scorned by society, shamed by family and friends. (Twenty years ago, they would have also been demoted at work.)

China's pragmatic—or, to use a marketing term, functional—approach to sex is reflected in attitudes toward homosexuality. Sexual orientation is almost beside the point. Gay clubs and prostitution were commonplace during the Tang dynasty, and they still are today. Society is less inclined to judge individuals for gay acts than failure to fulfill filial obligation to procreate. Marriage and fatherhood remain the societally defined foundation of respectability. Although the government is signaling a more tolerant attitude toward untraditional lifestyles, most modern Chinese, including the majority of middle-class young gays, are unable to conceive of a future without a wife and child.

UNHAPPY DESTINY?

The prevalence of loveless unions and cheating spouses begs the question: Are the Chinese unhappy? Do they yearn to buck demands to forgo personal gratification in the interests of social stability? Yes and no. On one hand, divorce rates have skyrocketed in the past twenty years. According to official statistics, more than 25 percent of Shanghai marriages now end in court, up from about 5 percent during the 1980s. Support groups, both online and off, are increasingly commonplace. Clearly, an economically empowered new generation refuses to put up with serial cheating, physical abuse, emotional abandonment, deadbeat dads, or domestic cold war. That said, Chinese and Western aspirations—emotional, spiritual, and material—are not, and never will be, the same. In the West, the pursuit of (individual) happiness is seen as an inalienable right, the fundamental purpose of life. The Chinese crave a *ta shi* future, steady and sturdy; so long as both husband and wife advance the clan's well-being, harmony will reign. In the aforementioned Durex survey, China placed second in terms of marital satisfaction.

True, the desire for romantic fulfillment is universal and ever more aspirational, even idealized, in a globally connected China. But 5,000 years of cultural truth—the supremacy of Confucian cohesion over Jeffersonian individualism—will not be swept away by ten years of Barbie and Ken fantasia. The Chinese will resolve, in their own way, on their own terms, the struggle between passion and pragmatism.

PART FIVE

CHINA AND THE WORLD

31

ICONS AND IDENTITY: AN INTRODUCTION TO CHINA'S ENGAGEMENT WITH THE WORLD

China does not boast many icons. But they exist—people who capture the public's imagination to such an extent they generate universal admiration. In China, an icon is, without exception, an individual who transcends conventional definitions of what it means to be Chinese. Icons reinterpret Chinese identity without abandoning it. In doing so, they bring glory to the country, enabling the masses to stand tall on the global stage.

Yao Ming. The Shanghai Sharks superstar was selected by an NBA team, the Houston Rockets, as their first-round draft pick in 2002. Despite an injury that ultimately brought his career to a premature close in 2011, Yao was selected eight times as a starter for the Western Conference in the NBA All-Star Game. In China, he is a megastar because he won big in the United States and did so by deploying a quintessentially Chinese style of play—*lingqiao*, or flexible skill. Yao did not emulate the style of NBA trash-talking but instead leveraged resourcefulness and understatement, two aspirational personality characteristics, to make his mark. On the basketball court, the new generation's altar of cool, Yao brought home victory and worldwide applause. (In contrast, sprinter Liu Xiang's iconic potential evaporated when he withdrew from the Olympic hundred-meter sprint in front of a global television audience.) By reinterpreting, not discarding, traditional Chinese values, Yao made the nation proud.

Zhang Yimou. He is the most celebrated fifth-generation film director, renowned in the West since his 1987 debut oeuvre, *Red Sorghum*, the first Chinese film to be nominated for an Academy Award. The Chinese themselves took longer to come around. Until recently, Zhang was often criticized for presenting a quaintly traditional view of China, predigested for foreign consumption. His acclaimed movies, such as *Ju Dou*, *Raise the Red Lantern*, and *To Live*, were said to romanticize feudalism. Stories of concubines and landowners, saturated with color, reinforced an archaic view of China. Public indifference toward Zhang began to change when *Hero*, a 2002 epic martial arts masterpiece, became an international hit, particularly in the United States. The eponymous protagonist, a master swordsman who prevents the assassination of China's first emperor, represented an incarnation of the ultimate Chinese truth: the sublimity of unity versus the evil of chaos. Zhang did not approach deity status, however, until he staged the opening ceremony for the 2008 Beijing Olympics. The three-hour extravaganza, broadcast to billions, was a declaration of China's emergence as a twenty-first-century *cultural* power. For the first time in modern history, the world understood that China's values—and not just its economy—would be a force to be reckoned with.

Bruce Lee. He is the closest thing Chinese men have to a spiritual savior. He developed his own kung fu philosophy—Jeet Kune Do, or The Way of Intercepting Fist—by fusing various schools of classic martial arts techniques. Lee's style, a quintessentially Han combination of defensive power and under-the-radar masculinity, elevated the chop-socky Hong Kong martial arts flick to a new level of international popularity. The fame of Lee, who was born in San Francisco and raised in Hong Kong during the 1940s and 1950s, made Chinese feel big. He died in 1973, just as the country was about to emerge from its darkest period in history, an era of political and economic emasculation. Inured to, but powerless to counter, impotence in the face of Western hegemony, Chinese males needed a role model who personified masculine grace: lithesome agility, "defensive offense," the ability to transform harmony with the external world into explosive power. Today, almost forty years after his death, Lee almost transcends iconic status.

The idolization of Yao, Zhang, and Lee suggests a profound ambivalence in the Chinese people about the outside world. On one hand, the nation craves engagement with and acknowledgment from the international community. On the other hand, China has an inferiority complex, exacerbated by two hundred years of humiliating economic decline. Fiercely nationalistic and culturally absolutist, the country has a chip on its shoulder. The Chinese do not feel safe. They wonder whether the nation's economic ascent is sustainable and, if not, whether the world will gang up on them. To paraphrase Ronald Reagan, China needs to "trust but verify."

Image 31.1 Although he died in 1973, Bruce Lee, the quintessence of Chinese masculinity and dignity, remains both an icon and product spokesman. His image makes men feel proud to be Chinese. In this Nokia viral advertising campaign, consumers were invited to vote whether footage was genuine or fake. In two weeks, twenty million clicks were generated. (Courtesy Zhu Jinjing, director of JQK Production, and Nokia)

China's relationship with foreigners will always be paradoxical. Pragmatic engagement, ethnocentric isolation, and defensive offense will continue to uncomfortably coexist.

Pragmatic engagement. China has rejected isolationism. It has assiduously pursued leadership roles in multinational organizations such as the World Health Organization, the G20, the World Economic Forum, and, most recently, the International Monetary Fund. In return, many overseas companies, from mobile phone and auto manufacturers to airlines and hotels, have achieved sustainable profits and broad scale in the mainland market. Regulatory hurdles are simpler than in Japan, although still opaque. On the street, foreigners are pleasantly surprised by the friendliness and openness of ordinary Chinese.

However, multinational engagement—economic, political, or social—is purely practical. Joint ventures are meticulously negotiated; contracts demand technology transfer to domestic partners. (One example: foreign auto companies, none of which is allowed to own more than 50 percent of local joint ventures, have been strong-armed into deploying their proprietary systems and technology to launch "indigenous brands.") Affairs between foreigners and locals are rooted in material gain, not romantic bliss.

The pragmatism inherent in China's broadened worldview is reflected by a new passion for travel. According to the Chinese Tourism Authority, outbound departures reached 65 million in 2011, up 13 percent year on year. Despite limited incomes, figures will continue to skyrocket. By 2013, China will supplant Japan as the second-largest outbound tourist market. But the Chinese do not travel to discover cultural riches. Expensive hotels and restaurants are unnecessary extravagances, indulgences that yield no return. The real motivation is buying luxury brands. According Global Refund, a company specializing in tax-free shopping for tourists, the Chinese account for 15 percent of all luxury items purchased in France but fewer than 2 percent of its visitors. Trips to Paris and London are expensive, but they are not sunk costs; they are status investments. They reinforce identification with a sophisticated middle-class lifestyle. Today's Chinese collect destinations and post them on microblogs as ego boosters.

Cyclical destiny, ethnocentric isolation. Unlike Japan, a cocooned island nation, China is not set apart from the world. Indeed, the country fancies itself the center of the universe, a cultural supernova that sucks in anything in its path. China—as much a civilization as a nation-state—has endured for thousands of years, a feat attributed to natural order. China analyzes, dissects, and atomizes the political systems of other nations. It studies Western competitive advantages and applies them to local circumstances. But it is also a country in search of its own Copernican revolution. It remains unable to weave itself through the fabric of other societies:

- No Chinese consumer goods company has achieved significant scale in any developed market—Haier's 10 percent share of refrigerators in the United States is currently China Inc.'s biggest success story—because of, among other factors, the inability to balance marketing and sales functions.
- International cuisine is a hit in public settings where middle-class Chinese do whatever they can to project an image of cosmopolitan erudition. However, even sophisticated Shanghainese rarely eat foreign foods at home.
- Chinese expatriates, particularly men, do not assimilate well. They often return home with a simplistic view that the West looks down on them. But reality is subtler. At business schools and in offices in other countries, clusters of Chinese retreat into self-effacing, gun-shy cliques, reinforcing stereotypes of Chinese men as soft.
- Chinese students who attend university overseas are acutely aware of the deficiencies of China's memorization-based education system, but they nonetheless avoid Western liberal arts like the plague. The most popular majors are still engineering, math, and business.
- Starting in 2004, the government opened hundreds of Confucius Institutes to promote intercultural harmony. Because of political restrictions and a dearth of effective outreach ambassadors, institutes have become language schools.

Defensive offense. For three thousand years, China has felt exposed. During dynastic times, nomadic armies from the north repeatedly breached the Great Wall. After the Opium War, the nation was economically vivisected by Western powers through a series of unequal treaties, starting with the Treaty of Nanjing. During World War II, Japanese armies slashed and burned their way across broad swathes of countryside. Threats to unity, perceived or real, trigger alarm bells. Hell breaks loose when we touch the third rail of Chinese insecurity—fear of territorial disintegration. But what the West sees as offensive is, in Chinese eyes, defensive. Examples abound: China's adventurism in the South China Sea; anti-Japanese furor over the disputed Diaoyu islands; diplomatic lock-down each time America sells weapons to Taiwan; vilification of the Dalai Lama; hysteria in response to the accidental 1998 bombing of China's Yugoslavian embassy and the inadvertent 2001 downing of a Chinese plane by a US pilot off the coast of Hainan island.

So long as the international community acknowledges China's right to "rise peacefully," Beijing will not threaten other nations' sovereignty. China is pragmatic. It knows expanded global clout requires the support of other countries. China is also cautious. It fears upsetting the delicate geopolitical balance on which economic expansion depends. And China is proud. The nation craves global admiration and respect. It would never do anything to reduce itself to pariah status, for both emotional and economic reasons.

Will China emerge as a responsible stakeholder in global affairs, mutually accommodating on overlapping interests? Grudgingly, yes. It will do so reactively, and never without rigorous cost-benefit analysis. True, the Chinese are instinctively driven by self-interest. Beijing will vigorously protect access to natural resources. It will relentlessly pursue commercial engagement in Africa, granting concessions on human rights issues and corporate governance only if the international community makes a big fuss. But red lines of peaceful coexistence will not be crossed. Countries will not be invaded. Beijing knows it has a lot vested in the current international order and has no choice but to take responsibilities seriously.

The sections that follow explore on a more granular level how the Chinese, both as a people and as a government, are awkwardly yet inexorably adjusting to the country's emergence as an economic superpower. In particular, I will review domestic manifestations of China's stability-obsessed worldview; the country's ambivalent relationship with America; the person on the street's evolving opinion of Barack Obama; the irreconcilable differences between China and the West on human rights; the role of the Beijing Olympics in defining the country's place in the world; and the twitchy relationship with—as well as fundamental cultural differences between—China and its largest, most influential neighbors, India and Japan.

32

CHINA'S WORLDVIEW: DON'T ROCK OUR BOAT

Everything that registers on China's domestic and international radar does so because, directly or indirectly, it impacts stability. Pragmatic to the core, the country cherishes one thing above all else: order. Stability has always been, and remains today, the platform on which progress is constructed.

The Chinese are cautiously optimistic about their future, seeing a rising economic tide lifting many boats. People are thrilled by the nation's growing clout in global affairs and its destiny as a superpower. Thirty years of top-down orchestrated growth fuels hope and bravado: parents believe children's fortunes will exceed their own; even angry youth respect the central government's technocratic efficiency. But they take nothing for granted. Optimism can morph into infectious ambition only when the coast is completely clear. China's Everyman—from farmer to middle-class striver—is afflicted by an underlying anxiety it could all go wrong, that the fault lines in contemporary society will cause walls to come tumbling down.

A COMMON THREAD: FROM EGYPT TO JAPAN AND BACK TO CHINA

That stability matters above all else becomes clear once one considers reactions to certain events of 2011, seemingly unrelated but linked on psychoemotional levels: the jasmine revolution in the Mideast, resulting in a broad crackdown on human rights activists, artists, bloggers, and defense attorneys in China; the trial of Yao Jiaxin, a moneyed princeling who murdered a pedestrian; and Japan's concatenation of tragedy (earthquake, tsunami, and radiation).

The international community was taken aback by the breadth and depth of the Communist Party's spring 2011 crackdown on any voice not directly under the control of the government. But given the party's extreme sensitivity to even the slightest whiff of independent discourse, it should not have been a surprise. The authorities were extremely spooked by the jasmine revolution in the Middle East—so much so that, several months later, the word "jasmine" was still banned from local media and jasmine flowers were no longer sold in flower markets. The sensitivity of the upcoming leadership transition at the end of 2012 only reinforces China's conservative bent.

Ai Weiwei, the contemporary Chinese artist most familiar to overseas audiences, was the most prominent figure to be imprisoned and then placed under house arrest, his always-provocative work having become ever more critical of the government. But there were many others, including defense attorney Gao Zhisheng, human rights advocates Run Yunfei and Ding Mao, and democracy advocate Liu Xianbin, as well as countless bloggers. The party also began a new clampdown on any of its own members who fail to show sufficient support for the official line.

The jasmine revolution: Not our cup of tea. Perhaps more unexpected was the public's apathy toward both the democratic revolution in the Middle East and the rights rollback it triggered domestically. One restaurateur exclaimed, "The Chinese people are not stupid! Look at China—the *laobaixing* (common man) is doing okay. Over in the Middle East, everything is still backwards." My barber, a native of Fujian province, was dismissive of any connection between the revolution in Egypt and China's situation. "You've been here for thirteen years," he said. "You should know we don't like the central government. But we respect it. They keep everything moving." Calls from the blogging community for "silent walking" protests failed to elicit much of a response.

Domestic human rights crackdown: Tremors ahead? As for the domestic clampdown, sentiments were subtle, pragmatic, and stability focused. Few had heard anything at all, a testament to the government's success in framing public discourse. And those who had—English speakers who read foreign newspapers—were not up in arms about rights violations.

Nevertheless, some were unsettled by the party's ham-handedness. The breadth of the crackdown signaled a growing insecurity among political elites—typically rich, coastal-bred bureaucrats who may doubt their own ability to navigate the crosscurrents of Chinese society. Respect for the government rests on its ability to continue to deliver stability and prosperity; over-the-top repression weakens public faith in the ruling clique. The CEO of a large bank whispered to me, "Now they're arresting gadflies. It means they're afraid of losing their grip." Another friend, the boss of a local advertising agency, confessed, "I don't know if they can keep the good times rolling. I'm glad my family has Canadian passports." The Chinese general manager of a Western media company complained, "Hu Jintao and Wen Jiabao have never led economically powerful provinces. They were consensus candidates. I hope Xi Jinping [Hu's heir apparent] will be more effective. At least he succeeded in Fujian and Zhejiang. They have money there."

Death to Yao! Theoretical debates about human rights do not set pulses pounding. But the dark side of China's legal system—random, rigged against the little guy, manipulated by land-hungry provincial bosses, dysfunctional in advancing the interests of the small potato—triggers deep hostility and anxiety. On the surface, the nation's apoplectic reaction to the April 2011 trial of Yao Jiaxin was about justice. The defendant, a twenty-one-year-old music student and well-connected son of privilege, murdered a working-class pedestrian, Zhang Miao, to prevent her from reporting an accident to the police. Public cries for the death penalty revealed a strand of angry nervousness that infests everyday life. Yes, there was sympathy for the victim's family, and Yao, savaged by local media as an amoral princeling, made a great villain. But most of the virulence was directed at the inbred power structure, which protects itself at the expense of ordinary folk. To 99 percent of the population, Zhang's demise was a cautionary tale; without connections, life is precarious. As a colleague said, "The same thing could happen to my mother."

Judicial corruption is a violation of the covenant between the party and the people: political subservience in exchange for competent management and meritocratic opportunity. Few people advocated leniency for Yao, despite his youth, voluntary confession four days after the murder, and no previous record of misconduct. There was an overriding sense that if he wasn't executed, the government would be accused of protecting one of its own and, in the process, lose legitimacy. Confidence in the robustness of China's institutions, still strong at the national level, would drop, tainted by impressions that the government discriminates in favor of the wealthy or powerful. (Yao was eventually found guilty and put to death, his execution approved by the Supreme People's Court of the PRC and carried out with the tacit blessing of the Central Steering Committee.)

Japanese civility: Are we missing something? The Chinese are willing to forgo a civil society only if the lack of one does not impact an individual or household's material circumstances. An underlying anxiety that China lacks cultural and institutional building blocks to safeguard individual economic interests was laid bare after the March 2011 earthquake and tsunami in Japan, and the nuclear crisis that followed. Since 1949, the Chinese government has systematically transmogrified anti-Japanese sentiment—triggered by the invasion of northeast China and acts of barbarism during the thirties and forties—into fierce, pro-party nationalism. The people of Japan have been dehumanized in everything from elementary school readers to propagandistic media tirades, particularly during spasms of leadership insecurity. The Chinese were therefore surprised by Japan's post-disaster civility. There was no anarchy. The best aspects of Japanese society—graceful stoicism and dignity, consideration toward strangers, regarding patience as a virtue rather than a competitive weakness—were beamed across the nation. The Chinese were inspired by the sense of order. "They line up to make telephone calls. We fight over bags of rice," was one fairly typical online comment. For the first time, Japanese attention to detail, often derided as an obsessive-compulsive tick, suggested adaptive strength. Chinese looked across the East China Sea, saw qualities they lacked, and asked, "What if?"

THE WORLDVIEW: RISK AND RETURN

China's worldview is, paradoxically, both broad and parochial. Anything that promotes cohesion and stability—the creation of the G20, even American involvement in the Taiwan Straits—is appreciated, explicitly or tacitly. Anything that potentially militates against China's success—the US Federal Reserve's quantitative easing policy, interference in Chinese engagement with Africa, meddling in the South China Sea—is resisted. Anything that does neither is ignored. Foreigners who deal with the country must also remember the importance of stability. Leaders who preach values without defining achievable goals will quickly fail. Politicians who lecture about human rights without linking them to efficiency will be snubbed. Corporate chieftains who promote corporate environmental responsibility must talk about "green" in terms of family welfare and national productivity. The Chinese value engagement with the world—but only if risk and return can be meticulously prognosticated.

33

HOW CHINA SEES AMERICA: DANGEROUS LOVE

Most Americans, only marginally less chauvinistic today than twenty years ago, have a simplistic view of China and the Chinese people. Although apprehensive about the rise of an economic juggernaut and its impact on the American way of life, the images China casts are rooted in the past: dusty, robotic, gray, and ultraconformist.

The Chinese, on the other hand, are fascinated by America, although often perplexed by its inherent contradictions. The United States is both free and unfair, creative and fashion challenged (some Chinese describe blue button-down shirts and khaki pants as our uniform), sporty and grossly overweight, institutionally robust and politically dysfunctional, individualistic and self-deluded (they love to laugh at narcissistic, talent-free *American Idol* contestants). They are amazed that a nation of 300 million self-starters does not come apart at the seams.

THE FORBIDDEN FRUIT

On a personal level, the Chinese admire—are even intoxicated by—US-style individualism. At the same time, they regard it as dangerous, both personally and as a national competitive advantage.

In 1999, NATO bombed the Chinese embassy in Yugoslavia. Thirteen years later, the vast majority of Chinese still assume the act was not only intentional but also a murky plot by the United States, the leading power in NATO, to contain China. The nation erupted with rage, but it was the fury of betrayal, disorientation, and stunned rejection. No one chanted, "America is evil." Instead, there were tears of disillusionment. The United States, then widely perceived as a land of endless opportunity and noble ideals, was exposed as just another country where the powerful protect their interests at any cost. I had been in China for a year then and was always greeted with openness, curiosity, and warmth. When the news of my country's misdeed swept the airwaves, the lights went out. No one's eyes met mine. They wondered whether I too was a fraud, a commercial hack intent on profiting from China at the expense of China. After a week, tempers cooled, but a scar of regretful suspicion has since marred the cultural landscape.

Deep affection. Evidence of deep affection for the American way of life is everywhere. Illegal DVDs of US movies and television shows sell like hotcakes, especially ones such as *Friends*, *Sex and the City*, *Desperate Housewives*, and *The Big Bang Theory*, which celebrate a quintessentially American fusion of community and individual idiosyncrasy. The election of President Barack Obama, a black man with no dynastic credentials, is regarded with awe, a tribute to genuine egalitarianism. Every conglomerate wants to become the GE of China, while Bill Gates and Warren Buffett are role models of the highest order, respected for personal vision and achieving master-of-the-universe status. Among denizens of rural China, who are less worldly than their coastal counterparts, America is not only esteemed for its freedom; it is also described transcendentally as "a land of dreams."

The "Chinese dream" vs. American individualism. The American dream—wealth that culminates in freedom—is intoxicating for Chinese, young and old alike. But whereas Americans dream of independence, Chinese crave control of one's destiny and command of the headaches and vagaries of daily life. Americans fantasize about being "horizontally" apart—living a sequestered life on a tropical island, away from the rat race's hustle and bustle. Chinese dreams are "vertical," to be on top of a mountain, looking down, able to manipulate the complexities of human existence. But Chinese do not want to be sequestered from their world. In contemporary author Su Tong's book *My Life as an Emperor*, a fictional ruler, banished from his throne, fantasizes about being a high-wire artist, mastering every step, rising above the pettiness of quotidian concerns by dint of a broad worldview. The winner of a popular televised talent show had angel wings placed on his shoulders. Hoisted thirty feet above the studio audience, he became master and commander of the sky. The Chinese, unlike us, never want to escape but to float above. Their standard definition of having it all—the *wuzidengke,* or five benchmarks of money, sedan, house, wife, and child—is as compelling in the twenty-first century as it was during earlier eras. Without these manifestations of societally mandated achievement, mainlanders feel cast off.

Material similarities between Chinese and Americans mask fundamentally different emotional impulses, which are rooted in radically different social structures. China's admiration of the American can-do spirit springs, ironically, from its Confucian heritage. The Chinese value system is a quixotic combination of regimentation and ambition. The clan, not the individual, is considered the basic building block of productivity, and human rights are either a theoretical abstraction or, even in good times, luxuries to be sacrificed to pragmatism. But Confucianism has always espoused social mobility. By mastering convention, Chinese have been able to, at least hypothetically, climb the hierarchy, the shape and structure of which are socially mandated.

Confucian egos are huge, so American-style self-expression is all the rage. Brands that celebrate "me"—from Nike's "Just Do It" spirit to Apple's "Think Different" rallying cry—are embraced, particularly by the young urban elite. American universities have huge appeal. T-shirts sporting the latest hip hop slang are all the rage, and pop cultural divas who bow to no one—Lady Gaga, Beyonce, Madonna, and, in perpetuity, Michael Jackson—are revered. Sports figures such as NBA stars Kobe Bryant and LeBron James are idolized infinitely more than their Chinese brethren. Indeed, Yao Ming, still revered for his on-court exploits, is now referred to as "Boss Yao," a respectful but somewhat emotionally disengaged acknowledgment that the star-cum-businessman has been folded back into the system.

Yet these American icons, while adored, are rarely emulated. Few Chinese end up challenging the system. Tattoos are always discreetly placed on the ankle or shoulder. Dye jobs are never over the top, with colors ranging from red to blond and sometimes Japan-cool gray. Women who flaunt their sexuality, in dress or attitude, are never taken home to Mom and Dad. Even the most opinionated employees rarely muster enough courage to overtly challenge the boss. American individualism is, in short, forbidden fruit, dangerously tempting. The Chinese remain intoxicated by the allure of genuine American self-expression but frustrated by its ultimate impossibility in their lives. As a result, attitudes toward the country, and its character, are mixed.

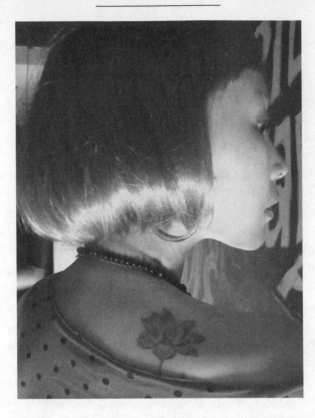

Image 33.1   Tattoos are trendy. But they are discreet. In China, where rebellion is frowned upon, self-expression is a dangerous game. Youth must "stand out by fitting in." (Courtesy Salome Zhang)

SEEDS OF UNCERTAINTY

Chinese ambivalence toward the United States will only grow as China emerges as a modern superpower, Herculean in ambition but still brittle politically and economically. As China confronts the challenges of sustainable growth, more people grasp the link—intellectually, at least—between American freedoms and the innovative spirit of the United States, between the right to challenge convention and high industrial productivity. Specifically, American freedom is underpinned by impartial institutions that protect individual interests. From an independent judiciary and wide availability of credit to self-correcting representative elections and a robust constitutional framework structured around checks and balances, the United States is a society balanced by rule of law. The Chinese, meanwhile, nervously abide by an intricate code of mutual obligations that keeps society from unraveling.

Chinese cycles vs. American reinvention. Instinctively and intellectually, China knows that limits on self-expression manifest themselves at the national level. It knows double-digit growth will not be sustainable if some sort of political reform—institutional responsiveness to society's fault lines—is not implemented within the next ten years. It knows its stock markets are closer to Macanese gambling casinos than temples of efficient capital allocation. It knows its courts are subordinate to the interests of the party, not the people. It knows the road map needs to be redrawn and that institutions require modernization.

But how? No leader has yet articulated a clear path forward. For the Chinese, America, and the political and economic systems that underpin it, is a mirage, not a destination. Vast cultural chasms exist between the United States and China. The American model, rooted in civil liberties, provides no blueprint for the future.

The Chinese have faith in the wisdom of their central government leaders and confidence in their ability to outline a series of incremental reforms that transform the PRC into a modern state. Unfortunately, this faith is beginning to wear thin; uncertainty expresses itself as anxiety on the most personal level. Real estate prices are skyrocketing, the supply of well-paying entry-level jobs remains vastly smaller than the number of new college graduates, and the Balkanized industrial chain is unable to ensure the safety of dairy and toy products. And provincial-level corruption of officialdom is now endemic, self-evident. Ever more people wonder how they will make ends meet for their families. The Chinese are optimistic about the adaptive strength of the people and nation. But their optimism is not absolute.

In this context, American resilience is a source of fear. Despite the tidal wave of schadenfreude released by recent economic setbacks and political immobilization, the Chinese, in their hearts, believe that the US system, built to last, is superior to theirs. As one client, an employee of a large state-owned enterprise, said to me, "America was born to be reborn. We exist in a cycle, one destined to repeat itself every few hundred years. "

National insecurities. Given an acute awareness of their system's limitations, the Chinese are hypersensitive to any perceived assault on their country's sovereignty. Nationalistic prickliness abounds, as does smugness vis-à-vis America's debt and currency challenges. When economic mandarins allowed the renminbi to rise against the dollar, cyberspace released a chorus of disgust. When a Chinese pilot was accidentally killed during the 2001 Hainan spy plane incident, most saw an American hegemonic plot to contain China. When the world protested the Chinese government's heavy-handed suppression of minorities in Tibet and Xinjiang, the nation was unified in protest, piqued by outside interference in its internal affairs. Perennial US weapons sales to Taiwan distress ordinary Chinese at the deepest level; the sales represent a direct assault on national cohesion, the ultimate safeguard against chaos.

More subtly, attacks on national potential also threaten self-confidence. Chinese ego repression ensures that individual identities are linked to national pride, exacerbating the impact of American condescension, real or imagined. All strands of Chinese culture—Confucianism, legalism, and Daoism—deemphasize the individual. Yet both Confucianism and Deng Xiaoping's "get rich" mandate put a premium on (state-endorsed) achievement. The vast majority of Chinese, particularly younger and wealthier ones, are caught between two mutually exclusive goals: standing out and fitting in. Chinese ambition is restrained by convention. Individual identities are smothered, burdened by layers of suppressed expression. Brand China—nationalism—is seized en masse as the ultimate identity surrogate.

TWENTY-FIRST-CENTURY HARMONY

Is all lost? Will China's love-hate relationship with America result in perpetual conflict, an ingrained win-lose approach to twenty-first-century affairs? I don't think so.

First, the Chinese, despite their insecurities, are eminently pragmatic. They realize that their economy is inextricably intertwined with that of the United States. They know they are—and will remain—dependent on the American market. Furthermore, China, fiercely self-protective, paradoxically relies on Uncle Sam's military might to maintain order in today's multipolar world.

Second, the vast majority of Americans are not anti-China. There is no shortage of admiration for the scale of Chinese ambition, not to mention respect for citizens' individual drive. A fascination with all things Han, emerging only now, is reflected by the 100,000 young Americans who will study on the mainland during the next few years.

China, a country that has been both intoxicated and repelled by America for more than one hundred years, knows we have no choice but to build win-win platforms. If it can successfully implement a crash-resistant growth paradigm, China will, for the sake of its children, continue to nervously embrace the United States as a parallel universe of double-edged desire.

34

THE OBAMA BRAND IN CHINA: BEWARE OF COOL CAT

China has long been Bill Clinton country. The forty-second president of the United States was seen as handsome, charismatic, and virile, and his efforts to build a strategic partnership with China were embraced by a population aching for acceptance as a global player. Clinton was able to articulate an American worldview as a moral imperative to embrace individualism and human rights without talking down to people from different cultures. And no one, from neighborhood grannies to slick entrepreneurs, understood the fuss whipped up by Monica Lewinsky's blue dress. Bill's narcissism never registered. Yes, he was a cad, but his conquests were part of his charm, not to mention the spoils of power.

Hillary Clinton also has long been admired as a paragon of no-nonsense, grounded determination. Her autobiography, *Living History*, was an instant best-seller. Chinese, while profoundly patriarchal, admire strong females. It was Mao who declared that "women hold up half the sky" and demanded they contribute economic muscle to the glory of the motherland. Wu Yi, a former vice premier and one of the most powerful women in recent Chinese history, remains a role model for all women, a combination of grace and strength.

Until her defeat in the 2008 Democratic presidential primaries, Hillary Clinton was Beijing's preference. They perceived her as safe, despite her swerve to the left in matters of trade. The Chinese revere scale because it projects reliability and commands trust, and the Clintons had led the biggest, most powerful political franchise in the world. In an ever-changing universe in which yin shifts relentlessly to yang and back again, and in a global marketplace in which new rules are forever being written and rewritten, the quest for stable order is a primal urge. In this sense, Hillary Clinton was the prudent choice, the tried-and-tested formula.

Barack Obama, of course, was not. Despite his quintessentially American rise, he was uncomfortably exotic. His brand was too hip, launched with new-fangled Internet technology and targeted to dreamy youth. He was breezy but ephemeral, shiny but unsubstantial, a disarming political neophyte. He was interesting to look at but unfamiliar, not quite right for Mr. Zhang's kitchen or office. One friend of mine, a savvy media type who works for News Corporation, shook his head, insisting that America was, yet again, being "deceived and seduced" by a "flavor of the month."

Winds began to shift, however, well before the election. During a meeting with employees from a traditional state-owned enterprise, I probed preferences. Nine out of ten said they would vote for Obama over McCain, describing the former with adjectives such as *lihai* (a quintessentially Chinese expression meaning intimidating but impressive), *tupou* (breakthrough), and *liao bu qi* (incredible). Even taxi drivers, the canaries of Chinese public opinion, started giving Obama a cautious thumbs-up.

There were two reasons for this emerging pro-Obama sentiment.

Respect for winners. Chinese revere winners, not challengers. Obama, in vanquishing the mighty Clinton machine, won big. Before he clinched the nomination, Obama was a fool's gamble, but he broke through to become an icon, a successful game changer who won the endorsement of the establishment. Mold breaking is tolerated in China but only as a means to an end, a tool of advancement within an omnipresent, hierarchical order. And Obama has *become* the order. Bill Gates is popular because he too forged a new paradigm; he reordered the digital universe. Having the courage to drop out of Harvard became cool only after he became one of the world's wealthiest men.

Support for outsiders. The underdog status of Obama, a black man operating within a white political establishment, initially worked against him. After he won the election, however, his underdog status became a huge plus, a font of admiration. (It's true many Chinese are somewhat racist; skin whiteners sell very well here. That said, pragmatism always carries the day.) Obama was an untested commodity, but his triumph, not to mention an understated self-possession, is something most Chinese who operate outside the system relate to. Like Yao Ming, the Houston Rockets NBA superstar who deployed quick-witted resourcefulness to conquer foreign opponents, Obama vanquished an old guard by dint of razor-sharp intelligence and a dazzling personal narrative.

China is capable of lurching from self-flagellation to defensive, chest-thumping nationalism, seemingly in a matter of moments. The country's swings are driven, in large part, by a realization that, to continue rising, it must integrate itself into a culturally alien geopolitical superstructure. By ingratiating himself with the masses and penetrating upper echelons of power, Obama had achieved what a sometimes-insecure China aspires for itself.

The ability to morph from nothing into a star, lauded by society, has always been at the foundation of American appeal. A national idealism, easily liberated through a structured system with checks and balances, impresses ordinary Chinese who view their central government as fair but provincial organs as inherently corrupt. As one participant in the 1989 Tiananmen protests whispered to me, "I loved America. When I was in college, I believed in America. As an adult, I awoke from my dream. But maybe it wasn't a dream after all." He then continued: "Obama's election could never happen in a country with a history as long as China's."

STANDING UP TO CHINA

China's passive-aggressive behavior on the world stage is unfortunate but not unexpected. President Barack Obama is handling the PRC's noncollaboration with great skill and savvy, appreciating that ancient cultural imperatives and contemporary geopolitical objectives dictate a balance of caution and steely firmness. If he stays the course, push-me-pull-you tension between China and the West will continue. But strains will not erupt into full-blown crisis.

Global engagement, timeless truths. China's engagement with the world is driven by three truths. First, calls for constructive engagement will yield little if ties are perceived to violate Chinese interests. Despite the "One World, One Dream" sloganeering at the Beijing Olympics, warm and fuzzy notions of international brotherhood mean nothing. Issues must be framed and resolved pragmatically, as win-win opportunities. Everything in the PRC is a means to an end, and the most important end is continued economic growth.

Second, in China stability is paramount; gradualism, often imperceptible, is golden. The government believes there are two great dangers lurking on the landscape: unemployment or inflation triggered by abrupt shifts in macroeconomic policy and perceptions of affronts to Chinese territorial sovereignty. If the West pursues confrontation, it will trigger a deeply rooted anxiety of centrifugal disintegration, and the sky will fall. If not, China will continue to behave in a relentlessly incremental manner. It will, with empirical precision, test the limits of newfound economic prestige. But it will not upset the apple cart. It's worth noting that China has never been an expansionist power. Even at the zenith of imperial clout, it controlled pan-Asian trade through economic tributaries, not military conquest.

Third, and fortunately, China knows its ascent will not continue without Western complicity. No matter how successful the central government is in rebalancing the economy toward domestic consumption, exports to Western markets, which have fueled more than 60 percent of economic expansion since 1990, will determine growth rates for decades to come. It is important to note that China has always productively engaged with other cultures, from Indian Buddhism to American capital markets, absorbing new influences and applying them in Chinese contexts. It has also learned from the thirty years of economic and social disaster triggered by the postrevolution isolation that preceded Deng Xiaoping's assumption of power in 1978: walls, at least outside cyberspace, are counterproductive. In China, there is no desire, even among reactionary military factions, to become divorced from global forces of progress. As one street-smart sixty-year-old confided, "We're afraid of not having any friends."

China's twenty-first-century anxiety. The government has been intractable on a number of issues: opacity on currency reform; reversion to platitudes of six-party "talks" after North Korean military provocation; hysterical reaction to the assertion of American interest in the South China Sea and to US weapon sales to Taiwan; castigation of countries attending Liu Xiaobo's Nobel Peace Prize ceremony; and reluctance to address Sudanese sponsorship of genocide in Darfur, Iran's nuclear weapons program and Syria's ruthless suppression of dissent. All can be understood in the context of China's timeless protective, don't-rock-my-boat modus operandi.

Twenty-first-century phenomena also reinforce traditional go-slow obstinacy. The country stands on an unfamiliar threshold of superpower status but has not figured out how to apply its weight. China knows it is not in a position to supplant the United States in terms of hegemonic or cultural influence. Furthermore, the expansion of an economically vested middle class challenges social cohesion, ensuring continued focus on domestic issues. These stresses militate against diplomatic adventurism; there will be competition for natural resources but, assuming cool heads prevail, China will neither attempt overt power grabs nor be reborn as an angel of multilateralism.

How to deal with an insecure China. What can we do now to minimize the bombast of a newly assertive, but still insecure, China? Given that the gain and loss of face are regarded as the currency of forward advancement, only the most naive would resort to public hectoring. But neither should the West accept China's awkward attempts to impose its will on neighbors or cut its way to the front of lines.

Obama's Asia strategy has hit on the perfect pitch. From Japan to Vietnam to Singapore to India, he is strengthening relationships with China's neighbors, building or rebuilding partnerships with powers that crave American presence in the region. He is adopting a stronger, clearer line with the Chinese on issues ranging from human rights to currency appreciation, sending unambiguous signals that the West will not be intimidated by Chinese swagger. A classic example was the deployment, in response to North Korean bellicosity, of an aircraft carrier to waters claimed by Beijing.

At the same time, Obama is not encircling China. He voices respect for Chinese aspirations and views its success as fundamental to twenty-first-century prosperity. He has driven the creation of the G20, a much more representative economic forum than the G8, and has actively supported increasing emerging-market voting power at the International Monetary Fund.

The US president is projecting pragmatic steeliness, which the Chinese respect. His balanced demand at the 2011 APEC CEO summit, that China "play by the rules," was typical. He stated, "The bottom line is the United States cannot be expected to stand by if there is not reciprocity in trade and economic relations. We will continue to bring it up. There is no reason why this should inevitably lead to sharp conflict. There's a win-win opportunity there. In the meantime, where we see rules broken, we'll continue to speak out and bring action."

The Chinese know Obama is no fool. As one senior leader of a state-owned enterprise said to me, "I used to think he was nice. Then I realized he was intelligent. Now I know he's shrewd, just like President Hu Jintao. Your leader is a strategist."

Will Obama's approach work? Much depends on the rationalism of future leaders. Xi Jinping, Hu's heir apparent, has a tentative reputation as a man with whom we can do business. Still, given China's gradualist impulse, breakthroughs will be few and far between.

Propaganda organs will never acknowledge Liu Xiaobo, and China will never publicly admonish Iran, but progress is possible. The renminbi will appreciate, although at a slower pace than the West would like. China will further isolate North Korea if, and only if, North Korean belligerence poses an immediate threat to regional stability. If America avoids military provocation, territorial disputes in the South China Sea will not disrupt international sea lanes.

If, in the words of Teddy Roosevelt, the American people and politicians are wise enough to "speak softly and carry a big stick," the world will be a more stable place and China will be a more accountable, more noble, global competitor.

OBAMA POST-OSAMA: TWO CHEERS

The Chinese have always had a grudging admiration for Barack Obama. After the death of Osama bin Laden, a global black sheep, their respect has been significantly less unequivocal. In record time, his speech justifying the American government's decision to eliminate its adversary was faithfully translated by state-controlled media. Obama is, finally, the quintessence of China cool. He treads softly, then pounces, and never loses his composure.

Post–bin Laden, Obama's brand equity has likely reached an inflection point. The laconic chief of one of China's largest apparel manufacturers and proud Communist Party member said to me, "Your president is good for America." The popularity of Shanghai's Obama Club, serving cocktails with names such as the Obamatini and Barack Rocks, is one signal that the American president now has mass market cachet.

That said, the Chinese have been unimpressed with his ability to shape the American political agenda. How, they ask, can such an intelligent guy fail to resolve basic domestic conflicts, particularly given an unhinged Republican Party? Pragmatic to the core, Chinese citizens tacitly acknowledge the United States is still the only nation capable of safeguarding geopolitical stability. So our reluctance to tackle national debt and repair crumbling infrastructure does not stir Chinese souls.

Nevertheless, the style with which he orchestrated bin Laden's demise constitutes a master course in advanced Chinese survival skills. Obama was silent but deadly, and the Chinese revere leaders who deploy absolute power sotto voce. Until the time came to pounce, he was understated and resourceful, a must in a regimented society loaded with political booby traps and murky regulation.

Before bin Laden's demise, Obama was a worthy adversary. Now, he is both respected and feared. If he rides this wave to reelection, the president will possess the power to awe even wary, phlegmatic Chinese. Of course, few will utter this heresy aloud. But, from Shanghai to Xinjiang, the country may be ready to, against the odds, tip its hat to a US leader.

DEALING WITH DISSENTERS: PRAGMATISM, NOT PASSION

The December 2009 conviction of Liu Xiaobo, who was jailed for up to eleven years for his role in the Charter 08 petition that demanded the right to free speech, open elections, and the rule of law, was deeply disappointing. Most observers believe Liu did not advocate the overthrow of the Communist Party; his actions therefore were not seditious. Furthermore, the nature of his trial—suddenly announced, quickly executed, and closed to foreign observers—makes even pretense of due process risible. Critics of the Communist regime are right that Liu's draconian punishment is indicative of a fear-based, insecure power structure that is awkwardly wielding a Leninist iron fist at home while striving to become a power broker abroad.

The party's hypersensitivity to even the slightest whiff of dissent undermines its own legitimacy in the eyes of mainland citizens. And, in this respect, it does seek to cling to power irrespective of people's will. For the time being, fueled by clear-eyed pragmatism and the lack of an alternative governing apparatus, the masses have no choice but to hope that the party succeeds.

No moral absolutes. Many Chinese might shake their heads at Liu's conviction, ruing the distance the country must travel to achieve global standards of civil rights and decency. But others believe China is not yet ready for free expression, even the nonviolent, nonsubversive sort. Their reservations are not the product of brainwashing; rather, they reflect certain truths regarding Chinese culture and the relationship between individual and state, reinforced across millennia.

Chinese have no conception of moral absolutes. Their worldview is cyclical, with the forces of yin and yang, light and darkness, positive and negative rebalancing themselves across time and space. Furthermore, social structures are characterized by an intricate interconnectivity. Without whipping up an algebraic lather, suffice it to say that Chinese philosophy and morality frown upon rights that exist independent of context. Torture, or even murder, facilitated through a compliant judiciary subordinated to the party, will be defended, and there is still wide public support for the death penalty if it militates against chaos. Order is a prerequisite to advancement, so universal rights, while appreciated as lovely ideals, are seen as impractical given China's current stage of development.

Liu's methods are nonviolent and benign; he is simply advocating what he believes to be in the best interest of China, but most Chinese fear their society is not mature enough to even debate, let alone digest, Charter 08. A minority of citizens probably suspects Liu's undeclared end objective is, in fact, to overturn one-party rule. If this were true, he would be denigrated, even by those who have not yet benefited from economic reform.

How the West should respond. In light of this fear of instability among the ranks of government and citizenry, how should Westerners respond to a conviction that violates our sense of decency? Above all, we should not wag fingers or patronize. We must acknowledge that China's stage of development and large population pose challenges America and Europe do not fully comprehend. Chinese are, if nothing else, supreme pragmatists. We should adopt measured tones and empirically based polemics. We should focus energies on persuading the country's leaders that gradual political reform—implementing judicial independence, clarifying antisedition laws, expanding elections of local and provincial leadership posts, and instituting intraparty checks and balances—would make China more, not less, stable. It is also important to suggest that the country's middle class will ultimately demand a level of democratic responsiveness the party is currently ill equipped to deliver.

Barack Obama's nonhectoring approach, almost quantitatively analytic, is pitch perfect. The State Department called on China to release Liu, saying that the "persecution of individuals for the peaceful expression of political views is inconsistent with internationally recognized norms of human rights." A clear-eyed, nonfiery response is just what the doctor ordered.

The administration forfeits brownie points at home for not stridently espousing moral absolutes, unlike, say, German Chancellor Angela Merkel's dismay at the sentence or the UN's rumbling that Liu's punishment had thrown "an ominous shadow" over China's commitment to human rights. But in China, Obama's calm, methodical approach to conflict resolution generates respect. If the country's leaders do not feel threatened or misunderstood by outside forces, they will, over time, bend to global and domestic reality. The Western goal should be to apply just enough fact-based pressure for rulers to conduct objective cost-benefit analyses regarding their own short- and long-term interests. Only then will we be able to bridge the cultural chasm.

35

THE BEIJING OLYMPICS
AND SHANGHAI EXPO:
PARTY POWER PLAYS

The importance of China's successful Olympics is difficult to overstate. Despite challenges during the lead up to the Games—anger provoked by international opprobrium after Tibetan unrest, heartbreak following the Sichuan earthquake—China emerged as a more self-possessed nation. And the central government strengthened perceptions that it has what it takes to confront epic challenge.

THE TORCH RELAY: FRIEND OR FOE,
CHINA PERSEVERES

Lenovo, an Olympic sponsor and one of JWT's clients, invited me to participate in the 2008 Beijing torch relay. As I ran my one hundred meters in Minghan, an outlying industrial district of Shanghai, it was difficult not to be moved by the emotion and unity of ambition on display. Despite China's awkward progress on many issues of concern to Westerners, its resolve to confront operatic challenges—from natural disaster to economic crisis—is inspiring. That's what the domestic torch relay was ultimately about.

Meticulous planning. Everything leading up to the event was exquisitely planned. Runners, selected from the public at large, were vetted during a six-month process to ensure proper motivations and political appropriateness. I was provided with an identification number, the exact location and time of my

Image 35.1 In the lead up to the 2008 Olympic Games, Anta's nationalistic website was a hit. National glory lifts repressed-but-ambitious egos. "China is great, so I am too." (Courtesy JWT)

run, detailed instructions on what must not be worn (no logos), and a list of food that would and would not be allowed in the meeting hall (only items provided by event organizers). We were deposited at departure points three minutes before our moment in the sun and picked up thirty seconds after the eyes of onlookers had moved on to the next runner among the 20,000 who participated. Not a beat was missed when, after the Sichuan earthquake, the entire event was pushed back seventy-two hours to avoid overlap with an official three-day grieving period.

Disciplined communication. The Chinese know how to manage a message. Responding to the earthquake, Beijing's propaganda machine changed the Olympic torch run tagline from "Ignite the passion, spread the dream" to "Spread the sacred flame, spread caring love." Identical headlines appeared everywhere, framing the torch relay as national resolve, a tribute to Sichuan. At Lenovo's press conference, each bearer was given sixty seconds to express pride in being selected to participate and concern for the victims and hope for their families. For the group photo, we were adorned with yellow sympathy ribbons. In the middle of preparation drills—Flame held high! Logos forward! Dignified facial expressions!—a mourning video appeared on two large screens. Everyone stood up, instantly, silently, and bowed their heads.

Unbridled passion. Political pageantry notwithstanding, there was nothing programmed about the enthusiasm. Every torchbearer—peasant, police officer, politician, or industrialist—was thrilled to be participating. One multimillionaire, a garment factory owner, whispered to me that representing his country was "the greatest honor of my life." As we got off the bus, we were cheered by other torchbearers, and crowds exploded with patriotic frenzy. China has its shortcomings, as do all nations; the propaganda organs were instructed to pump up the passion, and the quasi-evangelism recalled Cultural Revolution hysteria. But the pride and joy was real.

Epic mobilization. The importance of the Olympics to the Chinese is difficult to overstate. In a society in which individualism is suppressed but ambition is rampant, the nation serves as a surrogate identity. Emotional investment in the 2008 Games therefore was deep. The torch relay resonated for two reasons. First, its sheer scale and logistical complexity reflected China's ambition and how far it has come. Second, it was an acknowledgment of a long road ahead, filled with unpredictable, but surmountable, obstacles. When the earth shook in Sichuan, killing more than 80,000, the Olympic flame morphed into a symbol of China's resilience, its ability to rally.

Throughout history, mobilization has been tantamount to survival. Cohesion ensures continued existence, as a nation and a culture. In the fifteenth century, immediately after Emperor Zhu Di suspended his ambitious maritime expeditions, 250,000 soldiers from all corners of the country were plucked from villages to cross the Kerulen River and defeat the Mongols. The fourteen-year construction of Beijing engaged 100,000 artisans and one million workers. Five million were harnessed to construct one of the greatest engineering feats of the preindustrial age, the Grand Canal, more than 900 miles long. More than three million were dispatched to rebuild the Great Wall during the fifteenth and six-teenth centuries.

More recently, thirty million were sacrificed in the Great Leap Forward, Mao's misguided attempt to industrialize the countryside. During the Cultural Revolution, sixteen million youth and intellectuals were sent to the countryside to learn from the peasants. The containment of SARS in 2003, a crisis unfore-seen by the developed world, was probably the latest example of mass mobiliza-tion and a vivid demonstration that the Chinese, when unified, have a unique ability to grab triumph from the grip of disaster.

In the end, the torch relay was not a self-congratulatory victory lap. It was an entire nation's primal declaration, in the face of adversity, to survive. Defensive nationalism, conspicuously on display after the pro-Tibetan protests, was not the key driver.

AT THE OPENING CEREMONY: CHINA REVEALS ITS SOUL

In my 2005 book, *Billions: Selling to the New Chinese Consumer,* I asked whether Beijing would summon enough courage to show the best side of itself at the Olympics. "Will the opening ceremony be a rousing release of national pas-sion or an Orwellian propaganda spectacular? Will the awe-inspiring zip, zing, and pizzazz of the Chinese people be overshadowed by an insecure government apparatus paranoid about lost face? Will an instinctively self-protective China open its doors to the unfamiliar, or stage a well-rehearsed Beijing opera sure to leave most of us cold? Time will tell."

Three years on, as I witnessed the opening ceremony of the Games, alongside 100,000 individuals, both Chinese and foreigners, the question was answered emphatically. In the majestic Bird's Nest stadium that August evening, China bared its soul to the world, and perhaps also to itself.

Some inauspicious omens. As we waited for the show to begin, not all signs were positive. B-list local celebrities spent half an hour teaching spectators how to deploy cheaply produced patriotic paraphernalia. Hyperfriendly supporting cheerleaders, college students who were also party members, were deployed every ten rows. Security clearance, an hourlong marathon, took place in a ram-shackle lot more than a mile from the main venue. The gargantuan Olympic

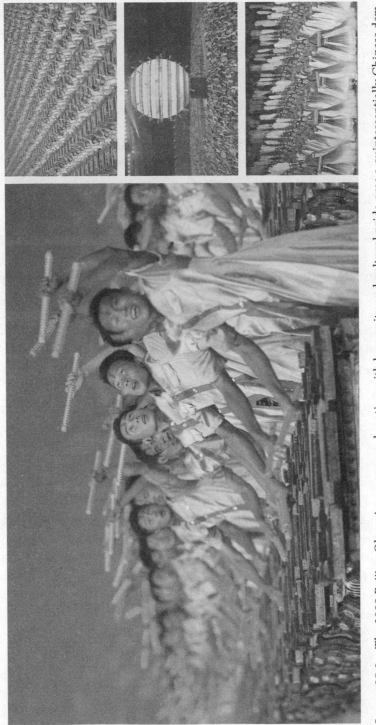

Image 35.2 The 2008 Beijing Olympics ceremony, bursting with humanity and cultural pride, was a quintessentially Chinese demonstration of mobilized scale (meticulous and swift construction of large-scale projects). (Courtesy ImagineChina)

Park, four square miles of solidly constructed athletic infrastructure and commercial pavilions, lacked touches of humanity. And grim-faced, stiff-backed
security personnel were everywhere, reminding everyone that the government's
hyperdefensive "safety first" rallying cry was no laughing matter.

And yet, among those in the stadium, there was still warmth. Locals were
curious, eager to ask where a foreigner was from, what he thought of Beijing,
why he had come, and what he expected of the opening ceremony. When different countries' athletes entered the stadium, applause was genuine—particularly
for Brazilians, Argentineans, Australians, and, yes, Americans. Proclamations
of China's intention to promote "international friendship and mutual understanding" were greeted with thunderous—and sincere—ovation.

A spectacular production. No one doubted the production—helmed by
director Zhang Yimou of *Raise the Red Lantern* and *Hero* fame—would be
world class. Within seventy minutes, 20,000 performers had graced the field.
A huge screen on which the nation's artistic heritage was vividly brought to
life enveloped the entire stadium. During a jaw-dropping fireworks display,
milelong "heavenly footprints" strode, Thor-like, from the Forbidden City to
the Olympic park to welcome the world to Beijing. Hundreds of meticulously
choreographed drummers launched the show; multistory, dragon-emblazoned
pillars extended across the field. The lighting of the Olympic flame was nothing short of volcanic. When giant Olympic rings formed from stardust, many
gasped, then cried.

The essence of China. Many expected the extravaganza to be a chest-
thumping, unadulterated totalitarian tribute to a nation committed only to
generating industrial power and legions of gold medalists. Happily, this was
not to be. I was struck by the combination of scale on one hand and depth
and thoughtfulness, even intellectualism, on the other. The ceremony, surpris-
ingly and touchingly, was about Chinese culture—and its ability to resolve the
various conflicts percolating within the country: between growth and stability, progress and tradition, East and West, and past, present, and future. More
ambitiously, Zhang interpreted the Games' tagline, "One World, One Dream,"
as China's life force, *harmony*: between individuals (Confucian sociology) and
with the universe (Daoist cosmology). Dancers became brushes to create a sev-
enty-yard natural landscape scroll painting; life-size printing blocks/Chinese
characters morphed into a human sea of wisdom.

Who was watching? The night had two audiences.

Domestic. Most important, the ceremony was targeted to the Chinese.
Zhang, a victim of Cultural Revolution abuse, was pleading with the nation to,

finally, stand up with pride. Today's China, he believes, springs from a rich cultural heritage and a timeless worldview, one in which all elements are elegantly interconnected, always in motion. China's profound respect for intelligence has created a country that reveres the scholar, emphasizes knowledge over might, defense over offense, skill over brute force, concentration over impulse. These qualities, he insists, must be venerated. In this respect, the event was a resounding success. In the stadium, on the street, and in hotel lobbies, many locals were moved, describing the show as perfect and meaningful. People streamed out of the stadium beaming with pride.

The performance was also politically correct. The government hopes to evolve from a guarantor of double-digital GDP growth into a protector of Chinese values and builder of a harmonious society. But, once in a blue moon, political correctness and wisdom align. The party does encourage mainlanders to define themselves as more than agents of economic productivity and to balance materialism and civility for the sake of sustainable development (as well as the ruling elite's hold on power).

International. China was also reassuring the rest of the world that its rise would not threaten geopolitical order so long as its olive branch was reciprocated. In this respect, the show fell short. While the staging was exquisite and its message of geopolitical harmony was uninterrupted by political posturing, many of the themes were probably too esoteric for Westerners to grasp. More important, everything was one way. The entire event, though steeped in declarations of universal brotherhood, may have reinforced perceptions that China, so skilled in absorbing foreign influences and applying them in a domestic context, is not yet capable of reaching out or understanding what makes other societies tick. National glories were not presented as part of a global tapestry—Chinese culture was framed as the quintessence of human civilization and China, as always, its epicenter.

There were African drums and Scottish bagpipes, and costumes from every corner of the world. But Western civilization—from Renaissance art and modern American technology to rock music and free-style soccer—did not even score a courtesy mention. There was no fusion of China and the world's other centers of gravity. Foreigners remained, in the purest sense, spectators, on the outside looking in. Consequently, parts of the show intended to represent the benefits of mutual understanding lapsed into propagandistic cliché—astronauts drifting in space, doves in flight, and legions of smiling children.

Their night. International concerns aside, the night belonged to China. The nation articulated its spirit with brio, proclaiming its strength, values, and culture to be worthy of respect. After decades of trauma and self-doubt, a more confident China suggested that, finally, it might be willing to embrace the world.

SHANGHAI'S WORLD EXPO: AN INTERNAL AFFAIR

Like the opening ceremony of the Beijing Olympics, the Shanghai World Expo was a domestic power play. Speaking at the close of the Shanghai World Expo on October 31, 2010, Chinese Premier Wen Jiabao expressed lofty sentiments regarding the event's impact: "Only when the ideas behind the accomplishments of civilizations are shared can they become treasures for all of humanity and be carried on forever."

Judging by these poetic, open-armed standards, the expo was a colossal failure. Despite the official tally of 73 million visitors, the vast majority of them mainland Chinese, the world's response to Shanghai's self-proclaimed moment in the sun was a gigantic, collective yawn. And no wonder. Those who visited the site were impressed by the architectural marvels of the 250 or so corporate and country pavilions. (China, Spain, the United Kingdom, Sweden, Denmark, Saudi Arabia, Italy, among others, hit the mark. The US effort, on the other hand, was compared to a suburban office complex.) But the combination of interminably long lines, few sparkles of on-the-ground humanity, and limited green space left many visitors, local and foreign alike, underwhelmed.

Furthermore, the Shanghai government did precious little to entice foreign travelers. Its public relations efforts—a bizarre fusion of bureaucratic propaganda and brain-dead imagery dominated by an omnipresent pale-blue creature named Haibao—ensured foreign visitor attendance figures remained below projections of (only) 5 million people.

According to meticulously orchestrated closing-day news reports, the expo was all about a twenty-first-century global village for which China had morphed into a beatifically smiling citizen. As *Shanghai Daily* wrote, "For the past six months, the Expo site was a place where people could see rare cultural treasures from around the world—such as the Bronze Chariot and Horse sculpture from China's Qin Dynasty, the statue of Athena from Greece and the masterpieces of French Impressionist artists—and also get a taste of the world's diverse cultures through more than 20,000 events."

There is little to credit this view. The central and municipal governments, despite pervasive bilingual signage and visitor booths scattered throughout the city, had their eyes focused squarely on domestic concerns. With the following objectives as benchmarks, however, the expo *was* a success.

Primary objective: Forging order from chaos. In China, everything is a means to an end. The expo was conceived and executed to catalyze a host of internal breakthroughs. Most important, in a system dominated by political factionalism and ever-present fiscal competition between central, city, and district-level organs, the event forged order from chaos. Petty, bottom-up, back-room infighting was supplanted by top-down, command-and-control decision making. In the years leading up to the event, infrastructural breakthroughs—ten subway lines, several bridges, a new ring road, high-speed trains between Shanghai and neighboring cities, and massive commercial developments for which eminent domain concerns were swept aside—were unveiled with clocklike efficiency. In addition, an extensive clean-up effort left behind a more sparkling urban landscape. Store signage has been upgraded, roads have been repaved, and sidewalks are infinitely more user-friendly than even a year earlier.

China's Everyman has been impressed with the government's ability to, yet again, mobilize resources for large-scale projects. Despite clumsy efforts at behavior modification—illegal DVD shops went further underground, cigarettes (well, at least ashtrays) were banned from many restaurants, slogans promoting civilized behavior were everywhere—the population fell in line. Work units, government teams, senior centers, and high schools made pilgrimages to the expo by the busload. Very few grumbled. Opening and closing ceremonies, bereft of spontaneity or joy, nonetheless rivaled Beijing 2008 in terms of scale and pageantry. And the site itself, if sanitized, was epic in every sense.

Domestic takeaway: Foreigners fall in line. Chinese citizens were also impressed with the government's ability to cajole foreign leaders to acquiesce to its demands, a harbinger of the country's twenty-first-century superpower status. Every nation—from America to Russia to Croatia to Nigeria—fell in line. No one dared not to participate. China's ability to coerce foreign leaders to bend to its will, even for a second-tier international event, reassured the hoi polloi.

In the end, Shanghai's World Expo was not an international event. It was orchestrated as a domestic power display, in the same vein as the 2008 Beijing Olympics, the country's sixtieth anniversary military parade in 2009, or the 2010 Asian Games. The government's goal was a Herculean projection of organizational mettle and global stature. Despite acute awareness of the game their government was playing, the Chinese—even, grudgingly, the anti-Shanghai Beijingers—acknowledged the job got done.

36

CHINA AND ITS NEIGHBORS: COLLEAGUES, NOT FRIENDS

America will always play an important role in maintaining the balance of power in the Pacific for the simple reason that Asia's major economic powers do not like each other very much. It's true that pragmatic young Chinese are fond of Japanese and Korean brands, but beyond consumerism, there is no love lost. China resents Japan for its failure to apologize abjectly enough for the sins committed in the name of Japanese imperialism during the first half of the twentieth century, particularly the rape of Nanjing. Japanese accuse Chinese of being loud and uncouth, a sentiment bound to deepen as cash-rich mainland shoppers invade elegant Tokyo and Kyoto in search of luxury bargains, not aesthetic inspiration. Chinese sometimes unfairly accuse South Koreans, their Confucian cousins, and perhaps the hardest-working people in Asia, of being arrogant, perhaps because of the contrast between South Korea's high living standards and smaller economic heft relative to the mainland. China and India are repelled by unresolved border conflicts as well as profoundly different worldviews.

JAPAN AND CHINA: CONTRASTING RESPONSE
TO THE FINANCIAL CRISIS

Many Americans are unable to differentiate Chinese from Japanese, both physically and culturally. True, both are influenced by Confucianism and Buddhism. But, as divergent reactions to financial crises and natural disasters illustrate, the two nations are almost parallel universes, yin to each other's yang. In both China and Japan, there is much talk of harmony. In China, it is a means to an end: Advancement, either individual or national, is the ultimate objective. In Japan, the emergence of relatively more individualistic younger generations notwithstanding, harmony—that is, fitting in—remains an end in itself: primary satisfaction derived from consensus.

Given this fundamental difference, the contrasting way in which ordinary Chinese and Japanese people responded to the global financial crisis is not surprising. While Chinese are supreme pragmatists, Japanese often seem stunned and helpless in the face of crises that do not pose an immediate threat to national cohesion.

The Chinese: pragmatic to the core. In China, the crisis was met with reassessment and recalibration. Government planners reviewed risk exposure and considered potential opportunities. State-owned enterprises revised their five-year plans. While state-owned behemoths shuddered slightly but stayed afloat, some elements of the private sector were sunk. But even this was handled with speed and pragmatism. The export-oriented manufacturing sector shed jobs and consolidated, laying the groundwork for a subsequent revival.

The 20 million migrant workers who returned to the countryside without jobs were not without hope. "We have been through much worse" was a refrain often heard. "I'm sure something will come up in six months' time and, until then, my family has saved some money," a lanky, bright-eyed young man from Anhui province said to me. Shanghai taxi drivers saw their incomes cut by about 25 percent, primarily because of fewer airport fares, but they remained clear-eyed, betting that passenger loads would pick up within a year. Even the penny-pinched middle class began to reopen its wallets as 2009 wore on, encouraged by a raft of tax breaks and subsidies on everything from cars to rice cookers.

JWT, like many multinationals, had to "de-risk" budgets throughout Greater China. The Chinese accepted the relatively minor staff cuts with minimum fuss. There was concern and sadness, but so long as decisions were based on individual performance, workers did not suffer major morale crises. I once asked a few employees whether we should meet budget requirements by firing a few people or lowering salaries across the board. The answer was unanimous: trim headcount, please.

The Japanese: numbed anxiety. Japan has risen from the ashes before, reshaping its society and reinventing itself as a value-added global force, in cultural as well as high-tech terms. The grace of the people and their focus on innovative detail remain significant, albeit latent, competitive advantages. But, in 2009, the Japanese were loath to accept a new reality. This crisis, unlike the "lost decade" that followed the deflation of the Japanese real estate bubble back in the late 1980s, was a foreign creature. It landed on the country like an unfamiliar alien invader.

Several months on, the magnitude of Japan's predicament still had not sunk in. Their anxiety was largely silent, buried in layers of bureaucracy. Euphemistically branded "voluntary retirement schemes" occurred with unaccustomed frequency, making men in their fifties fearful of being laid off but loath to talk about it. (Most social security is connected to employment.) Consumers pulled back even more than their American counterparts. But on the street, there was no panic, only resignation.

If the crisis has fundamentally challenged Japan's economic model and way of life, change is imperceptible to Westerners. The patriarchal model that underpins Japanese society—leader protects underling in exchange for consensus—is still considered the right way. The public was in denial about the gravity of the challenges confronting the nation. When some companies rescinded job offers extended to third-year university students, citizens and editorial pages protested. Japanese labor laws are as rigid as ever. Once-in-a-generation layoffs at Toyota and Sony seemed to come as a bolt from the blue; people were shocked that the pillars of Japan's industrial complex had been so compromised.

JWT's "voluntary retirement scheme" targeted nonperformers who were offered generous severance packages. In one-on-one conversations, there was some anger but, more often, stunned grief. A chorus of "This is not the Japanese way!" rose from the ranks, orchestrated by union leaders. To keep spouses from discovering jobless status, it was agreed that severance to former employees would be paid in twelve monthly installments.

There are several factors that explain the aforementioned discrepancies. First, China's economy is in an earlier stage of development, so growth, although it slowed during the crisis, is still relatively strong. Japan, on the other hand, remains too dependent on exports for a mature economy.

Leadership. The Chinese also believe in their government. China, a Confucian society, reveres strong central leaders who are capable of efficiently, sometimes ruthlessly, mobilizing resources for the greater good. Eminently pragmatic, mainlanders still feel relatively protected by the power structure. Japanese, on the other hand, are dismissive of their politicians—the country is on its sixth prime minister in as many years. The bureaucrats who control institutional levers of power are regarded as old guard, out of touch.

Culture. Confucian and Buddhist thought are present in the societies of China and Japan—but Confucianism dominates in the former and Buddhism in the latter. It is telling that the two countries, both anti-individualistic, express the importance of collectivism in subtle but significantly different ways. The Chinese say: "The leading goose gets shot down." It is an ambitious statement, recognizing the impulse of forward advancement, albeit within a regimented structure. The Japanese say: "The nail that sticks up gets hammered down." The sentiment is altogether more collective and harmony driven.

Japanese society, as a result, is characterized by exquisite traffic etiquette; sparkling streets with neat neon signs flush against buildings; cleanliness as a primary urge (people wear masks when they have hay fever); young men who shape their eyebrows; a surreally slow pace of change reinforced by an instinct for unanimity; a superior service culture with genuine satisfaction derived from pleasing others; door-to-door auto salespersons; inconspicuous demonstration of wealth (titles on business cards are more important than salary; big diamonds are worn infrequently because of the attention they draw); a highly creative design community that glorifies detail; an assertive ecoconsciousness.

In China, however, harmony means order and stability, not peace and mutual respect. It is pragmatic and often messy. Hierarchies are everywhere, but everyone wants to climb the ladder of success. Crossing the traffic-laden streets is dangerous, with auto accident settlements resolved in the middle of the highway; title inflation is endemic, with high staff turnover a constant challenge; service is mechanically scripted and product quality is slapdash; elevator talk is deafeningly loud and advertising blares from all corners; business people who "forge new models" are revered. Tellingly, joy, frustration, despair, pride, and glory are on public display; and China's spontaneous humanity, both admirable and self-serving, is accessible to foreigners.

What does all this mean for the fortunes of the two countries in the twenty-first century? China is already adapting to a new global economic environment, although some of the more fundamental reforms—many of which relate to the transition from investment to consumption-driven growth—will be hard won. Relentless pragmatism and faith in the wisdom of leaders should help. And Japan? Twice in the past, the country has redefined itself without abandoning its cultural moorings: at the beginning of the Meiji era and again after World War II. But, after seventy years of postwar introspection, the daunting challenges should not be underestimated. A new, more liberal generation must assume the reins of power but, by then, will it be too late?

JAPAN AND CHINA: CONTRASTING RESPONSE TO NATURAL DISASTER

China and Japan have both recently experienced disasters of the century. In 2008, the Wenquan earthquake in Sichuan province killed more than 80,000 people, including many children who died in the rubble of poorly constructed schools. In 2011, Japan's northern prefectures were obliterated by earthquake and tsunami, and then radiation leaked from damaged nuclear plants in Fukushima.

Top down. The countries' responses to tragedy reveal fundamental cultural differences. In China, everything was top down and pragmatic. The central government sprang into action, orchestrated rescue attempts, whipped provincial and local party organs into line, and told the nation how and when to mourn. For seven days, national television stations broadcast all programming in black and white. Media coverage was micromanaged. For two months, focus shifted with tick-tock exactitude from reports on the scale of destruction to stories of heroic rescue. Criticism of corruption and shoddy materials was allowed but for only two weeks and not on the front page. The Communist Party's technocratic mastery—an ability to marshal resources—was on full display and applauded by the masses. (Three years later, lawsuits by parents who lost children have been squelched. Defense lawyers have been silenced or arrested.)

Conditioned to submit to a central mandate during crisis, people were practical. Grief was channeled into productivity. There was no national day off for mourning. When the leaders gave eulogies, staff gathered in front of televisions, shed quiet tears, and went back to work. A groundswell of charity carried a whiff of political correctness. Undercurrents of nationalism rose to the surface, with Internet users castigating multinational corporations for stingy donations. At many companies, employees posted rankings of individuals' contributions. Expatriates were taken to task if their sympathy was deemed not sincere.

And bottom up. In vivid contrast, the Japanese government froze after Fukushima. There was no leadership, no coordinated information flow or cheerleading. The bureaucracy, a sclerotic by-product of toothless consensus, failed the people. Mumbling administrators exacerbated radiation fears.

But Japan still impressed. Bottom-up proactivity and civility inspired the world. There was no looting. People waited stoically to use public phones. The generosity of Japanese corporations kicked into high gear. Sony, along with countless other enterprises, organized relief drives. JWT employees spontaneously established task forces to ensure all employees, including their family members, arrived home safely. Members of the creative department organized clothing donations, transporting goods to the edge of the disaster zone.

The earthquake and its aftermath crystallized anxiety about the country's ability to escape a two-decade decline. (According to JWT's Anxiety Index, a global survey that tracks economic insecurity, 91 percent were "not confident" about the nation's future.) But the resilience of individuals and corporations was on vivid display. Families were succored by the comfort of home and hearth.

Intimate neighborhood restaurants quickly reopened, even after foreigners fled. Japan demonstrates that genuine collective spirit exists independent of the government. Solace came from the beauty of small things: Häagen-Dazs sales spiked, and citizens were furious when the authorities suggested staying home during cherry blossom season.

Global engagement vs. splendid isolation. China was acutely aware the eyes of the world were upon it. Japan was not. In Beijing, editorials highlighted American and European admiration of the party's efficiency. The media reprinted favorable press coverage to bolster Communist Party legitimacy, reinforce superiority of the Chinese model, and stir patriotism in advance of the 2008 Olympics. Emotion morphed into status projection. In Japan, people were stunned by foreign respect for local people's grace under pressure. They were also surprised by overseas offers of assistance.

To advance its own interests, China enthusiastically engages with the world. Japan is content with blissful isolation. It is difficult for outsiders to grasp the island fortress mentality that pervades Japanese daily life. On the surface, the country is modern and international. The majority of talent in television ads is Caucasian. From Hokkaido to Kyushu, Apple-mania sweeps the nation. However, deep down and in vivid contrast to the Chinese, Japan has never embraced other cultures. Westernization, from the Meiji restoration to the present, feels like a compromise to keep the devil at the doorstep. Few corporations are willing to work with multinational advertising agencies, and businesses never hire foreigners. Very few college graduates speak passable English. Even nightclubs decline entry to non-Japanese patrons. In Shanghai, there are at least 100,000 expatriate Japanese, but they are invisible, clustered within Japanese villages where residents dine and socialize among themselves.

Some implications. China and Japan's divergent postdisaster impulses are fundamental:

- Japanese society is harmonious on a granular level. People derive genuine satisfaction from fitting in. In China, harmony means order and is imposed by the government.
- Japan does not rely on economic growth and wealth to define progress. Quality of life, spiritual enrichment, and balance are treasured. The Chinese, never taking survival for granted, cherish safety, rudimentary material stability, and status—the latter a currency of hierarchical advancement.
- Japan will stay a wealthy country, albeit in gentle decline, even if its government does not undertake structural reform. The people

are resourceful and innovative, despite dysfunctional isolation and a consensus-obsessed bureaucracy. China, on the other hand, will always depend on top-down technocratic management to generate growth. If economic and political reforms designed to ensure more efficient allocation of resources are not undertaken within the next several decades, growth will stop and crisis will erupt.

- The Chinese economy will be buttressed by an impulse to establish useful partnerships with other countries and multinational corporations. For better or worse, Japan recedes into exquisite seclusion.

Japan and China are, in many ways, polar opposites. They will never be friends. There are few cultural bridges, so America, admired in China for ambition and scale and in Japan for humanist ideals, will be an important intermediary.

A NOTE ON SOUTH KOREA

Unlike Japan, South Korea does not capture the Chinese imagination. This is likely because of its relatively small size. Despite significant investment in the PRC by corporate Korea, and the popularity of brands such as Samsung and LG, Seoul is not top of mind. (North Korea has been relegated to nuisance status. Diplomatic ties are vestiges of the Cold War, sustained by fears of having to manage the detritus of a failed state on its border.)

Apathy is unfortunate. Given South Korea's economic development, a closer bilateral relationship could be beneficial. Despite high annual per capita income and representative democracy, it remains China's closest neighbor, culturally speaking. The countries share a Confucian core ethos that drives filial piety and education obsession; top-down, patriarchal corporate governance; hierarchical conservatism that reduces self-expression and creative breakthrough; government interest in strategic industries; latent racism; an ambitious new generation; and preoccupation with business cards, the first and most basic way to project professional status.

But, despite a long and intertwined history, the countries are cousins, not siblings:

- South Korea, despite high digital penetration and diplomatic ties with the West, is more isolated, both geographically and attitudinally, than the mainland. Trade barriers are omnipresent. English is rarely spoken and foreigners are treated very warily. America, the country's putative protector for decades, is regarded with profound ambivalence. Our continued military presence remains an indignity, particularly among the young generation.

- Trust facilitation, critical in both countries, is trickier in Korea. When establishing collaborative business relationships, the Chinese are pragmatic and flexible. Round tables in private rooms are sites of friendship lubrication and deal making. Koreans can be clannish, an intimating characteristic to outsiders of any stripe and, for that matter, locals without the right educational or family background. Relationships must be reinforced by blood or time, lest they whither. Everyone seems to be beholden to a second cousin once removed, high school classmate, or a former professor. Much of this is because of the continued dominance of a small number of families who own *chaebols,* conglomerates that, directly or indirectly, account for as much as to 70 percent of the country's economic activity.

- Korea, economically vibrant and homogeneous, thinks of itself as a big family, not an aggregation of distant clans. As a result, the country is more civil. Codes of conduct are meticulously obeyed. Behavior in stadiums, bars, and karaoke parlors is courteous and restrained, unless drinking spins out of control.

The mainland and South Korea will never be adversaries. Chinese passion for Korean soap operas even suggests that mutual affection, if properly harvested, could blossom. But the PRC is too preoccupied with its standing vis-à-vis the world's powers to invest much energy in a multidimensional relationship. And the Koreans are too inward looking, not to mention wary of China's emergence as an economic colossus, to extend a firm hand of friendship.

CHINA AND INDIA: A MATCH MADE IN HEAVEN?

Were there ever two countries more yin and yang than India and China? On every dimension, in every sphere, their strengths and weaknesses are complementary, ripe for a commercial partnership that could—theoretically—alter the twenty-first-century global order. China, overflowing with technocrats, could build the factories. The business of building and managing global companies and brands could be turned over to India, a country of tremendous intellectual and strategic energy.

Compared to China, India is a manager's nirvana but for the lack of investment capital. Its service sector, representing well more than 50 percent of output, is light years ahead of its Asian counterpart's. Ditto the emergence of world-class multinational corporations led by seasoned management. These companies are fed by universities producing legions of inventive, conceptually driven, English-speaking professionals. And India's economic emergence has come despite dysfunctional state organs and petty political infighting.

China, meanwhile, boasts formidable production capability but has yet to fully nourish its consumer markets. Fueled by armies of well-trained workers, the country is a powerhouse, ruthlessly propelling its way to the top of value chains. During the past two decades, in spite of rampant corruption and few checks and balances, China's massive, technocratic bureaucracy has engineered a stunning industrial infrastructure. A dynamic private sector has been built upon these foundations by a Chinese people equipped with an expansive world-view and great ambition.

Hurdles to overcome. Engagement between the two powers has begun. Bilateral trade has jumped twentyfold in a decade to $61.8 billion in 2010, hinting at a new age of cooperation. It looks like a match made in heaven, but strategic collaboration will not come easily.

From a Chinese vantage point, there are three barriers that preclude symbiosis, that is, actual integration of economic and corporate structures. First, the sovereignty disputes from the 1962 border war have not been resolved, and, more critically, India's embrace of Tibet's Dalai Lama hits the paranoid third rail of centrifugal disintegration.

Second, India's most exportable products—services such as education and software development—have limited entry to the mainland. NIIT, the world's largest technology institute, has struggled valiantly to operate freely in China, despite a severe shortage of qualified Chinese IT professionals. China's own service sector—banks, travel, financial services—is nascent. Beijing is obsessive about controlling political dialog, shying away from industries driven by free expression, despite an oft-proclaimed need for innovation. Leaders are schizophrenically torn between learning from the world and insulating state-owned enterprises from the claws of foreign competition.

Third, China and India spring from two radically different worldviews. Confucianism, China's cultural blueprint, dictates that individuals accept their place in, and then advance through, an intricate societal hierarchy. Chinese adhere to a striving, pragmatic, morally relativistic code of conduct. Hinduism and Buddhism, in contrast, reject materialism and embrace cosmological transcendence. The love of debate that springs from Brahminic restraint—primary satisfaction derived from intellectual exchange—is also at odds with the Chinese inclination just to get on with it.

Are the China and India destined to deal with each other on tenterhooks, confounded by motivational discrepancies? Both are gigantic, emerging economies with complementary strengths and weaknesses, but any marriage must be built on trust. Unless the countries' respective leaders encourage people to celebrate cultural diversity, the potential for the Sino-Indian collective greatness will be capped.

PART SIX

EPILOGUE

37

THE MYTHS OF MODERN CHINA

China will become an economic superpower. In real terms, its economy will become larger than that of the United States within the next ten to twenty years, depending on whom you ask. A cash-rich Beijing—the nation currently holds more than $3 trillion in foreign capital reserves—will increasingly strut its diplomatic stuff. It will be less apt to compromise on anything it deems a vital interest. China will more firmly entrench itself as the world's supplier of value-added goods, dramatically shifting the balance of industrial power between East and West. As more Chinese citizens become middle class, they will spread across the globe, just as they have done for hundreds of years, in search of opportunity and riches. Our hotels, schools, and entertainment complexes will become more "Sinicized" as institutions adapt to the epic rise of a gargantuan consumer class, one that did not exist until the late 1990s. The twenty-first century will not be an American century.

But much of Western analysis has been overly alarmist. Yes, the world must adapt to China's economic and cultural heft. For the first time in modern history, two fundamentally different yet influential worldviews—one rooted in institutional protection of individual interests and the other in top-down Confucian patriarchy—will coexist. However, competition is not destined to devolve into a Manichean struggle between darkness and light, good and evil. China, nonhegemonic to its core, must continue to make its peace with an established geopolitical and economic order. It has served the country's interests for the past thirty years and will continue to do so for the next several decades.

Nor will China implode. Its road to superpower status will be bumpy, even rocky in parts, but the fundamentals of sustained macroeconomic expansion are in place and, for the large part, enduring. Societal tensions—between rich and poor, urban and rural, young and old, cadres and noncadres—can be managed for the foreseeable future. Pragmatism and incrementalism are bulwarks against extremism. Chinese society has evolved since the misadventures of the Great Leap Forward, perhaps the most destructive and colossal misallocation of resources in human history, and the Cultural Revolution, Mao Zedong's megalomaniacal and ill-fated attempt to reshape the nation in his image. China's postrevolution leftist lurches were historically anomalous, instigated as a dazed country emerged from 150 years of decay into an unfamiliar Western hegemony. Today, Beijing's power structure has returned to form. It dismisses breakthrough as destabilizing, inherently counterproductive. The body politic prizes consensual moderation, and this instinct is now institutionally embedded in the party's decision making and leadership minuets.

We still don't "get" China. (Do we even want to?) We swing violently from slack-jawed wonder to geopolitical nihilism. The truth is far grayer. It is worth our while to highlight some of the myths that color people's preoccupation with the enigmatic ascendance of China:

1. Populist anger means the party's power is weakening.
2. American-style individualism is taking root.
3. Contemporary Chinese have no beliefs.
4. The Internet will revolutionize China.
5. The China market is, like Europe, many countries.
6. The Chinese consumer is inscrutable.
7. The Chinese growth model is in critical danger.
8. China Inc. will eat America's lunch.
9. China will become *the* twenty-first-century superpower.
10. China is militarily aggressive.

MYTH 1: POPULAR ANGER MEANS THE PARTY'S POWER IS WEAKENING

The relationship between the people and the Chinese government is, to say the least, ambivalent. The country's wealthiest citizens scurry to obtain foreign passports as a hedge against future uncertainty. The little guy rails against bureaucratic corruption, particularly when his interests are affected. The number of small-scale protests (mostly local disputes) has steadily climbed; according to official statistics—surely conservative—more than 150,000 "public disorder events" occur each year. Rampant land seizures, with the owners compensated at fire-sale prices, represent abuse of eminent domain on a massive scale. The dramatic restructuring of state industries has dislocated many urban workers, stripping them of the dignity provided by a job. And the Internet, particularly microblogs, provides further grist for the mill—concerns about government impartiality and favoritism have been digitally fanned. Bureaucrats who protect unsavory types or lead fat-cat lifestyles disgust the public.

And yet, the party is in firm control and will not lose its grip any time soon. First, the government has become ruthlessly efficient in nipping dissent in the bud. Every housing complex pays one or two underemployed residents to snoop on neighbors and report suspicious goings-on to authorities. (These people are usually unassuming and older, and belie impressions of China as Orwellian. They also handle complaints about uncivil behavior, including overflowing trash, construction dust, and paint fumes.) According to foreign estimates, more than $100 billion is spent every year maintaining public order, using both low- and high-tech means. The Ministry of State Security employs at least 100,000 individuals and has deployed sophisticated algorithms to monitor—and censor—sensitive online chats, BBS forums, and microblogs.

Second, the West vastly underestimates of the power of the Communist Party as perhaps the strongest, most enduring brand in China. Why is Mao Zedong, the father of new China, still idolized by the majority of the population despite colossal mistakes during the Great Leap Forward and the Cultural Revolution? Because he, under the banner of the party, liberated China from foreign invasion and civil war and unified the country. Propaganda organs proclaim Mao's actions were "70 percent positive and 30 percent negative." Most agree. Mao still undergirds party's legitimacy—to wit, former Chongqing Party Secretary Bo Xilai's 2011 revival of revolutionary "red songs."

The prosperity covenant. When Deng Xiaoping rose to power, the Communists rejected cultish hagiography in favor of future focus. Deng was a quintessentially Chinese pragmatist; his maxims about "black or white cats" and "crossing rivers by feeling stones" resonate deeply. He imposed a scientific economic model—central management of key resources, liberalization of non-strategic industries, gradual urbanization, solicitation of foreign investment, and mercantilist foreign policy—that is still effective. Despite the naysayers, Deng's "socialism with Chinese characteristics" continues to work. According to the United Nations' International Fund for Agriculture Development, between 1978 and 2008, average annual per capita income increased six times, and the number of rural residents living in absolute poverty—that is, on less than US$1.50 per day—decreased from 260 million to 16 million. China is creating a middle class that will reshape twenty-first-century industry and commerce. The Communist Party, despite its heavy hand, has street cred. Unless growth collapses, citizens will grudgingly support national leaders.

Sublime stability. Third, the Chinese people crave order—stability is the platform on which progress is built. Confucian society is patriarchal, at peace with top-down compliance. The son/subject does not exist independent of his obligations to the father/ruler. Democracy in China is tantamount to responsiveness, not representation. Individual rights are abstractions, unless linked to immediate economic or family interests. There were reports of "walking protests" in response to the Arab Spring, but the government effortlessly squelched disturbances. People do not feel safe—China is not yet harmonious, and the social safety net is in tatters—but there is no plan B. The foundation of party legitimacy remains the masses' faith in their mandarins' ability to—somehow, someway—guide China's long march to prosperity. Father knows best, even if he sometimes makes mistakes.

Into the future: The Singapore model? What is the future of China's governance? Reform will come from within the party, and it is conceivable that Singapore's Confucian, self-monitoring model of administration could transplant itself in China. Experimentation would start in major cities. Debugged, the model could replicate itself across smaller urban areas. Does anyone know how to get from here to there? No, but Singapore's passion for technocratic competence, bottom-line accountability, and meritocratic advancement are compatible with the party's underlying pragmatism. And the Chinese are stunningly efficient at adopting preexisting models. Of course, there are many hurdles. Official pay must rise before corruption can be rooted out; an interconnected web of the interests of local, provincial, and national officials must be shredded; and a win-win relationship between urban and rural areas must be forged. But the future of China's political system will not be made in America or Europe.

MYTH 2: AMERICAN-STYLE INDIVIDUALISM IS TAKING ROOT

A Chinese new wave? China's rock scene, underground but dynamic, is loaded with bands that suggest a new, post-1990s rebellious spirit. Their names fly in the face of collective harmony: Hutong Fist, Tomahawk, Catcher in the Rye, Twisted Machine, Queen Sea Big Shark, and Wild Children. Indie singers are, collectively, a huge force on Douban, China's leading cultural and artistic website. Performers such as Jay Chou, known for nonconformist lyrics, and Hong Kong's Edison Chen, a "real guy" despite being driven out of the city because of a pornography scandal involving several Hong Kong starlets, are embraced by the new generation. Lady Gaga is an icon. Subculture tribalism is the rage for local fashion brands such as Metersbonwe. The nation cheers self-determination; when an armless twenty-year-old won *China's Got Talent* by playing piano with his toes, many cried. In coastal cities, tattoo joints, purveyors of indelible badges of individualism, are as ubiquitous as massage parlors.

Surely the forces of change are reshaping the Chinese psyche. Surely people once suppressed by colorless conformity are embracing individualism.

Sorry but no. Self-expression is not equal to independence of thought. Chinese society has never celebrated the liberation of individual potential that, in any way, smacks of rebellion. Creativity—and, make no mistake, mainlanders are capable of wonderful originality if they feel safe enough to pursue it—exists in a bottle, placed up high, out of reach of ordinary citizens. Underground musicians never achieve mass popularity, and not only because of draconian censorship laws. The Chinese, despite the rise of alternative music, still gravitate toward headliners who sing sweet melodies. Although the glow of regression-to-the-mean Cantopop stars such as Aaron Kwok and Andy Lau is fading, no home-grown individualistic superstar—that is, the Chinese Madonna—has emerged to capture imaginations. Chinese sculptors and painters sell their works mainly to investors, foreign and domestic, with eyes on artistic arbitrage. Chen Danqing, a well-known artist and intellectual who lived in New York for twenty years before returning to Beijing ten years ago, said in a recent interview, "None of us in today's China is a genuine intellectual. None of us."

Instinctive anti-individualism. Westerners sometimes have difficulty grasping the structure of Chinese society, so radically different from their own. Individuals are never encouraged—by parents, teachers, bosses, or leaders—to define themselves as independent of society. The basic productive unit of society is the clan, not the individual. Free thought is inherently destabilizing, a threat to conventional order. Institutions designed to protect the interests of individuals, both political and economic, have never been developed. Courts serve the interests of the state. In hierarchical settings, few dare to overtly challenge the boss's opinion, particularly in front of peers. Fathers are uniformly respected by even the hippest new-generation types. Teachers, feared by both pupils and parents, are agents of the power structure, vested with the authority to determine who advances within it.

Ego gratification, as opposed to self-driven individualism, is a primary urge for an ambitious, upwardly mobile population. But success is still synonymous with societal acknowledgment. Although entrepreneurial achievement counts—owning a business suggests control of one's destiny—nontraditional career paths such as advertising or charity work are abandoned by the age of thirty-five, particularly by men responsible for an extended clan's material security. The pursuit of happiness, a tempting but forbidden fruit, is an adolescent fantasy, best forsaken by the time the pressure of marriage, mortgage, mother-in-law, and auto ownership come into play.

Human rights: No passion. This instinctive anti-individualism also means that human rights will never be the driving force of China's evolution. The passions of morally relativistic, pragmatic Chinese are not roused when another's liberties are infringed upon. The Chinese greeted the recent arrests of Nobel Laureate Liu Xiaobo and renowned artist Ai Weiwei with sadness but not righteous indignation. Concerns that do not directly impact "my family" quickly dissipate. The exception is cases wherein ordinary people can easily see themselves in a victim's shoes. For instance, "nail house" owners—stubborn folk who refuse to relinquish their homes to real estate developers—are local heroes. In the end, though, the desire for a stable, if imperfect, future stirs the soul. To quote a famous maxim: "If you are standing upright, don't worry if your shadow is crooked." Pragmatism is king.

MYTH 3: CONTEMPORARY CHINESE HAVE NO BELIEFS

China was founded to ensure survival, not as an earthly manifestation of God's moral covenant with humans, the latter blessed with a divine right to pursue happiness. Indigenous schools of Chinese philosophy—Daoism, Confucianism, and legalism—are mechanistic, concerned with values as a means to an end—that is, social and cosmological stability. To the extent morals exist, they serve a greater purpose of aligning heaven and Earth. Inherently relativistic, China's moral topography shifts to address external circumstances. (It is *not* always wrong to murder.) And pragmatism is, again, a key driver. Religious practices— meat and potatoes Buddhism, originally imported from India but adapted to accommodate secularity—focus on gods of wealth and kitchens, not spiritual enlightenment. The Chinese do not obsess about higher meaning. They are concerned with today, not eternity.

Secular spiritualism. Although Chinese and Western religious orientations do not intersect, it is incontestable that Chinese spiritualism—if defined as pursuits beyond material gratification—is in the midst of transition, particularly among the overworked, overstressed middle classes.

For millennia, Chinese contentment has been rooted in external endorsement. During dynastic times, mastery of Confucian canon was the ticket to transcendence. Knowledge, acquired through classical Chinese texts, theoretically yielded a government post among the ruling scholar-noble elite. (Even during the Song dynasty, when Zhu Xi and other scholars incorporated Buddhism into a neo-Confucian ruling framework, officialdom resisted. Neo-Confucians did not believe in an external world unconnected with the world of matter.) After 1949, command of "Mao Zedong thought" defined the new man, a leader of masses. Political correctness, elevated into cryptoreligious truth in millions of Little Red Books, enabled people to scale party hierarchy. When Deng Xiaoping toured Guangdong in 1992, he made a new imperial proclamation: "To get rich is glorious!" In one swoop, he defined the production of capital as the ultimate contribution to the nation. Given the poverty of the times, the person-on-the-street's interpretation of Deng's mandate was simple: money is success.

Deng dogma. Of course, the Chinese have always used material display as a surrogate indicator of worth. But since the 1990s, things have spun out of control. The quest for prosperity, unattainable chimera for the vast majority of penny-pinched mainlanders, has turned into a rat race. Apartments, now a prerequisite for marriage, are so stratospherically expensive they require multi-generational pooling of resources. Addiction to luxury brands results in sales growth of 50 percent per annum, despite 53 percent import tariffs. Matchmaker talk shows produce legions of gold-digging femme fatales, one of whom set chat rooms ablaze because she "would rather cry in the front seat of a BMW than be in love on the back of a bicycle." An automobile, on average 100 percent more expensive than in the United States and costing more than 120 percent of buyers' annual income, is a must for anyone aspiring to be labeled middle class—hence China's emergence as the world's largest car market. Fixation with flat-panel TVs makes American couch potatoes seem Spartan in comparison.

The discovery of tradition. To the Chinese, materialism is not superficial. It is meaningful, tantamount to advancement within society and faith in the future. Run amok, however, it corrupts ambition and threatens the country's social fabric. Extreme competitive materialism, exacerbated by acute economic insecurity, has led even upwardly mobile arrivistes to doubt the Deng Xiaoping dogma. China appears to be finally rediscovering the utility of Confucian ideals. According to a study conducted by the advertising agency TBWA, the appeal of traditional values such as loyalty, moderation, and respect for elders made modest comebacks between 2002 and 2009, while personal success and rights have slipped as aspirations. Is China abandoning an achievement ethos? No. But record viewership of Professor Yu Dan's lecture "Confucius from the Heart," broadcast nationally on China Central Television, hints at a budding realization that there is more to life than an Audi and a nice apartment. The popularity of *Golden Marriage,* a television series extolling commitment, not romantic passion, as the secret sauce of love, also suggests a reemergence of Confucian ideals.

It is worth mentioning the spread of Christianity in both rural and urban areas does not represent a rejection of traditional values. During the Tang dynasty, Buddhism was embraced as complement to, not repudiation of, material secularism. (On the mainland and in Taiwan, a traditional Chinese society that was not disoriented by Mao's utopian experimentation during the Great

Leap Forward and Cultural Revolution, Protestantism and Catholicism provide similar balm today.)

Chinese society is not in the throes of a spiritual crisis. Instead, it is on the threshold of reclaiming values that have always set it apart. The Cultural Revolution did not purge traditional morality: the sanctity of clan and nation has never been challenged; societal harmony is still noble; anti-individualism is still pervasive; fulfillment of mandate still defines success. Contemporary Chinese, however, are unable to articulate the country's cultural DNA. Dazed and confused, they have yet to leverage their unique worldview as a defense mechanism against disorientation. As the new generation passes through collective adolescence, however, it is finding a new balance. It is, slowly but surely, achieving harmony with a new order.

MYTH 4: THE INTERNET WILL REVOLUTIONIZE CHINA

Change...Make no mistake. The Internet is changing China, and mostly for the good:

- Emotionally, the Internet has been manna from heaven. Stifled by real-world restriction, more than 500 million Internet users are free to indulge in violent computer games, free music downloads, illegal access to thousands of boot-legged movies, and an infinite array of chat rooms with interests ranging from heavy metal music to exotic fish.
- Transactionally, e-commerce transparency has shifted the balance of power between retailers and consumers. And online megamalls such as Taobao.com compensate for the scarcity of high-quality brick-and-mortar destinations.
- Politically, digital technology has narrowed the chasm between rulers and ruled. An army of anonymous sentinels stands ready to relay reports of official corruption, particularly at local levels. Of the 130,000-plus accusations of corruption said to have been reported in 2010, many came by means of Weibo—China's Twitter clone— and websites sporting names like ipaidedabribe.com, a knock off of an Indian site.

But "revolution" is a strong word. There are four reasons why the Internet will not fundamentally change China's landscape and upend the relationship between people and government.

First, digital behavior here is, by Western standards, conservative. "Release" is not the same as "freedom." Even the most opinionated, angry youths are anonymous, shielded by avatars. Most Internet users just want to play games or chat, not organize dissent. Not rebellious, and concerned for the welfare of their families, few would-be agitators are willing to risk getting in trouble with authorities.

Second, the party has the technological sophistication to block searches or messages on sensitive topics. When former president Jiang Zemin was rumored to be terminally ill, censors halted searches containing the character for "river," which is also Jiang's surname. Only a small fraction of the population was aware of dissident Liu Xiaobo's arrest or his Nobel Peace Prize. It's worth noting, however, that there are some instances in which digital snoops have lost control. After a high-speed train accident in Zhejiang province, Chinese posted an astounding 26 million tweets on Weibo complaining of cover-up and corruption. "I eagerly await the US embassy asking for an explanation from the authorities—paying close attention!" wrote Weibo user jemmba. "Would it be possible to send the CIA or FBI over to investigate?" asked another.

Image 37.1 Blog postings are one of the only ways to vent antigovernment sentiment. This posting, executed in a style similar to a nationalistic Adidas ad that ran during the 2008 Olympics, demands accountability for a 2011 high speed train crash in Wenzhou. The headline demands, "Hold up the truth!" (Courtesy Lu Ming)

Third, foreign companies are often complicit in enhancing the party's monitoring capabilities. The *New York Times* reported that Cisco Systems was one of several firms working on a government project in Chongqing that includes creating the biggest police surveillance system in the world. A year and a half after Google relocated its search services from the mainland to Hong Kong to avoid censorship, Microsoft's Bing still restricts some searches in China. It has also agreed to provide search results in English for Baidu, China's leading—and heavily censored—engine.

Fourth, Chinese cyberspace is a walled garden. People look out at the world but are not allowed to really engage with it. All international social networking sites are banned, and the Chinese equivalents of Facebook and Twitter—Renren and Weibo, respectively—both bend to Beijing's will.

Harmony from cyberspace? The party has also been clever in using the Internet to advance social harmony.

- It knows the masses need to let off stream. After disaster or scandal, the censors open a release hatch out of which diatribes spew. Then it slams the door shut and life moves on.
- E-commerce platforms, supported by the government, have expanded the supply and quality of consumer goods available in lower-tier markets, right down to the rural fringe.
- Digital technology facilitates party responsiveness. At least fifty thousand net police monitor bulletin boards and chat rooms to not only expunge discussion of sensitive topics but also alert leadership about unharmonious rumblings before they become incidents. In this sense, China's digital revolution represents one of Communism's biggest polling breakthroughs ever.

In the end, China's digital era remains quintessentially Chinese. The government has granted the people a blank canvas for self-expression and material gratification, but it retains the wherewithal to frame and control public discourse. Internet users, prone to grumble, are still in no mood to rebel. In the future, assuming the government loosens up a bit, boundaries will expand, but they will not go away.

MYTH 5: THE CHINESE MARKET IS, LIKE EUROPE, MANY COUNTRIES

The biggest cliché repeated by newly arrived foreigners is that China is not a country but a continent. This is false, and not only because massive infrastructure investment has accelerated interregional collaboration and operational synergies. Han Chinese take great pride in their unified culture. There are no political or cultural divides as pronounced as those in Europe—lackadaisical Italy versus industrious Germany, and socially liberal, anti-institutional Protestants versus morally conservative, statist Catholics. Within China, differences do exist but largely because business and political environments are not the same. The north, dominated by Beijing and the largest state-owned enterprises, is bureaucratic. The south, close to the sea, is entrepreneurial, less encumbered by government hierarchy. In Beijing, luxury brands are purchased as status projectors—flashy Rolexes are huge sellers. In Guangdong, luxury brands are exchanged as gifts; they lubricate business relationships and facilitate trust—cognacs are big. Climate differences are also important. Northern shampoo users worry about dryness; southerners worry about oiliness.

A unified worldview. But these are nuances. Ethnic Chinese are unified by an identical worldview: a fatalistic, cyclical view of time and space characterized by meticulous interconnectivity of things big and small; a morally relativistic universe in which the only absolute evil is chaos and the only good is stability, a platform on which progress is constructed; and the family, not the individual, is the basic productive unity of society. (Fifty-six minorities that account for 8 percent of the population remain outside the Han cultural footprint.)

Economic disparity, cultural cohesion. Most transregional differences are driven by variations in economic development and per capita income, not culture. (Millward Brown, the leading research company specializing in advertising effectiveness, has not cracked the code that explains geographic inconsistencies in scores measuring change in brand preference. The problem probably has more to do with poor fieldwork and lack of normative data than shopper motivations.) Inland provinces, still relatively poor, are physically isolated from both rich China and the rest of the world. Although infrastructure development and communications penetration is accelerating, consumers in underdeveloped areas are less experienced than in more prosperous regions. They are apt to be more suspicious of new brands, place an even greater emphasis on in-store service, focus on family harmony, and reject complicated messages.

China is Balkanized. The challenges of unifying distribution networks, sales channels, retail presence, and sourcing standards remain monumental. But operational hurdles, not culture, are what stand in the way of the country's becoming the world's biggest single market.

MYTH 6: THE CHINESE CONSUMER IS INSCRUTABLE

The Chinese are cautious, loath to lower guards in unfamiliar circumstances. They crave security. When I moved into a traditional Shanghai lane house development, it took six months before (elderly) neighbors smiled. The biggest management challenge continues to be encouraging self-expression within hierarchy. At American universities, Chinese students rarely speak up for fear of lost face. Oversized conference rooms are cold zones of frozen facial expressions and icy stares. Domestic CEOs are self-protective—they consolidate power through ambiguous edicts no one knows quite how to interpret and encourage rival power factions beneath them.

And yet, the Chinese are very warm, realistic, and direct. Once trust is established, and common cause is identified, relationships are straightforward and fun. Laughter is loud, cigarettes are offered, and language becomes spicy. Business negotiations speed up, feedback loops quicken, and friendships form.

The omnipresent Confucian conflict. The Chinese are not complicated. The contrasts that confuse foreigners—respect for tradition and conformity on one hand, and irreverence and boldness on the other—are manifestations of a homogeneous worldview. Chinese culture, reinforced for millennia but reinterpreted to accommodate contemporary circumstances, continues to bind the nation together. At all levels of society, there is a unifying Confucian conflict, a tension between ambition and regimentation. Practically everyone wants to stand out while fitting in.

Resolution of the Confucian conflict is at the heart of all effective marketing strategies:

- Women want to reconcile achievement and traditional feminine grace, and therefore like to buy themselves diamonds, which sparkle but don't glare.
- Men must win—that is, claw their way up the ladder of success—without transgressing the rules of the game, hence a preference among wealthier individuals for Audis or BMWs instead of flashy Maseratis.
- Middle-class consumers must simultaneously project status and protect hard-won gains, hence savings rates in excess of 35 percent, aversion to car loans, and down payments on real estate that average 50 percent of the selling price.
- Luxury buyers want to demonstrate mastery of the system but remain understated, hence the appeal of Mont Blanc's six-point logo and Bottega Veneta's elegant cross weave, both conspicuously discreet reflections of inner substance.
- Youth want to be both individualistic and accepted, hence the draw of conventionally hip fashion brands—for example, Converse, Uniqlo—and discreet tattoos.

The Chinese are knowable. Once foreigners appreciate China's unique characteristics, the mists evaporate.

MYTH 7: THE CHINESE GROWTH MODEL IS IN CRITICAL DANGER

When it comes to prognosticating the future of China's economy, critics swing from starry-eyed wonder to end-of-days doom. The truth is surely somewhere in between. No matter what, China's emergence will not be smooth. It faces many challenges: rising inflation; skyrocketing commodity prices; wage increases that weaken its position as a low-cost manufacturer; bureaucratic conservatism that militates against bold, and necessary, structural reforms; an urban-rural income gap that threatens social harmony; and an education system that squelches creativity and innovation.

Not overheating. In the short-term, China's economy is not overheating. Although postfinancial crisis investment skyrocketed, few believe the banks are critically overextended, especially at the national level. GaveKal-Dragonomics, a Chinese-focused research house, estimates that government debt amounts to about 80 percent of GDP—a sustainable level, even after accounting for central and local government projects, bank restructuring costs, and other liabilities. Investment in infrastructure is yielding lower productivity gains than several years ago, but as a nation, China has not overbuilt. The *Economist* notes that China's accumulated investment in fixed assets is still low and real wages have been rising strongly, which should help boost consumption in the medium term. Despite unaffordable property in major cities, talk of popping bubbles is confined to high-end neighborhoods in coastal capitals.

An enduring model. In the long term, China's growth model still has legs. There are various components, including aggressive attraction of foreign technology and management expertise; integration with international financial institutions to improve compliance with global standards of governance; top-down management of strategic industries; minimal interference in private enterprises, many of which are dynamic but starved for capital; ruthless control of capital flows; a gradual shift to domestic consumption, one that has not yet begun in earnest; and regional specialization. Different regions now specialize in different sectors, facilitating the formation of supplier-and-producer clusters that slash operating costs. What's more, the emergence of China's middle class completes a successful investment-production-consumption circle, the same one that allowed America to become an industrial powerhouse in the twentieth century.

The grand urbanization and job creation paradigm. The most important element, however, is rapid (but steady) urbanization, the ultimate catalyst for higher productivity and disposable incomes. In 1990, China's urbanization rate was 26 percent. By 2010, it had reached approximately 50 percent, and, if all goes according to plan, by 2035, more than 70 percent of the country's population will live in cities and towns. In many respects, the past two decades have been a successful Great Leap Forward. (Mao's 1958–1962 utopian folly was the most disastrous misallocation of capital in human history. Peasants, herded into collectives, focused on forging backyard furnaces, not rotating crops. By some estimates, thirty million people perished from starvation.) The countryside is becoming industrialized and urbanized. Boosted by infrastructural investment, towns have sprung up on what used to be farmland. Peasants, once toiling in fields, now work in factories, on construction sites and in hospitals, hotels, and airports. As people leave low-productivity agriculture jobs for higher-productivity ones in the manufacturing and service sectors, human capital is liberated. As a result, 250 million people have been rescued from poverty. Immense productivity gains mitigate inefficiencies, including poor innovation, creaky distribution networks, rampant corruption, excessive savings encouraged by frayed safety nets, and patchy tax collection. Urbanization is a rising tide that lifts many boats, even ones with holes in the bottom.

Image 37.2   China's countryside is being industrialized. The central government's Great Urbanization Paradigm has increased productivity, lifted hundreds of millions from poverty, and kept the PRC's economic juggernaut on track. Sustaining growth, however, will require major structural reform. (Courtesy ImagineChina)

Political wherewithal? Does China have the political flexibility required to sustain the paradigm? No one can say for sure. But policy makers are not naive—they know that reform is imperative. Without it, labor mobility, already slowing, as evidenced by rising wages, will stop. What does the party need to do? There must be a massive reallocation of wealth from the cities to the countryside so peasants feel secure enough to leave villages and settle in urban areas. This will require two fundamental changes: reform of the *hukou* system, which keeps migrant workers from collecting the generous benefits only city residents receive; and land reform. Regarding the latter, genuine change would involve gradually allowing farmers to buy, and cash in on, the farmland they do not yet own and relocate permanently to cities.

Real reform on both fronts has barely begun, impeded by left-wing dogma and fears of upsetting a middle class whose tax bills would have to rise to fund restructuring. But the world should not underestimate the technocratic savvy of Beijing mandarins. Rationalism, it can be hoped, will lead to a new deal between the party and the peasantry. When reform does come, it will be microscopically incremental, barely noticeable to outsiders. The Chinese are adept at experimentation. (Currency and interest rate reform seem to be further along the test-and-refine track than *hukou* and land reform; that said, Chengdu and Chongqing do appear to be laboratories for the latter.) It is unclear how much time remains before the rural-urban express train comes to halt, but there are legions of underemployed peasants out there. Farmers' incomes are approximately one-sixth that of factory workers. And infrastructural reform, plus the growth of inland cities, minimizes migrant dislocation. Peasants still have plenty of incentive to head for the bright lights; the party still has several years before the clock runs out.

The extraordinary Chinese. Perhaps the most powerful, albeit qualitative, argument in favor of sustained expansion is the uniqueness of the Chinese people. They harbor no illusions about challenges confronting the nation. They have experienced the agony of disintegration and will accommodate tough choices with more grace than the Communist Party supposes—or, indeed, than we in the West seem able to muster ourselves. During the past eighty years, the masses have persevered through Japanese invasion, civil war, revolution, the nightmare of a hundred flowers blooming, the Great Leap Forward, the Cultural Revolution, Deng Xiaoping theory, the Tiananmen Square massacre, the uncomfortable debut of global China, head-spinning urbanization, a digital big bang, and apartment price vertigo. Through it all, the Chinese have adapted. They survey the horizons for threats and opportunities and, mostly, thrive. They are still optimistic—and with good reason. Despite the tumult and awkwardness of economic adolescence, China is more stable, more integrated into a multinational framework, than at any time in history. The people crave stability and will, to a point, suffer in order to sustain the nation's precarious balance.

China has emerged, at all levels of society, as a nation of realists. What I observed in my last book, *Billions*, still holds true:

> The Chinese boast a broad (albeit ethnocentric) worldview and are fascinated with anything new. Anti-individualism fuels a patriotic fervor that unifies the nation behind a common goal of national advancement. A profound respect for intelligence, the ultimate weapon in a dog-eat-dog world, has created a country that reveres the scholar. Their mindset emphasizes knowledge over might, defense over offense, skill over brute force, and concentration over impulse. As a result, Chinese are analytically and tactically brilliant. While creativity is not China's forte, dazzling application is. The Chinese are, simply put, the most striving, ambitious yet clear-eyed people on the planet and that counts for a lot. They are pragmatic yet human, wary yet hopeful, patient yet quick to respond. They are the hope of their future. I'm betting on them.

I still am.

MYTH 8: CHINA INC. WILL EAT AMERICA'S LUNCH

Just because China will not collapse does not mean it will take over corporate America. Chinese corporations will continue to do what they do best: leverage colossal size to slowly but surely crawl up the value chain. Economies of scale, combined with a growing domestic market, will ensure that its price-value equation continues to outpace other countries' in the developing world. China does not want to be a sweatshop. A combination of affordable price and reliable performance explains why brands such as TCL (televisions), Huawei (telecom equipment), Haier (electronic appliances), and Midea (electronic appliances) are already reasonably well distributed in emerging markets such as India, Africa, Eastern Europe, and South America. Chinese corporations, most of them supported by the state, are already on the hunt to acquire foreign assets, including both resources and brands. On the manufacturing front, strengths in engineering and production, combined with downstream resource domination, will ensure no other nation supplants China as the world's factory.

The Chinese are (not) coming! It will be decades before Chinese corporations—even in strategic industries such as renewable energy or information technology—beat American, Western, and European companies on their own turf. Indeed, it may never happen at all. Indian companies have a better shot. Anyway, for the time being China is focusing energies on its expanding domestic market, a sensible strategy given its growth and price-conscious consumers. However, the single largest obstacle to the emergence of powerful Chinese brands is not tied to policy or preference. Put simply, the Chinese are great at application but lousy at innovation. Companies find themselves limited by inefficient investment in research and development; limited shareholder rights; ineffective corporate governance; zero protection of intellectual capital; capital markets corrupted by political favoritism; and CEO "kings" whose focus is split between the bottom line and political imperatives.

The trust deficit. Then there is the national trust deficit. China is a closed society and so are its corporations. The country lacks dynamic networks that stimulate new ideas and the dynamic collaboration required to harvest them. Columnist David Brooks, writing in November 2010 for the *New York Times*, puts his finger on an enduring American competitive advantage as a country of immigrants, a "crossroads nation." The United States boasts permeable global networks and has evolved to be a dynamic society with "high social trust." American companies therefore are more open and responsive to evolving market circumstances than Chinese enterprises. Brooks attributes this to Confucian values and China's hierarchical social structure. He states, "Americans...challenge their parents...underlings and are relatively free to challenge their bosses [rather than] submit to authority." New ideas can come from anywhere and anyone.

The Chinese, defensive and protective, are culturally and institutionally averse to ideas that buck convention. Chinese CEOs surround themselves with yes men, allied by blood or geography. Within organizations, territorialism is rife. Sales managers vigilantly protect turf, minimizing cross-department teamwork. Resources are rarely pooled for innovation, leading to chronic short-termism and minimal investment in value-added products or brands. Subordinates, anxious about losing face, never counter senior managers, particularly on subjective matters impervious to proof. Deals with foreign joint venture partners are tortuously negotiated because a win-win mind-set is never taken for granted.

Patents, not ideas. China's top-down modus operandi mobilizes resources to achieve economies of scale, an appropriate strategy for expanding into lower-tier cities. But imperial management is incompatible with creative expression, the latter a threat to established authority, hence China's woeful performance on the innovation front. Innovation is always incremental or feature driven, never a breakthrough. Jared Psigoda, the twenty-five-year-old American CEO of Reality Squared Games, an international online gaming publisher for Chinese titles, observes: "The vast majority of the games that come across our desk are *shanzhai*, fake with a twist. For most of them, they steal the codes, change a few pictures, and change the title." Weibo tweaked the Twitter concept by enabling photo posting. Haier, the nation's largest appliance manufacturer, reconfigures conventional washing machines into infinite variations, including one that washes potatoes. Food manufacturers add novel ingredients to expand product range—for example, Yinlu's peanut milk or eight-treasure congee. But the nation does not experiment with new models—China's Apple is not in the incubation stage.

And what about services? China boasts computer networks to process e-transactions, call centers run by automatons, and platoons of delivery boys on scooters. But its tertiary sector is rudimentary. For now, this is fine. Corporations deploy resources to succeed domestically—there are roads to pave and airports to build. Low price, economies of scale, and armies of sales personnel willing to tame a vast commercial landscape are the most powerful weapons on an expansive battleground. The West can continue to hone its own competitive advantages—innovation, dynamic capital markets, creativity, and responsiveness to individual needs—without fearing China.

MYTH 9: CHINA IS *THE* TWENTY-FIRST-CENTURY SUPERPOWER

In the narrowest sense, a superpower has the military might to force the world to acquiesce to hegemonic resolve (for example, the Soviet Union). Then there are economic superpowers that influence capital flows and global growth rates. When they struggle, the world does, too. Finally, there are soft superpowers, nations that own universal values.

American strengths and weaknesses. In response to the brouhaha about the American debt ceiling, a correspondent for the German newspaper *Die Welt* wrote in July 2011: "Out of the American twenty-first-century crisis could come the downfall of the dominant power of the twentieth century." His sentiments, perhaps overheated, are a reminder that nothing lasts forever. It is to be hoped that America's disorientation, triggered by the rise of China, political polarization, and a hangover of material self-indulgence, is not permanent. Even if GDP growth slows because of protracted deleveraging, the combination of a growing population and high per capita income ensures continued economic sway. America's military budget, currently eight times that of China, will continue to underpin geopolitical clout, even as the country's status as an 800-pound gorilla diminishes in a multipolar world.

American values—as opposed to its political system—will have global appeal for generations. Individualism—the encouragement by society to define oneself independent of society—does not travel well, but respect for the dignity of the common person touches all hearts. Iconic American brands such as Nike and Coke, vessels of hope to many consumers in the developing world, will never go out of style. American pop culture will not be challenged. Superstars—from Lady Gaga to Michael Jackson to Angelina Jolie to Johnny Depp—epitomize self-actualization, an aspiration that transcends culture.

China's soft power gap. China will undoubtedly evolve into an economic superpower. Its economy, within decades, will become the world's largest. Per capita disposable income will be constrained, but aggregate spending power will be massive. China's industrial tentacles will be felt everywhere; traditional Chinese medicine will become more popular; and university students will learn Mandarin.

But China will struggle to capture hearts and minds. Bluntly put, the Chinese are chauvinistic. In ways large and small, its instinct to narrowly defend interests is off-putting:

- The country maintains a chip on its shoulder regarding indignities suffered at the hands of foreigners between the Opium War and the establishment of Communist China in 1949. Strident outrage erupts whenever any country "hurts the feelings of the Chinese people," as the propagandists say.
- In a pinch, the government lapses into bullyboy petulance, throwing economic and military weight around the region. Diplomatic relationships with Japan and India are tetchy, largely because China remains brittle and insecure. Decades-long territorial disputes are unresolved.
- Although Chinese society is more civil than a few years ago, daily life is still dog-eat-dog. Charity organizations are underdeveloped because of the party's reluctance to grant authority to any entity not under its direct control. Families, unprotected by rule of law, fend for themselves at the expense of individuals outside the clan. Anyone who fails to conform to convention—for example, the disabled or mentally ill, homosexuals, and AIDS patients—is socially ostracized. Spitting and burping in public is commonplace. In crowded elevators and airplanes, mobile phone users lack volume control.
- Chinese, a language in which written and spoken forms are completely unrelated, remains a temple of linguistic exclusivity, a walled garden, frustratingly off limits to everyone but the most disciplined and determined foreigners. Every character requires memorization; every sentence must conform to structural imperatives.

When in Rome? Despite fascination with the world, the Chinese do not assimilate easily. China tries hard to be open—road signs are bilingual, English is a passion, trade links are robust, macroeconomic policies during financial crises were constructive—but, emotionally, the nation stands apart. Information is controlled. Again, the Chinese language is impenetrable to all but the most culturally adventurous. Defensive instincts militate against free and easy exchange of ideas. Until trust is established, foreigners are treated with polite suspicion. Manufacturers that acquire Western companies have difficulty integrating domestic and international management teams. The global footprint of China's state-controlled English-language news outlets is growing, but broadcasts are so dull that international viewers tune out. The opening ceremony of the 2008 Beijing Olympics, impressive in scale and moving in ambition, lapsed into mawkish cliché when gears shifted from celebrating China's glory to preaching "One World, One Dream."

China's ability to leverage the assets of other cultures is peerless. Its superhighways are modeled after America's, and major web portals are copycats of Western sites, tweaked for local users. The party has also integrated itself into the fabric of the global trading system as a check against domestic weaknesses (for example, poor corporate governance, pliable standards of financial transparency). But, unless deemed safe, foreigners are still confronted with awkward silences and robotic smiles. Bonding at the national level is a long ways off.

China will be an economic superpower only. There will be more than one tiger on the mountain.

MYTH 10: CHINA IS MILITARILY AGGRESSIVE

The list of military provocations grows longer: outlandish territorial claims in the South China Sea, and vilification of Hillary Clinton when she had the temerity to challenge them; installation of more than 1,000 ballistic weapons aimed at Taiwan; confrontation on the high seas with Japan, Taiwan, and the Philippines; year-on-year military spending increases of 13 percent since 1989, with defense budgets now approaching at least $80 billion; production of the nation's first national aircraft carrier and development of missile that can strike ships from 900 miles away.

China is ramping up military capabilities, but it will never invade other countries or challenge the military supremacy of the United States. Its primary concern is defense, an understandable one given its history. For a credible analysis of China's modern fighting force, scour Pentagon briefings. But to get a sense of the Beijing's pacifist instincts, come for a visit.

Every tourist monument built to last was built to protect. China offers little of transcendent delight. There is no Chinese Taj Mahal, no Eiffel Tower. The Great Wall was built to shield the nation from nomadic invasion. The Forbidden City, raised during the early Ming dynasty as a bulwark against the Mongols, is a fortress, replete with moats, turrets, and a labyrinthine inner structure. Beijing's magnificent Temple of Heaven was accessible only to emperors. Traditional Chinese homes ensured not only physical safety but also hierarchical and cosmological security. Southern Hakka clans constructed gigantic circular edifices that housed entire villages during attacks. Shi Huangdi, China's ruthless first emperor, carved thousands of terra cotta warriors for protection in the afterlife.

Even today, manifestations of China's protective instinct are everywhere. Thick walls topped with glass shards and barbed wire obstruct views of Shanghai's lovely French Concession manors. Inside luxury apartment buildings, the front doors of individual units are double gated. Safeguard, the leading soap brand for twenty-five years, is popular because of "germ protection." Engagement rings mean commitment, not romantic love. Lack of toxicity drives premium paint sales. Martial arts, a perennial passion, teach defense, not offense. Products, from bread to staplers, are sold triple-wrapped in cellophane. Taxi drivers steer from behind cages.

Chinese shield themselves from danger, real or imagined. They are not a people itching for war. They want unity. They will not support militarily aggressive governments, including their own. If Taiwan declares independence, the People's Liberation Army will invade the island. But, in Chinese eyes, this extreme act will not be perceived as aggressive—it is being done to defend sacred borders. Will forces of paranoia trigger an act of irrational, preemptive self-defense? If an ossified Communist Party invades Taiwan as a last-ditch effort to rally a low-growth nation, things could get ugly. But given China's penchant for incremental reform, it seems unlikely. If the United States accepts the inevitability of sharing the spotlight with a resurgent China, Beijing will keep cool.

In the end, how China behaves in the twenty-first century has a lot to do with the West. Many of the tensions of contemporary China—between rich and poor, city and rural, ruler and ruled, insiders and outsiders—are eternal. So is the country's resourcefulness. Geopolitical harmony is as much our choice as theirs. Given an adolescent economy and an immature body politic, China must focus on domestic imperatives. America also has work to do—the population is aging, generational and ethnic divides are clear cut, the economy is becoming ever more reliant on creative innovation. May both nations be blessed with leadership enlightened enough to embrace a new world order.

INDEX